אבבגדההוזח

טיככךלמם

נןסעפפףצץ

קרששת ‏ וו

ָ ‏ ׃ ‏ ֳ ‏ ֻ ‏ ֿ ‏ ֵ ‏ ֹ ‏ ֿ ‏ ֱ

CTIBOR
RYBÁR

**JEWISH
PRAGUE**

**Notes
on History
and Culture
– A Guidebook**

CTIBOR RYBÁR

JEWISH PRAGUE

Gloses
on History and Kultur
– A GUIDEBOOK

In cooperation with:
PhDr. Jiřina Šedinová, CSc. (Prague Hebrew literature)
PhDr. Gabriela Veselá (The Jews in Prague German literature)
PhDr. Arno Pařík (The Jewish Museum in Prague)

Drawings:
Dipl. Ing. Jaroslav Staněk

Photos:
František Přeučil (80), archives of Dr. Ctibor Rybár (46), Antonín Krčmář – Archives of the Municipal Museum of Prague (27), ČTK Press Agency (31), Museum of Literature – literary archives (11), archives of Dr. Helena Krejčová (9), archives of the Jewish Museum (4), Jiří Doležal (4), Zdeněk Paul (3), Z. Reach (2)

Translation:
Joy Turner-Kadečková – Slavoš Kadečka

PRINTED IN CZECHOSLOVAKIA
930-007-91
ISBN 80-85334-06-2

Contents

I.

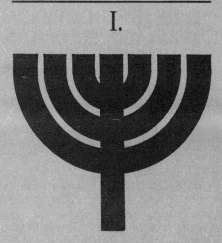

NOTES ON HISTORY

THE JEWISH TOWN
OF PRAGUE – ITS ORIGIN
AND SETTLEMENT

One thousand years ago a Jewish-Arab merchant by the name of Ibrahim Ibn Jacob said, among other things, the following about Prague:
"The town of Fraga is built of stone and limestone and it is the biggest town as regards trade. Russians and Slavs come here from the royal town with goods. And Muslims, Jews and Turks from the lands of the Turks also come here with goods and trade coins!"

How long have Jews lived in Prague? Ten centuries, or even longer? Let us content ourselves by saying that they have been here since ancient times and that it is impossible to determine exactly when they made their way to Prague and when they settled here.

After Jerusalem, Prague occupied a wholly exceptional place in the Jewish tradition. Although there were towns with far greater Jewish settlement in the medieval Jewish diaspora, places where whole generations of miraculous rabbis lived, nothing could equal the glory of Jewish Prague!

According to the oldest legend it was Princess Libuše who, with her clairvoyant spirit, prophesized that at the time of her grandson a foreign nation would arrive in Bohemia and bring the land good fortune if it were affably received. And so when the first Jews allegedly made their way to Bohemia in 860, during the rule of Hostivít, they really did receive an affable welcome along with an order to settle in the environs of Újezd.

The legend tells us that the Jews arrived here immediately after the demolition of the church of Jerusalem and that a ghetto existed here already before the arrival of the Slavs. Christian and Jewish chroniclers, among them Václav Hájek of Libočany († 1553) and David Gans († 1613), inform us that in the years 995–997 the Jews were granted permission to settle in Prague and to found their own township here – a ghetto – as a reward for the aid they had rendered the Christians in their fight against the pagans. According to Václav Hájek the Jews were also allowed to build their own school in Menší Město, the Lesser Town of Prague (now Malá Strana – the Little Quarter), on a site below the present Convent of Our Lady Below the Bridge. Similarly as in the case of other countries, the Jews made their way to Bohemia in the first centuries of the Christian era. They came as merchants, as intermediators of trade and exchanges of goods, and also to seek protection and security against the endless persecution and pogroms to which they were subjected.

In his History of the City of Prague V. V. Tomek states that Jewish merchants (negotiatores) may have been in Bohemia already at the time of the Markoman tribe and that "they were especially the chief entrepreneurs in trade with people", being also engaged in trade with slaves and prisoners.

In view of its closeness to the river and considerable number of small market-places and merchants' communities Prague was an important cross-road of trade routes. Two entirely different types of Jewish merchants and immigrants arrived in Bohemia from two sides. The original, older group – Jews of Byzantine origin, – came from the east and settled on the territory of the so-called Stará škola (Old Shul) then in the environs of Dušní Street of the present. A little later Jews arrived on the territory of the Old Town from the west. They settled round the present Old-New Synagogue and founded their town, later called a ghetto, here. It is in these places, then, that we can seek the beginnings of Jewish Prague, a special community with its own autonomy in the hands of its own representatives, Jewish elders (majores natu Judaei). However, Jews also lived in other places in Prague. Important settlement is documented in the present streets called Voršilská, Opatovická and V Jirchářích. Cosmas (c. 1045–1125), deacon of the Vyšehrad Chapter, wrote the following

---

✝ V

ROKU OD NAROZENÍ PÁNĚ 1097[cc]
Kníže Břetislav, povolav k sobě Oldřicha, syna Konrádova, dal ho zajmouti a poslal na hrad Kladsko do vězení.

ROKU OD NAROZENÍ PÁNĚ 1098
Doneslo se knížeti Břetislavovi, že jakýsi počet Židů uprchl a že někteří tajně stěhují své bohatství dílem do Polska, dílem do Panonie [Uher]. Kníže, velmi se proto rozhněvav, poslal svého komorníka s několika bojovníky, aby je od hlavy k patě obrali. Ten přišed povolal k sobě starší Židů a takto se jal mluviti k nim:

„ZPLOZENÝ Z KURVÍCH SYNŮ, TY NÁRODE IZMAHELITSKÝ, KNÍŽE VÁM POROUČÍ ŘÍCI, PROČ PRCHÁTE Z KNÍŽECTVÍ JEHO,
PROČ TÉŽ POKLADY SVÉ TEĎ MENŠÍTE, ZÍSKANÉ ZDARMA? COKOLI VE CHVÍLI TÉTO JEST MÉ, JEST ÚPLNĚ MOJE.
Z JERUZALÉMA ŽÁDNÉ JSTE S SEBOU NEVZALI JMĚNÍ.
TRICET ZA JEDEN PENÍZ VÁS ČÍTAJE, VESPASIANUS CÍSAŘ ZE ZEMĚ VYHNAL A TAKTO JSTE ROZSETI V SVĚTĚ. BEZ GROŠE PŘIŠLI JSTE K NÁM, BEZ GROŠE JDĚTE, KAM CHCETE!
VY ZE JSTE PŘIJALI KŘEST — AŤ BŮH JEST TOHO MI SVĚDKEM —
ŽE SE TO NIKOLI MÝM, NEŽ BOŽSKÝM PŘÍKAZEM STALO.
Že jste však opět upadli v židovství, ať biskup Kosmas hledí, co by v té věci měl učiniti."

Tak pravil jménem knížete, a oni hned vpadnuvše do domů vybíjeli je a pobrali poklady i z nářadí, co našli nejlepšího. Nezanechali jim nic leč zrní obilné, co by stačilo toliko na živobytí. Ó, co peněz toho dne bylo

cc] A3 zde uvedl pojednání o Děthartovi, opatu kláštera Sázavského. Viz dodatek III.

Cosmas's Bohemian Chronicle. Book Three, p. 147 (Svoboda, Prague, 1972)

✝ LVII

Téhož roku moc Krista Boha a moudrost Boží, řídící vše na světě svou vůlí, ráčila milostí svou vyrvati tuto zemičku z osidel satana a jeho syna Jakuba Apelly. Jeho usmolená pravice čeho se dotkne, poskvrní, a jeho dech, smrdutý jako baziliškův, usmrtí ty, jež ovane; o něm svědčí i velmi mnozí lidé pravdomluvní, že bylo častokrát viděti, jak mu po boku stojí a služby koná satan v lidské podobě. A tak ho svými lstmi strhl k takové smělosti, ba šílenosti, že onen ničemný zlosyn, povyšuje se nad svůj stav, zastával úřad místopána po knížeti; bylo to hrozné peklo pro lid křesťanský.
Tento člověk, stav se po křtu zase odpadlíkem, dal v noci rozbořiti oltář, vystavěný a posvěcený v jejich synagóze, a vzav svaté ostatky, neostýchal se hoditi je do svého záchodu. Kníže Vladislav, pln zpa Boha a horle horlivostí pro Krista, dal tohoto svatokrádce a zločince dne 22. července zatknouti a do těsného vězení zavříti. Ach, co mamonu nepravosti bylo z domu toho podvodníka pobráno a do pokladny knížecí uloženo! Mimo to Židé, jemu rovní v hříchu, složili knížeti, aby řečený kurvy syn nebyl sťat, tři tisíce hřiven stříbra a sto hřiven zlata; kníže pak z vnuknutí milosti Boží vykoupil křesťanské otroky ode všech Židů a zakázal, aby žádný křesťan u nich nesloužil. „Amen, amen," pravím; čím se kdy provinil, všecko tímto chvalitebným činem odčinil a jméno věčné si získal.
MARIE MAGDALENO, TY ZBOŽNÁ KRISTOVA SLUŽKO, TOBĚ VŽDY PŘINÁŠÍ POBOŽNÝ LID SVÉ SLÍBENÉ DARY za to, že o tvém svátku byl vyrván ďábelskému nepříteli.
Také téhož roku dne 11. srpna v jedenáctou hodinu denní bylo zatmění slunce a po něm přišel veliký mor na skot, brav a vepřový dobytek, mnoho včelstev pomřelo a nedostatek medu byl veliký. Obilí ozimé vyhynulo i jaré, jen prosa a hrachu se urodilo.
Téhož roku kníže Vladislav, muž přeslavný a ctihodný, slavil vánoce a Zjevení Páně [1125] ve vsi Zbečně. Potom, že byl nemocen, dal se převézti na hrad Vyšehrad a tam zůstal až do své smrti.

Cosmas's Bohemian Chronicle, p. 200

---

in his Czech Chronicle with regard to the year 1091: "Nowhere else can you grow rich better or elevate yourself more than in the outer bailey of Prague and in Vyšehradská Street. There are Jews there who abound in gold and silver, there are the wealthiest merchants of all nations there, there are the richest financiers there, there is a market-place there where your soldiers can gain an abundance of rich spoils". Cosmas expresses himself somewhat unfavourably about the Jews also in other places in his Chronicle. In 1098, when Prince Břetislav learned that the Jews were fleeing from Bohemia and taking their wealth with them he reproached them as follows: "Why are you also diminishing your treasures, gained for nothing? You did not bring any property from Jerusalem with you."

In 1096, at the time of the crusades, Prague's Jewish community in Vyšehradská Street became the victim of pogroms ... "On God's visitation some of those (note: i.e. Crusaders) passing through this country attacked the Jews and christened them against their will, killing those who resisted ..."

Two years later, in 1098, when the Jews decided to move out of Bohemia, "... the prince sent his valet along with several warriors to fleece them from head to foot." And Cosmas continues: "They left them nothing but a grain of corn, enough to keep them alive only. O, what a lot of money was taken from the miserable Jews that day, such wealth was not taken even from burned Troy to the Euboean coast."

From the few historical sources at our disposal we can presume that even though they originally arrived in Prague as free people of the most varied callings, the Jews were repeatedly exposed to crude humiliation and persecution.

An adequately expressive source lies in Cosmas's Chronicle, mentioned previously. With a considerable measure of hatred for the Jews Cosmas records one happening after another:

During the last few years of the reign of Vladislav I (c. 1124), when the Jews once again acquired great wealth, a christened Jew by the name of Jacob gained considerable power, perhaps also as the custodian of the prince's treasure. Although he was formally a Christian, he allegedly had the Christian altar in the synagogue secretly demolished and the holy relics contained in it desecrated. For this the prince had him thrown into jail and confiscated his property. For his redemption even the other Jews were called upon to pay a fine of three thousand pounds of silver and one hundred pound of gold. Furthermore, the prince ordered that from then on no Christian was to be employed in the services of Jews.

However, we have other sources from that time. According to the none too plausible chronicler Václav Hájek of Libočany (†1553) the Jews defended themselves so bravely when the fanatical sect of flagellants invaded Prague in 1150 that Prince Vladislav II permitted them to fortify the Jewish quarter and surround it with gates which were closed at night. Jewish butchers, who from then on were allowed to use the Czech lion in their emblem as a reward, showed particular bravery during the invasion.

In the 13th and 14th centuries the Jews were the servants-slaves of the royal chamber (servi camerae) and their fate was in the hands of the ruler, who applied his property rights to them. In view of their social and religious discrimination the Jews were originally excluded mainly from the production branch and the form of employment in which they were allowed to indulge was in the first place commercial activity – the lending of money and the realization of various financial transfers. For a long time this branch was a kind of Jewish "monopoly", because both the church and the nobility regarded it as undignified for Christians. ("The taking of interest on loaned money was regarded as usury and was forbidden by the church laws with the result that an agreement on interest was invalid. Only Jews were exempted..." V. V. Tomek: Dějepis města Prahy (The History of the Town of Prague), part II, p. 327).

Jews were often a sacrificial lamb which was obliged to take over the sins of others. If the ruler needed to turn the attention of the people away from unpopular measures he easily found guilt among those who were able neither to defend themselves nor rebel.

In different periods the legal status of Jews was modified on the basis of the most varied measures and privileges. Jews thus alternately enjoyed or did not enjoy the protection of the ruler. As a rule this protection depended on whether the ruler needed their money and assistance or not.

One of the first Jewish privileges known to us was granted by Soběslav II in the years 1174 to 1178.

Nearly one hundred years later, in 1254, Přemysl Otakar II (1253–1278) granted Jews a great privilege which, apart from other things, bestowed limited civil rights on them. On the basis of a number of measures their status and the attitude of the Christian population towards Jews were modified. The privilege even laid down that if a Christian killed a Jew the murderer was to be put to death and "if a Christian injures a Jew with a dry blow he shall give the king four mites of gold and the Jew four mites of silver and if he does not possess them he shall lose a hand". The same sentence was to be passed on a person who attacked a Jewish cemetery or Jewish school. (He who dissolutely threw something at a Jewish school was to pay a fine of two mites to a Jewish judge. He who took away a Jewish child (perhaps for education in the Christian faith against the will of its parents) was to receive the same punishment as a thief). As a measure against the widespread rumour that Jews used Christian blood the privilege laid down the following principle: "A Jew may be accused of washing in Christian blood or of drinking it only if the Christian accuser can produce three Christians and three Jews as proof." To this Otakar added: "if the Christian cannot produce proof he shall suffer what awaited the Jew, that is, death."

Přemysl II's privilege also contained a number of civil and legal regulations and principles concerning public law. The basic decree was that the supreme judge of Jews in disputes with Christians was the king, who in the case of less important cases transferred his authority to a special clerk bearing the rank of "judex judeos" – Jewish judge. These decrees did not concern disputes inside the Jewish community, disputes between Jews. In such cases the recognized, even if unofficially, arbitrator was the rabbi. The Jewish judge (magistrate), who held court in a Jewish school or synagogue, did not always have to be a Jew. The ranks of Jewish magistrates also included Christians. Sometimes one Jewish and one Christian magistrate jointly fulfilled their function. The Jewish judge-magistrate exercised his judgement perhaps in the case of disputes among Jews, while the Christian one judged disputes between a Jew and a Christian. Jews took oath by placing their hand on the Old Testament and in less serious cases they took oath at the door of their synagogue. (See also the chapter entitled "The Jewish Community"). The privilege was to specify the binding rules of a kind of statute of the Jews, the Jewish community and the mutual relation between it and the rest of the population. A paradox lay in the fact that these rules were most frequently broken by the rulers themselves. After the relatively liberal reigns of Přemysl Otakar I and Václav II (1278–1305) chroniclers recorded how in 1336 King John of Luxembourg (1310–1346) plundered the Prague ghetto, "had the school excavated and luckily found some thousand mites of precious metals." After that he had all the Jews in Prague and the kingdom as a whole caught and let them go only if they paid him large sums of money. Charles IV adopted a grandiose approach towards the Jewish population, but he succumbed to the pressure of the Church when he ordered Jews to wear a degrading tall hat in public. On the other hand, however, he allowed them to move (with the exception of those who lived in the Jewish Town) to newly founded Nové Město (the New Town). Only very few of them took advantage of this concession. Some of them built several houses in the vicinity of the "Jewish garden", the Jewish cemetery to which "the bodies of deceased from the whole country were taken."

From a certain document preserved from the first years of the reign of Charles IV it is clear that one of Prague's richest Jews was Lazar, son of Mann, from whom the sovereign often borrowed money. As a reward Lazar was freed in 1350 from many taxes for a period of two years and when he was to marry in 1351 all the guests and invited persons who wanted to attend the wedding received a special permit guaranteeing them a safe journey and the possibility of remaining in the town for fifteen days or more. It was just the house of this Jew by the name of Lazar that, after his death, Charles IV bestowed on the masters of Prague University as the seat of the first university college.

In 1393 Václav IV extended the old privilege of Přemysl Otakar II of 1254 and in 1410 issued a special confirmation in respect of the Jewish cemetery in the New Town, including the houses adjoining it.

If we seek Jewish sources of the Early Middle Ages we shall find them in the work of the rabbi Isaac ben Moses (Moshe), who was born in Prague about 1180 and also worked in the town for some time. His Hebrew work OR ZARUA (Sown Light), a commentary to the Talmudistic rituals, not only reflects the mentality of the Jewish population, but also contains certain practical hints and life advice.

* * *

The Vyšehrad Jewish community most likely ceased to exist after the pogroms of 1096. After the great fire in the Little Quarter in 1142 the local synagogue was destroyed and the Jewish settlement of the Little Quarter patently became extinct. The Jews deserted the outer bailey and began to concentrate on the right bank of the River Vltava. This was at the time when the whole of the right bank of the river and its numerous scattered settlement wholes acquired the character of a settlement of the town type, the time when international trade also began to be concentrated here. The nearness of important trade routes, the ford later replaced with stone Judith's Bridge over the river, merchants' stone houses, at least thirty church buildings, the presence of foreign and home merchants and craftsmen, the transfer of the community of German merchants from the Poříčí Church of St. Peter nearer to the centre, to the market-place, the locality of Havelské město (Gall's Town) – all these factors were responsible for the Jews moving here from the near and far environs. As has already been said, the first to settle here – round the synagogue called the Old Shul – were Jews who came from the east. Another Jewish district sprang up in the environs of the present Staronová (Old-New) Synagogue where the Jews who came to Prague from the west set up their homes. Not only their special economic function and their own system of autonomy, but especially their religion and forced isolation from the Christian population, outwardly manifested also by the fact that Jews had to wear a special mark (from the 16th century a yellow circle and previously, during the reign of Charles IV, a tall hat) were the reasons why they did not merge with their surroundings, but formed a kind of separate town in the town – a ghetto.

At first the territory as a whole was called V Židech (inter Judeos), while the northern part was known as V Podžidí (in Subjudaea). As said previously, it was divided into two parts. In his Dějepis města Prahy (History of the Town of Prague) Václav Vladivoj Tomek writes: It is not wholly incredible that in ancient times, perhaps at Cosmas's time, before the first persecution of the Jews by the Crusaders passing through Prague (1096) which he described, the two parts were mutually connected." It is most likely that this intimation concerns Vyšehrad. The oldest documented Jewish settlement was thus concentrated round the so-called Old Shul, round the territory which was later separated by Christian houses from the ghetto proper and formed a separate Jewish enclave.

The territory in question can be precisely located in the vicinity of the Church of the Holy Spirit and the oldest synagogue – the Old Shul – on the site of the Spanish Synagogue of the present.

The heart and centre of the ghetto proper was the Old-New Synagogue and the district which can very roughly be said to be demarcated by the street called Židovská (Široká or also Josefská) and the greater part of Zlatá ulička (Golden Lane), the two short and narrow little streets running to the butchers' shops and the Old-New Synagogue (also called the Big Jewish School), from here to Rabínská Street and through three more little streets to the Old Jewish Cemetery.

The whole area of the ghetto was separated from the Christian streets by gates or gate-houses (porta Judaeorum) for the protection of the Jews. The number of these gates changed from six to seven. At the time of Charles IV specific mention was made of six, located as follows:

1. at the end of the main Jewish street near St. Valentine's, opposite the courtyard where the house of the Provost of Chotěšov stood,
2. by the entrance to the Jewish Golden Lane
3. on the corner of the short street running from the Maisel Synagogue to Široká Street
4. at the entrance to Široká Street from the east side, opposite the Church of the Holy Spirit,
5. in the middle of Rabínská Street,
6. near Rabínská Street by the side street to the so-called Clamps.

The last two gates were popularly referred to as being "near the brothel". Jews were forbidden to buy houses beyond the gates, but, on the contrary, Christians could acquire houses inside the ghetto on the basis of a special permit.

V. V. Tomek provides us with the following information about some of the most interesting Jewish houses:

Next to the gate behind St. Nicholas's stood the house of Lazar (Lazar the Jew), which in 1366 Charles IV presented to Prague University or to Charles College, which had its seat here until it was moved to Rotlev's House in the street Nové tržiště.

Mention is made of a Jewish garden – (Hortus Judaeorum) – in the vicinity of this house and this is particularly interesting due to the fact that there were no gardens in the Jewish Town. The Old Cemetery was in fact the only one.

In view of the fact that the king regarded the Jewish houses in the ghetto as his property, he often did what he liked with them. For example, in 1404 he bestowed house No. 87 in the neighbourhood of the Maisl Synagogue, which belonged to the Jew Pinkas (of the Pinkas family, founders of the Pinkas Synagogue?), on his scribe – illuminator Frán. Similarly, house No. 124, which belonged to the Jew Jonas, became the property of a nobleman by the name of Smil of Sulevice. And so we could continue and mention other houses which the king presented to persons who enjoyed his favour: "the house of Michal the Jew (No. 230) was gained as a gift by the royal secretary Jan of Smržov."

The original Jewish settlement of the Old Town, initially called V Židech (In the Jews) – only from the 16th century did it use the name geto nuovo, ghetto, after the Italian, Venetian model – was, apart from the Old-New Synagogue and present-day Široká (formerly Židovská) Street, only a kind of mixture of small houses, extensions and arcades without numbers and names. The medieval Gothic Jewish community called "V Židech" formed only one half of the later Jewish Town. Proof of what the later Jewish Town of Prague looked like – in the context of the Old Town – lies in the oldest preserved plan of Prague drawn about the year 1640, probably by Matouš Unger. (The property right pertaining to the individual homesteads or houses was exceptionally complicated. Later, in the 18th and 19th centuries, the houses standing here were divided, so that one family owned only a part of a given house, while another had possession of the staircase, cellar or other part of the house.)

The main street was Josefovská Street, whose environs were the scene of a rich and busy commercial life and in time a small square came into being round the Old-New Synagogue.

Apart from the principal, Old-New Synagogue the Late Gothic period provided Prague's ghetto with several more public buildings. In the late 15th century the private synagogue of the Horowitz family originated in the vicinity of St. Valentine's Church. Later Aaron Meshulam Horowitz extended it on the northern and western sides. Another modest synagogue, the so-called New Jewish School, stood in Rabínská Street, but no detailed reports about its existence are available.

$$* \quad * \quad *$$

In the ghetto the Jews, whose religion, way of life and especially economic status, which according to then contemporary morals was socially considered to be undignified, found themselves in a state of isolation. The abusive mark which distinguished them from the rest of the population at first sight was intended to draw attention to their human and work inferiority.

Where and when should we seek the source of the enmity shown towards the Jews? In the ancient belief that the Jews were responsible for the death of the Lord Jesus Christ, in the later wide spreading of baiting pamphlets containing the most shameful statements about the contents of Jewish religious writings, or simply in economic, social or political reasons?

The official standpoint of the Church against the Jews, which best expresses the medieval approach to the "Jewish question, or the problems connected with Jews in the Czech Lands", was stated by the Prague synod convened in 1349 by Archbishop Arnošt of Pardubice. The framework of our brief historical mosaic makes it impossible to deal in greater detail with the arguments of the synod, which were based on the libel and prejudices of the time and the medieval anti-Jewish attitude towards and hatred for the Jews as the nation responsible for the death of the Saviour. The synod adopted a number of anti-Jewish measures which included one preventing Christian women from serving in Jewish families as wet nurses and midwives, while others forbade free movement on Good Friday, the holding of public offices and the building of new synagogues (those already in existence could only be modified, but not beautified or enlarged). The Jews had to differ from Christians also outwardly by wearing tall hats, Jewesses being obliged to cover their head and allow one lock of hair to hang over their forehead.

On the other hand, the synod (in 1252) confirmed the decree of Pope Innocent IV concerning the Jews according to which they were not to be forced to

neficia (privatio beneficii) i dle okolností wypowědění z dioécezí. Mladší duchowní we službě kostela Pražského, zejména
vikáři kanowníků a žáci kůrní, být měli i swěcení za jahny,
ne wšak na kněžstwí, směli býti za wýtržnosti při službách
božích trestáni také třeba metlau od kantora.

Klatbau rozumělo se wyobcowání z církwe, netoliko potud,
že postiženému jí zbraňowal se wstup do kostela a přijímání
swátostí, nýbrž zakazowalo se wšem wěřícím wšeliké s ním
obcowání, poskytowání jemu jídla neb pití neb jiné lidské pomoci, když pak we klatbě zemřel, tím samým zbawen byl křesťanského pohřbu. Wyhlášení klatby arcibiskupem wyrčené
ukládalo se obyčejně farářům míst, we kterých se ten zdržowal, a stáwalo se w kostele čtením rozkazu u welkého oltáře
nebo s kazatelnice při zwonění zwonů a při rozswícených swíčkách, kteréž kněz po přečtení klatby wzal a zhasil i powrhnul na zem. Setrwal-li odsauzený w klatbě do určité lhůty,
nehledaje propuštění, přikročilo se k stížení klatby (aggravatio)
wyhlášením *interdiktu*, to jest stawení služeb božích w místě,
kde se zdržowal, čímž pak obywatelstwo, zejména představení
obce neb jiné swětské wrchnosti nuceni byli, kletého wypuditi z místa, aby se toho sprostili.

Klatba mohla se jistým spůsobem wztahowati také na
Židy. Když se totiž některý z nich prowinil něčím, co se týkalo práw církwe, zakázal arcibiskup křesťanům wšeliké obchody neb jiné obcowání s ním, až se Žid podrobil wýroku
saudu duchowního. Tak se stalo w neznámém roce někdy
w prwních časích arcibiskupa Jana z Jenšteina Židu Pražskému Dawidowi z neznámé příčiny; i musil se poddati. [8]) Krom
takowého pokutowání bylo křesťanům zacházení se Židy powšechně dowoleno. Toliko zakazowalo se statuty arcibiskupa
Arnošta, aby nesměli Židé najímati křesťanek za kojné, čehož
příčinau byly jisté ohawné zwyklosti židowské; [9]) k zachránění
pak, aby newědomky Židé nesmilnili s křesťankami neb kře

---

[8]) *Form. Joh. Przimdæ* fol. 99.

[9]) Accepimus, quod Judæi Christianas puerorum suorum nutrices .. cum illas recipere corpus et sanguinem Jesu Christi contingit, per triduum,

sťané se Židowkami, bylo týmiž statuty nařízeno, aby Židé zacho-
wáwali rozdíl od křesťanů w oděwu, který býwal w obyčeji již
we starším čase, totiž Židé aby nosili zwláštní široké klobauky,
Židowky pak jakausi wywýšeninu wlasů čauhající wen přes
čelo pod záwojem neb pod jiným přikrytím hlawy. Také bylo
u welký pátek zakázáno Židům wůbec weřejně se ukazowati
pro zamezení ausměšků, kterých si jindy dowolowali; měliť
w ten den celý zawírati dwéře a okna domů swých.

Wšeliké powinnosti a práwa úřadu swého wykonáwal arcibiskup dle příležitosti swé buď sám buď prostředkem duchowních úředníků swých, o kterých jsme wětším dílem již učinili
zmínku na rozličných místech jiných. Ti se sauborem nazý-
wali jeho *konsistoři*. Nejpřednější z nich byli official a generalní vikářowé arcibiskupstwí. K úřadu *officiala* náleželo sauzení práwních pří jak mezi duchowními o jmění neb o bene-
ficia, tak také mezi duchowními a laiky, pokud takowé pří-
slušely k saudu duchownímu, rowněž pří we wěcech manžel-
stwí. *Generalní vikářowé* sprawowali wěci nesporné, jakož
stwrzowání k beneficiím, zřizowání nowých beneficií neb jiných
pobožných nadání, poněwadž k tomu bylo potřeba swolení
arcibiskupowa, udělowali dispensí w rozličných potřebách osob
duchowních i swětských, a konali sprawedliwost, pokud se týkalo zamezowání neb trestání win. W časích owšem, když official
arcibiskupůw byl zároweň také jedním z generalných vikářů,
splýwaly obadwa úřady poněkud dohromady. Wedlé úřadů
těchto starodáwných zřídil arcibiskup Arnošt hned někdy
w prwních létech spráwy swé úřad zwláštní tak zwaného *kor-
rektora* (corrector cleri), na nějž wzneseno jest sauzení a ká-
rání duchowních pro přestupky proti kázni. [10]) Prwní w úřadě
tom připomíná se bratr Albert kanowník řeholný, neznámo
z kterého kláštera, od roku 1357. Po něm následowali Přibi-
slaw arcijahen Horšowský (1363), který byl později jedním

---

antequam eos lactent, lac effundere faciunt in latrinam, alia insuper
contra fidem catholicam detestabilia et inaudita committunt. *Stat. Arne-
sti* rúbr. 66.

[10]) *Series episcop.* 440.

1388 brák (27 Dub.). Stáleji však přebýwal i toho času w Praze, kdež se nalezal u něho opět bratr jeho Sigmund zároweň s markrabím Joštem a zawřeli oba smlauwu s králem o spolek proti Baworům (17 Dub.).

Odboj Markwarta z Wartenberka byl teprw w letě toho roku přemožen dobytím jeho hradů a zajetím jeho samého. W Němcích však wedlo se králi Wácslawowi proti mysli. Města říšská, jichž se ujímal, utrpěla od knížat porážku w bitwě u Döffinka (24 Srp.), což krále uwedlo w takowau rozmrzelost, že se zanášel některau chwíli se zámyslem, odříci se Římského králowstwí. Odebraw se w měsíci Čerwnu opět z Prahy na Křiwoklát, zůstal tam celý ostatní čas až do konce toho roku, a oddal se we zlém rozmaru swém nejspíš docela zase rozkoši lowecké.

Za jeho nepřítomnosti byl w Praze legat papežský, kardinal Filipp z Alençona, o jehož jednání však nic jiného newíme, nežli že dal králi powolení k žádosti jeho, aby směl s dwořany swými w dni postní požíwati krmí z mléka a z wajec (27 Srp.).

1389   Teprw w měsíci Dubnu roku 1389 opustil král Wácslaw swá tehdejší obyčejná sídla, a odebral se do Cheba, kdež položen byl sněm říšský k účelu obnowení míru w Němcích. Král zůstal tam přes welkonoce. Tu se za jeho nepřítomnosti w Praze stala příhoda strašliwá z podnětů náboženských. Poněwadž tehdejší bydliště *Židů Pražských* na Starém městě skoro na wšech stranách byla křesťanskými domy obklopena a s nimi bezpostředně se dotýkala, nemohlo jináč býti, nežli že kněží z okolních far, zejména od sw. Walentina a od sw. Kříže wětšího, musili někdy se swátostí k nemocným jíti okolo samých domů židowských. Tu se stáwalo, že jim Židé činili na cestě wšelijaké obtíže neboli příkoří. [19]) Tak se přihodilo také jednoho dne odpoledně práwě w týden před welkonoci, že když šel kněz okolo s tělem božím, Židé sběhli se a po-

---

[19]) Že takowých případů bylo wíce, wychází ze slow Beneše minority (u Dobnera IV. 63), ktcrý prawí: quia sucerdotes corpus domini nostri portantes ad infirmos impediverunt.

křikowali naň, rauhali se Kristu a prawíce: kamenujme toho, 1389
jenž se wydáwal za syna božího, jali se házeti kamením na
kněze, až mu swátost wyrazili z rukau. Přirozeně strhlo se
z toho welké pohoršení w lidu a w duchowenstwu. Winníci
byli sice hned zatčeni, aby se nad nimi wykonal trest, jehož
zasluhowali. Ale na tom nebylo dosti. W neděli welkonoční
(18 Dub.) jali se duchowní na kázaních mluwiti o tom a po-
puzowati lid ku pomstě. Jestli prý nepomstíte pohanění, které
se stalo našemu pánu Ježíši, budete musiti wšichni snášeti
hanbu a potupu, prwé než jeden rok mine. Tu se začal ještě
téhož dne lid sbíhati na rozličných místech, ozbrojen kopími,
oštěpy, šípy a kamením. Konšelé snažili se lid wšemožně ukro-
titi, ujišťujíce, že budau wýtržní Židé náležitě ztrestáni. Ale
lidé si nedali říci, až jistý Ješek Čtyrhraný zwolal: Raději ať
wšichni Židé umrau, než aby křesťané zhynuli. Byla již prwní
hodina wečerní.[20]) K tomu slowu zdwihl se lid, a dawem
hrnuli se do ulic židowských, zapálili domy, jali se wražditi
Židy napořád, a kteří z nich utíkali z domů hořících, ty zase
honili zpět do ohně. Tak zahynulo Židů dílem w ohni dílem
násilným usmrcením přes tři tisíce. Jen některý počet žen
a dětí bylo přineseno do radnic, a tam jsau ihned pokřtěny,
aby jim lid rozwzteklený spíše odpustil.

Král Wácslaw obdržel w Chebě zpráwu o wýtržnosti Židů
proti knězi nesaucímu swátost patrně dříw než o strašliwém
wraždění, kterým byla opowážliwost jejich pomstěna, a uza-
wřel, wykonati za to nad nimi pokutu citelnau. Neb již na-
zejtří po ukrutné příhodě w Praze (19 Dub.) wydal z jeho
rozkazu podkomoří králowský Huler, tehdáž na Křiwokláté
přebýwající, nařízení přísné ke wšem purkmistrům, rychtářům
a konšelům měst králowských, aby wšecky Židy we městech
swých zjímali a u wězení chowali, jmění pak jejich mowité
i nemowité zabawili.[21]) Po pohromě, která na Židy přišla,
učiněno jest opatření, aby wšecko zlato a stříbro, které při-
tom lidé w domích židowských pobrali, odwedeno bylo na

[20]) *Breve Chronicon Lips.* (ap. Höfler 7.)
[21]) Palackého *Formelb.* II. 150.

22*

submit to a christening ceremony, not to be punished without a proper trial and not to be disturbed during their divine services. Furthermore, their cemeteries were not to be desecrated. The official standpoint of the Church was strongly oriented against the Jews and afforded priests the possibility of free interpretation. Indeed, it encouraged open hatred and attacks, which were not long in forthcoming.

The history of the Jews is one of pogroms and horrifying methods intended to draw attention away from other real problems. After the pogrom of 1096, when, on their way to the Holy Land, the participants in the first crusade also plundered other ghettos and when they murdered Prague Jews as well, another pogrom took place in Prague's ghetto during Easter of 1389. The excuse for the bloody attack against the Jews lay in an incident in the ghetto according to which a Christian priest was alleged to have been mocked by young Jews, who perhaps even threw stones at him, while he was walking through the Jewish Town. The fanatic crowd attacked the gate of the Jewish Town and the result was burned Jewish houses and three thousand dead Jews. Even though King Václav IV (1378–1419) was not present in Prague on the day of the pogrom and, after his return, tried to lessen the consequences of the pogrom by imposing a high fine on the Old Town of Prague in order to compensate for the damage done, he was unable to prevent the sad thing that usually followed pogroms. The Jewish children who survived their killed parents were placed in Christian families, which immediately had them christened. The guilty persons were called upon to hand over all the things, property and money stolen in the ghetto to the Town Hall. This property was not returned to its original owners, but fell into the possession of the king.

A relatively large number of reports about the Prague pogrom which took place at Easter in 1389 has been preserved. We can read about its course and tragic consequences in the Hebrew elegy of the scholar Avigdor Kara who died in 1439, and in the chronicle ZEMACH DAVID, written by the astronomer and historian David Gans (died in 1613). A Christian source about the pogrom lies in the period Latin publication Passio Judaeorum Pragensium (The Passion of the Jews of Prague). Mentions of the pogrom are also contained in the work of Aeneas Silvius Piccolomini (later Pope Pius II, died in 1464) Historia Bohemica and in The Czech Chronicle of Václav Hájek of Libočany (died in 1553).

The forced isolation of the Jews naturally had an influence on the formation of the Jewish mentality, which sensitively reacted to even the smallest signs of persecution and antisemitism. The Jews acquired a clear-cut complex which kept them on the defensive and aroused their caution and wariness against everything that arrived from outside their ranks. Their outer physical supremacy evoked a strong, mutual feeling of solidarity inside the ghetto as well as an endeavour to equalize the situation by increasing spiritual capacities. The main source of knowledge for the Jews was the Torah and its commentaries in the Talmud.

It is said that the Jews are a nation of books. They educated themselves

The Old Jewish Cemetery in Prague, the tombstone of Avigdor Kara, 1439 (modern replica of the oldest tombstone of the cemetery; original in the Jewish Museum)

even in the unfavourable conditions of the ghetto, because the gaining of knowledge and study of the Torah and Talmud ranked among the duties of every Jew. From their earliest childhood children were taught their letters, to meditate and to fulfil the strict Jewish religious rules. Although the Jews lived in an unimaginable state of want in the ghetto, they abounded in nobility of the spirit and their culture and thirst for knowledge often sufficed to overcome the feeling of injustice and fear in which they lived continuously. When studying the life customs of the Jews one gets the impression that they engaged in constant research and deliberation on religious matters. Abstract thinking led them from reality to another, better world.

The synagogue was the centre of spiritual, intellectual and all other spheres of life in the ghetto and the rabbi was the central figure. Even according to the words of Prague's present rabbi, "he is not a priest, a mediator between Man and God. His duties are many – he is a teacher, he has certain legal authority, he is the guarantor of religious matters, preaches sermons and also functions as a counsellor in family matters. His tasks also include the teaching of children."

In view of his profound education and culture and his knowledge of God's and human laws the rabbi always headed the Jewish community as its spiritual leader. Not in vain did people speak of the wisdom of a rabbi, wisdom which culminated in the life and history of Prague's ghetto in the figure of the miraculous rabbi Judah Loew ben Bezalel.

And so the synagogue was not only the scene of religious happenings, but also a centre where everyone obtained knowledge, education and practical advice necessary for life. Simple daily matters were dealt with just as thoroughly in synagogues as the eternal learned disputations on religion, philosophy and natural history were led.

The history of the culture of Prague's Jewish Town reaches back to the 12th and 13th centuries and it is symbolized by the names of the first scholars, the rabbis Isaac ben Mordecai, Eliezer ben Isaac and Isaac ben Jakob ha-Lavan.They wrote short texts in Hebrew and Aramaic as well as supplements and commentaries to the Talmud and because such commentaries are called "tosafot" in Hebrew, the whole group of the first scholars of the Prague ghetto are spoken of as the school of Prague "tosafists". Perhaps they can be regarded as the beginning of the tradition which began to manifest itself more strikingly in the mid-14th and the early 15th century in the teaching of Avigdor Kara and Yom Tov Lipmann Mülhausen. The religious poet, rabbi and physician and member of the rabbinical court in one, the scholar Avigdor Kara, died in Prague in 1439. He is buried in the Old Jewish Cemetery and his tombstone is the oldest preserved tombstone there. The inscription on it says that "he was a man who understood sweet songs, taught the Torah to many and to individuals and was well-versed in learning, in all books of wisdom and books of literature."

Avigdor Kara's work has remained vital to the present and his elegy (seliha) describing the bloody pogrom of 1389 is still read in the Old-New Synagogue every year during the Day of Reconciliation (Yom Kipur) service. It is

most likely that Avigdor Kara experienced the Prague pogrom as a child and witnessed the martyr's death of his father, Rabbi Jitshak Kara. Through its artistic and poetic form this elegy affords shocking testimony to the pogrom:
"Many were killed, they cannot be named,
youths and maidens, old men and babies.
You, Lord of all souls, do not need to be reminded of them,
you will judge all, you will investigate everything.
. . . . .
They even demolished the cemetery, the place of eternal freedom where the bones of my illustratious ancestors lie at rest.
They uncovered these, my treasures, they destroyed tombstones in anger to humilitate my pride.
How long still, o Lord, has there not yet been enough?!

✳ ✳ ✳

In the latter half of the 14th century Rabbi Yom Tov Lipmann Mülhausen, a man of learning who also probably experienced the bloody pogrom, lived and worked in Prague. However, he did not lose his life during the terrible event and he is not even buried in Prague. He concerned himself with religious, philosophical and cabbalistic matters and in his work "SEFER NIC-CACHON" (The Book of Victory) he defends Judaism and polemizes with the Christian evaluation and interpretation of the Torah.

✳ ✳ ✳

The Hussite and post-Hussite periods were times when the problems of the Jewish Town made way for social, political and religous struggles in which the whole country swayed. Only the voice of the Hussite preacher Jakoubek of Stříbro (died in 1429), calling at least for partial economic equality of the Jews, remained unique. The reasons why he defended the Jews did not spring from a special sympathy for them. In fact, quite the contrary was the case. In his Latin tract De usura – Jakoubek of Stříbro argued that the main cause of the hatred of the Christians for the Jews lay in the fact that the Jews did not work with sweat on their brows in the fields like the Christians and neither did they breed cattle or work in trade or the crafts. He wrote that the only way to prevent the hatred of the Christians for the Jews was to allow the latter to work in the same way as the Christians. Chroniclers record the anti-Jewish unrest which broke out after the execution of Jan Želivský in 1422, again in 1448 during the conquering of Prague by Jiří of Poděbrady and yet again in 1483.
The attitude of the Hussite movement towards the Jews can be expressed by means of the words of the historian Dr. Jaroslav Prokeš to the effect that "from the religious standpoint the Hussite movement had no reason to change anything in the attitude which Catholicism adopted towards the Jewish faith." The position of the Jews in the Hussite period can be characterized

The oldest view of Prague, anonymous, 1493

as the position of a group not involved in the conflict, because in its spirit the Jewish faith was as equally remote from Catholicism as it was from the Hussite movement." The reason why the Jews experienced a time of relative calm during the Hussite period can be seen in the fact that Jewish sympathies were not on the side of the Catholics either during the Hussite wars as well as in the fact that during the Hussite storms the Old Town community took upon itself the political and legal authority of the royal Jewish magistrate and also the right to collect Jewish taxes. And these Jewish taxes were indisputably also a reason why the position of the Jews remained unshaken in Hussite Prague. Even the high Jewish interest rate (one groschen per sixty groschens a week) remained unchanged, i.e. on its pre-Hussite level.

The old Jewish settlement – the Jewish Town – likewise remained more or less unchanged. During the anti-Jewish manifestations in 1422 and 1448 it was confirmed that the gates separating Jewish houses from Christian ones were an inadequate means of defence.

The two centres (the Old School opposite the Church of the Holy Spirit and the Old-New Synagogue) were increased in number by the addition of a private synagogue, later called the Pinkas Synagogue, standing near St. Valentine's Church. In the middle of the Hussite wars the Jewish property was

24

increased by the addition of the garden Christian land lying to the west of the Jewish houses. Its area was gradually occupied by the new Jewish cemetery intended to replace the old cemetery, the New Town "Jewish garden".

* * *

In 1497 the Jews also attended ("with broken voices they allegedly sang beautifully") the solemn entry of King Vladislav Jagiello into Prague. In fact a Jewish officer even headed the procession on horseback.

In 1501, at the Diet, the king took the Jews under his protection, but for this they were obliged to pay 3,000 groschens of silver a year.

It seems that the king and the burghers had enough problems of their own (the country was considerably desolated by the Hussite wars and conflicts), but the Jews did not stand aside even then. In essence it was the question of a dispute between the ruler, the nobility and the burghers as to whom they should pay. A paradoxical situation arose according to which the king "competed" against the nobility and the burghers for the favour of the Jews. In 1502 representatives of the Old Town burghers requested the councillors to secure the banishment of the Jews. However, the councillors tried to bring about just the opposite. They wanted the Jews in the ghetto to become "burgher Jews" in order that they might be at least partly removed from the king's authority. The disputes ended in a compromise. As long as the Jews paid everyone they were left in peace and so in 1510 the king once again confirmed the old privileges of the Jews. In 1511 the Jews received special praise for their assistance in quenching a great fire.

The new king Ludwig Jagiello (1516–1526) placed great hopes in the Jews and when he arrived in Prague in 1522 six hundred Jews, headed by the rabbi and council representatives, were on the spot to welcome him. A similar welcome was accorded to Ferdinand I (1526–1565) of the Hapsburg dynasty. "Jews numbering about 300 persons in magnificent garments with priests at their head, with singers who sang in Hebrew in their own special way. Carrying a beautiful standard and baldachin on which there was hung a panel containing God's commandments in beautiful writing they tried to get the king under the baldachin and to carry him on high, but the king refused to agree to this and merely assented to their plea that he confirm their faith and order according to the Old Testament." (V. V. Tomek, part XI, p. 37). Ferdinand's promises were not of a long duration. In 1541 the Czech Diet adopted a resolution (with the substantial assistance of the king) concerning the expelling of all Jews from Prague. Only fifteen families were supposed to remain in the ghetto. Two years later, in 1543, a mass exodus occurred (the gratest number made their way to Poland) with the exception of the richer Jews who purchased for money and held the right to remain in Prague.

The inadequate state of the royal revenues was clearly the reason why the question of increasing the number of Jews who could remain in Prague after 1543 was considered (their number was officially increased to thirty), but also

Ferdynand z Božij Milosti / Rzijmsk...
španij / Arcy Knijže Rakauské / a tMargkrabě tMorawské / Lucemburské a S...
Panuom / Rytijruom / Wládykám a tMestuom / y ginym wšem Obywateluon...
žetstwij Slézského / a tMargkrabstwij Hornijch y Dolnijch Lužic / tMilost na...
denkaždy z wás / o tom dobřau wědomost má / yak časuow předešlých na Sn...
ské / na Hradě Pražském držán byl / geden Artykul námi a wšemi Stawy Kr...
z yakých znamenitých a mnohých tehdáž vznalých přijčyn z tohoto Králows...
céni gsau se byli z tohoto Králowstwij giž y wystěhowali. Wšak na weliké / p...
se chtěgij wšeliyak dobře a chwalucbně chowati. Ráčili gsme ge do wůle naš...
šoš / kdyžbychom gim Rok napřed wěděti dáti ráčili / aby byli powinni podle p...
skrze tayž Národ židowský wšeliyaké nešlechetnosti / w špežých / w Pagamen...
paušstěgú / a mnohými Lichwami a půgčkami / pod rozličnými obyčegi / kteréž y...
toho podlé gegich předešslé přijpowědi a podwolenij / ničehož newmenšsugú / ...
ponijžené proseni / abychom ge z tohoto Králowstwij zase wypowěděti ráčili.
do wšeho délegij w Králowstwij našem Cžeském trpěti / Ráčili gsme gim po...
Statky swými / z tohoto Králowstwij / y z Zemij k němu přijslušsegijcych k od...
ssy Králowskau / aby se tak stalo / držeti ráčijme / Wšak předkem poněwádž tijž
Cžeského nenálo powinowati gsau / poraučeti ráčijme / Aby gedni druhým / co...
Byli. A kdyžby tijž Židé za bodomožénij dluhůw swých kteréhožkoli Obywatel...
dluhuow powinni byli / aby jez před wygitijm Roku ohoto zaplatili / a wijcegi...
dany / mezy sebau aby neciinili. Pakliby yaké dluhy / Bud Křestiané židuom /...
dau powinni platiti / než cožby dluhuow starých bylo / a na Roky se platiti mag...
Druhé / yakož gmenowitij Židé z Králowstwij Cžeského / wijc než gedna...
tMargkrabstwij tMorawského / Knijžetstwij Slézzkých / a tMargkrabstwij H...
lowském se stěchowati Budau / abyste wšyckni / y gedenkaždy z wás / sami na ně...
obyčegen gim neciinili / ani komu koli ciiniti dopaussteli / Uybrž ge pruowoden...
odebrati mohli / ssedrowali / A to pod vwarowánijm skuteéného trestánij /...
nij a Glaythu našemu dopuštil / a gim yakaužkoli překážku ciinil / nes ci...
nij a Glaythu našeho / přikročiti. Protož wědauce o takowém porucé...
tMeste našem Wijdni / w Pátek po Swatém Bartholoměgi. Létt...

Ferdinand

Decree of Ferdinand I of August 27, 1557, on the eviction of the Jews from Bohemia.

...erſký/ Cžeſký ꝛc/ Král: Jnffant w Hy-
...ꝛe/ a Luʒické Margkrabě ꝛc. Uroʒeným/Statečným/Slowútným/Opatrným/
...Stawuo̅ Králowſtwij naſſeho Cžeſkého/Margkrabſtwij Morawſkého/ Knij-
...eꝛſtau/a wſſecko dobré wʒkaʒugem. Wěrnij milij/nepochybugem že wſſyckni y ge-
...m/kteřýž w Králowſtwij naſſem Cžeſkém péi přijtomnoſti Oſoby naſſý Králow-
...ohoto/co ſe Zidůw wypowědènij ʒ Králowſtwij toho dotýče/ſwolen a ʒawřijn gè/
...ypowědënij byli/ podle kteréhožto Sněmownijho ʒuoſtánij/na wětſſým dijle wſſy-
...laĉtiwé proʒby gegich/y také přijmluwy/kteréž gſau ſe ʒa ně dály/připowijdagijce že
...počtu a čaſu ſem do Králowſtwij ʒaſe přigijti/a gijm Glayth náſs na takowý ſpů-
...Sněmownijho ʒuoſtánij/ʒ Králowſtwij Cžeſkého ſe wyſchowati dáti/y ʒnagijc že
...ý ſtřijhánij/ſſalſſe y ginaké proti Křeſtianuom ſwau liſtiwoſtij prowoʒugijc/a ſe do-
...mègij/ſtěʒugij. Y ač gſau mnohokrát pro to na Hrdlijch y ginak treſtáni byli/ wſſak
...dále wʒdy wijce přiwětſſugij/Tak že gſme mnohokrát od Poddaných naſſých/ʒa to
...my ʒ tèch napředpſaných y giných ſluſſných a hodných přijčyn/ tehož Národu Ži-
...Glaythu od nás gim daného / Rok napřed wèdèti dáti/ aby ſe wſſyckni Oſobami y
...gim wèdèti daného w plném Roce pokad ʒběhlého/wyſchowali/nad čijmž ruku na-
...ſto Králowſtwij/nemálo dluhů magij/y také ʒaſe oni Obywateluom Králowſtwij
...edliwě dlužni a powinni gſau/konečně pred wygitijm Roku tohoto ʒaplatili/a práwi
...llowſtwij žádali/aby gim dopomoʒno bylo/a ʒaſe komužby tijž Židé ſprawedliwých
...ʒidé Křeſtianuom/a Křeſtiané Židuom přes ten ſwrchu pſaný Rok/napřed wèdèti
...Křeſtianuom přes wygitij toho Roku meʒy ſebau ʒdělali/Tehdy gedni druhým nebu-
...tirom aby gedni druhým platiti powinni byli/ʒuoſtawuge.
...Solnicy ſe ſchowati budau/Proležž weſſem Obywateluom Králowſtwij Cžeſkého/
...odlnijch Luʒic/přijſně přikaʒowa... ...áčime/poněwadž geſſtě w Glaythu naſſem Krá-
...nižádné ſſkody a překážky w tom win ʒ Zemij ſchowánij/pod žádným wymyſleným
...aby ſe pokogně a beʒpečně/ʒ Králowſtwij tohoto/a ʒ Zemij k němu přijſluſſegijcých/
...i naſſý Králowſké. Neb geſtližeby k kdožkoli toho/proti takowému giſtěnu poruče-
...u každému/táčilibychom ſkutečným treſtánijm/yakož přeſtupiteli/a ruſſyteli poruče-
... /nepochybugem že ſe gedenkaždý ʒwás poſluſſně a poddaně ʒachowá.   Dán w
...wij naſſých/Ržijmſkého XXVIIͦ. Jginých XXXIͦ.

considered was the revoking of the original decision to expel the Jews from Bohemia. It is alleged that the intervention of Queen Anne and Sigismund, the king of Poland, also aided the Jews.

Moreover, in order to preserve life in the ghetto "two teachers, three school caretakers, four night watchmen, one butcher and another for the preparation of kosher meat, one grave-digger and two males and two females to attend the sick" were allowed to remain. In view of the fact that the residing of Jews in Prague and the issuing of special privileges – rights – meant financial gains primarily for the king, the councillors of the Old Town complained that Jews were appearing in Prague again and also that they could not be distinguished in any way from the rest of the population. In 1551 (17 November) the king issued a decree concerning the obligatory marking of Jews in Prague and Bohemia: Jews had to wear a round piece of yellow cloth at chest height on the left side of their top garment.

Later the Jews were even obliged to attend a Jesuit sermon in the Church of the Holy Saviour and to send their children to Roman Catholic schools.

If someone encountered a Jew who was not wearing the obligatory piece of yellow cloth he was given one half of what the Jew concerned had on him. A Jew who walked outside the limits of the ghetto without a cloak and hood had to pay a fine of two groschens.

When the Jews began to return to Prague again without permission to do so the Archduke Ferdinand, then governor of Bohemia, succumbed to the pressure of the Old Town councillors and persuaded King Ferdinand I to have them expelled again (1557) from all the lands of the Czech Crown.

All Jews were given a year (1558) in which to move, their synagogues were to be converted into Christian churches and Jewish houses were to be sold to Christian craftsmen. Furthermore, a cannon foundry and other workshops were to be transferred from the Castle to the ghetto.

When the newly elected Roman Emperor Ferdinand I made another visit to Prague at the end of 1558, the Jews also welcomed him – ("they sang and applied their own special methods of welcome") – in an endeavour to postpone their banishment.

A somewhat more liberal approach to the Jews came about during the reign of Maximilian II, who on the occasion of his coronation in 1562 had the expelling of the Jews postponed for one year. The Jews were now supposed to leave by St. George's Day 1563.

At that time the Jews exploited all their (particularly economic) influence to get the royal decision annulled. According to certain reports Mordecai Zemach ben Gershon, son of the rich owner of a printing house, Gershon Katz, even left Prague in order to visit Pope Pius IV to beg for his intervention.

The terms were continuously prolonged and in 1567 Maximilian permitted the Jews who were already in Prague to remain here. In an Imperial Charter of 4 April, 1567 Maximilian II decreed that the Jews were not to be banished from Prague or from other Czech towns. With certain limitations, this Charter

confirmed the previous Jewish privileges. Apart from others, the limitations concerned the following matters:
- Jews with their wives, children and descendants who had lived here up to the time of Maximilian's privilege could remain in Prague as well as elsewhere in the country,
- from then on no Jew – except those with a special royal permit – could move here,
- in future no Jews were to gain new Christian houses with the exception of those who already owned them,
- Jews were not to "deceive or trick" in deals with Christians.

The Diet also laid down that every Jew over ten years of age who lived in Prague or another royal town was to pay 24 groschens every six months and those up to ten years of age 10 Czech groschens. Jews living on lordly or yeomens' estates were to pay the same taxes as all other serfs.

In spite of all the described restrictions, the Jews gained relative peace. However, they lost an important source of livelihood, no longer monopolized finance and had to resign themselves to lower interest rates, because they were now allowed to take only twenty per cent.

Orientation towards other kinds of employment proceeded in the ghetto, but a craft could be practiced only within the framework of the place of residence of those concerned. A ban was also placed on participating in the town markets and the Jews could in exceptional cases offer their products in certain places only. In the course of the following century one of these places was the legendary "tandlmarkt", a kind of junk market in the Old Town (on the site of the present Kotce) where Jewish merchants, middlemen and dealers gradually gained prevalence over their Christian partners.

In 1571 the emperor, accompanied by his consort, visited the ghetto and "walked on foot there. It is certain that a lot of cleaning was done there so that there was no filth there like at other times."

THE RUDOLPHIAN
GHETTO

Rudolph II (1552–1612), who succeeded to the Czech throne in 1576 and ruled until 1611, was, after Charles IV, one of the most remarkable personages who resided at Prague Castle.

"Rudolphian Prague" is a concept in Czech and world history of science and art. The colourfulness and picturesqueness of the time, the facts, and sec-

Prague Castle by an anonymous author, according to F. Hoogenberg from the publication Civitates orbis terrarum, c. 1593.

rets of the then world, the legends about Faust and Golem, the sojourns of famous painters, artists, astrologists and alchemists in Prague, all this combined with the melancholic and art-crazy emperor still forms a lasting background of Prague as a city of fantasy and mystery.

However, such a picture of Rudolph and his town is somewhat distorted, tributary to later legends. Nevertheless, the fact remains that in spite of the complicated political situation of the time relatively good conditions existed here for the development of the sciences and arts. Contrary to his predecessors, Rudolph resided almost permanently in Prague. Prague became a kind of European centre and a place of refuge not only of scientists, but also of many charlatans and tricksters.

Rudolph himself was on the whole an unhappy person and as we know for sure today he was also seriously mentally ill. He inclined away from his duties as a ruler and found a place for himself in other worlds – art, magic, horoscopes and miracles. In the political sphere he waged a hopeless struggle against his brother Matthias on whom he gradually bestowed power in Moravia and whom he made his successor in view of his not having any direct offspring. In 1611 he abdicated from the throne in his favour.

Historians who claim that Rudolph was not interested in public matters are wrong. The truth was different. In his History of the City of Prague Václav Vladivoj Tomek writes: "At that time (1585) the Emperor Rudolph began to show signs of a melancholic nature which made communion with him difficult inasmuch as he avoided people, was less diligent in his statesman's calling and devoted himself to an ever greater extent to his scientific interests and doubtful art values."

Rudolph fell sick. In those days psychic lability, melancholy and depression were probably incurable. And so he appears to us in his other form. The form of a sick eccentric, a sometimes shy and sometimes excessively aggressive person who avoided people and finally his duties as the sovereign as well. He made people wait whole days before receiving them and convened and then cancelled Diets, preferring to devote his attention to his likings and passions. The supernatural and the mysterious had a great attraction for him. And this also explains his attitude towards everything Jewish. Jews attracted and repelled him, representing for him a different and, in its way, secret, mysterious world. Rudolph surrounded himself with artists whose traces have remained in Prague to the present. Prague was a place of art and science, the cradle of modern astronomy. More than one renowned artist (and also trickster) came here from the whole of Europe in search of help and money. On the recommendation of his physician and astronomer Tadeáš Hájek of Hájek he invited the famous Dane Tycho Brahe and the German scholar Johannes Kepler to Prague.

Not all those who lived in Prague at Rudolph's time left such permanent marks on science as these two scholars. Apart from astronomy, Rudolph was also greatly attracted by alchemy. Alchemy brought more than one interesting personality into Rudolph's circle. As examples can be mentioned the Pole Michal Sendivoj and the Englishmen John Dee and Edward Kelley, whose sojourn in Prague is connected with legendary Faust's House in the square Karlovo náměstí.

✳ ✳ ✳

The period of Rudolph's reign is alleged to have been marked by a more tolerant attitude towards the Jews, sometimes even being referred to as a golden period. However, this does not correspoond to reality. The game with Jews and their property had established rules during the reign of Rudolph II similarly as at the time of his predecessors and his successors. It is true that the ghetto experienced a relatively peaceful period during Rudolph's rule. According to the previously mentioned historian Tomek, representatives of the Old Town approached the emperor once again with the request (how many had there been before it?) that the Jews be expelled from Prague. At first the emperor gave the burghers a little hope, but later he allowed them to remain in Prague after all, referring to the privileges granted them by Maximilian in 1567 and by himself in 1577. The Old Town councillors made it clear that they were displeased with Rudolph's decision. They argued that the old privileges related solely to the Jews who were already settled in Prague, but not to those who had moved back to the town from various countries. The people of the Old Town once again drew attention to the tendency of the Jews to expand and to the fact that they purchased houses and enlarged their territory by buildings reaching as far as the Church of the Holy Spirit.

In spite of this pressure the Jews were not expelled from Prague during the reign of Rudolph II. "Allegedly they always won by means of bribes and gifts."

The stream of spiritual revival – the Renaissance – left its mark also on the ghetto. For the first time in the history of the isolated ghetto strong personalities asserted themselves, and not only in religious life. Building activity increased, but unfortunately some of the buildings of that time are now known only from old records and chronicles. On the corner of the cemetery (on the site of the Klausen Synagogue of the present) there once stood a building where rabbi Löw established a Talmudistic school called YESHIVA – BETHAMIDRASH. A separate part of the building contained a small synagogue, while another part perhaps housed a hospital and ritual baths. The whole was composed of three small interiors called cells (klausen – hence the later name of the synagogue).

On the opposite, south-west side of the Old Cemetery, where a small private synagogue belonging to the Horowitz family had stood since about 1490, the new building of the Pinkas Synagogue was connected with a ritual bath from 1535.

The area of the ghetto began to expand also in the direction of the embankment due to the purchasing of new houses on the site formerly occupied by a monastery and the Church of the Holy Rood. About the year 1613 the first synagogue, called the "Cikán" Synagogue (Zigeuner Synagogue), originated here. In 1627 Jacob Bassevi of Treuenburg built another synagogue in its vicinity. It was called the Velkodvorská Synagogue (Great Court Synagogue) and it stood in Rabínská Street.

These two synagogues, the "Cikán" Syngogue and the Great Court Synagogue, were destroyed by the fire which occurred in the ghetto in 1689. An exceptional place among all the builders and personalities of the Renaissance ghetto was held by two persons representing both the public and the church sphere, They were Mordecai Maisel and Jacob Bassevi and the latter was the first Jew to be raised to the nobility, a fact witnessed by the addition of the attribute "of Treuenburg" to his name.

The intellectual world was represented by another two personalities. The polyhistor, mathematician, astronomer and geographer David Gans (1541–1613), who was in contact with Tycho Brahe and Johannes Kepler, was one of them. He left behind him a chronicle entitled ZEMACH DAVID – Offspring of David – as well as other works concerned with astronomy and geography. Joseph del Medigo de Candia (1591–1655), a philosopher and physician who had formerly resided in Padua, also spent the last part of his life in Prague.

However, the renown and glory of Prague's Renaissance ghetto were won far beyond the boundaries of Prague and Bohemia as a whole by the "miraculous" Rabbi Judah Loew ben Bezalel, known as the Maharal.

✳ ✳ ✳

Marcus Mordecai ben Samuel Maisel (Mayzl, Maisl),
the later mayor of the Jewish Town, a financier, builder and patron, was born in the ghetto in 1528. His parents, Samuel and his wife Dubra, accumulated some small property through trade which was inherited by their first-born son Mordecai. We can assume that Maisel had a really extraordinary talent for finance and also for dealing with people. According to the inscription on his tombstone in the Old Jewish Cemetery and to the testimony of his contemporaries we may judge that he was really a noble-minded man, benefactor and patron of the arts who used his enormous property mainly for public purposes.

The inscription on his tombstone characterizes Mordecai Maisel as a man whose
"mercy knew no boundary
and who showed charity with his whole body and soul.
He built a shrine, a temple on a small scale
in honour and praise of the Lord in a magnificent robe,
baths and hospitals, he paved the streets with stone
in our Jewish town.
And he purchased a garden for the cemetery, built a house
for the gathering of the wise,
and he bestowed his grace on
tens of thousands of scholars of the Holy Script."

The inscription also tells us how he gave alms and gifts to the poor and with what wealth, property and gifts he endowed his relatives. We also learn that he redeemed prisoners with his power and loaned twenty thousand to two illustrious communities in foreign lands.

Of his contemporaries expressive testimony is given by his friend, the mathematician David Gans, in his chronicle ZEMACH DAVID in 1592:

The Old Jewish Cemetery in Prague. The tomb of Mordecai Maisel (d. 1601).

"... With his wealth he built the High Synagogue, a temple on a small scale to do honour and to beautify. He also presented numerous rolls of gold and silver temple decorations, some of which fell to our community, others to the Polish land and still others to Jerusalem, the Holy City. He also built baths: public baths and baths for women and a hospital for the poor and sick ... He then built a magnificent synagogue whose beauty is unrivalled by any in the whole of Israel and the rest of the world. It rests on twenty columns of hewn stones and now, when my book has been written, all these tasks have been completed." Finally, David Gans poses the question:" You reader understand and ask the past. Can a man be found like him, whose charitable deeds and justice stand for ever?"

Above all Maisel's wealth flowed from his financial contacts with the imperial court. He lent Maximilian money and, after him, Rudolph. He was granted the privileges of a "court Jew" and was so prudent that he lent the court and the emperor money under very advantageous conditions and certainly made up for it elsewhere! He was granted several privileges, even as a reward for affording financial support to the struggle against the Turks. He could do what he liked with his property and if he died without leaving a will – he had no children – his nearest relatives could inherit his property. That did not happen, however. Maisel was married twice. His first wife was named Chava and the second Frumet. David Gans wrote that both women were religious and god-fearing and that their hands were always open to satiate the hungry. Maisel had very good connections with representatives of the Czech Estates (he himself spoke Czech) as well. He lent them money to finance the wars and also to pay their debts to the emperor. Thus it is not surprising that they kept him under their protection. According to an Imperial Charter of 1592 he was given the task of securing obligations and of recording entries in the Land Rolls. For a Jew of that time these were unprecedented advantages. A record exists to the effect that in 1578 he lent the empress "... two thousand thalers for kitchen appliances and ... in 1588 the Emperor Rudolph II ... two thousand five hundred thalers for a gold cup ...".

Mordecai Maisel died childless in 1601 at the age of seventy-three. What happened to the enormous wealth he left behind him? No privilege nor Imperial Charter was of any good. A letter from Fugger-Zeitungen of 9 April, 1601 contains a detailed report which informs us about what happened after his death, about the confiscation of his wealth and property:

... "In spite of the fact that he bequeathed ten thousand gold coins to his imperial majesty and a great deal of cash to the hospital and poor Christians and Jews, His Imperial Majesty ordered, through the mediation of Jan of Šternberk, then president of the Czech Chamber, that his house be broken into and everything in it taken away. The widow of the deceased Maisel willingly handed everything over, because she had previously chosen the best pieces and hidden them. Apart from things like silver vessels, obligations, jewellery, clothes and coins of all kinds approximately 45,000 gold coins were taken away. However, later on, when Jan of Šternberk, against whom Maisel's wid-

Mi-Sheberah (in memory of Mordecai Maisel and his wife Fruma) commemorating his merits.

מִי שֶׁבֵּרַךְ אֲבוֹתֵינוּ אַבְרָהָם יִצְחָק וְיַעֲקֹב
משה ואהרן דוד ושלמה הוא יברך
המעכימ׳ ללכת לבית הכנסת קודם שילכו א
אחר עסקיהם ואת השומר פיו מלדבר דברים
בבה בעשת תפלת צבור משהתחיל הש׳צ ברוך
שאמר עד גמר התפלה עד קדיש האחרון וגם
בשעה קראת התורה ובשכר זה הקבה ישמע ת
תפלתו ויעשה בקשתו וימלא חסרונו בכל אשר
יקרא אליו ויקום בו אז תקרא יי יענה תשוע ו
ויאמר הנני ומי שגער באותם העוברים עד נזיפה
ומוכיח אותם למוכיחים ולמקבלים המצוה זאת
יגעם ותבא עליהם ברכת טוב וישמרם ויצילם
מכל רע ויתן להם חיים ברכה ושלום עד עולם
עם כל ישראל אחיהם ונאמר אמן

מִי שֶׁבֵּרַךְ אֲבוֹתֵינוּ אַבְרָהָם יִצְחָק וְיַעֲקֹב מ׳
משה ואהרן דוד ושלמה הוא יברך את

ow and the sons of his two brothers lodged a strong complaint and placed a charge with the Privy Council, was not satisfied with the money and things he had previously stolen he once again broke into the house in the night hours, undoubtedly on the order of His Majesty. One of the sons was seized, taken away in secret and interrogated in such a way by the master executioner that he gave testimony to his henchmen, whereupon the cash in question (here a precise list of all the stolen items and the cash) "amounting to 516,250 gold coins was confiscated!"

Such, then, was the end of Mordecai ben Samuel Maisel's inheritance.

* * *

The greater part of the inheritance fell to the emperor and the Royal Chamber. Apart from the imperial magistrate and mayor of the Old Town Jiří Heidelius of Razenštejn, the emperor's notorious valet Lang also participated in the theft. The court dispute with the heirs over the immovable estate left by Maisel lasted nearly one hundred years and in 1684 everything fell to the state.

* * *

Mordecai Maisel held an important function in the ghetto. He was the mayor of the community and, along with his friend rabbi Loew also represented the whole Jewish population in the Czech Lands. However, it was chiefly as a builder that he inscribed himself in the history of the ghetto. He also laid the firmer foundations of Prague's religious community as a secular organization which had, it is true, existed previously although its influence and importance were not felt beyond the boundaries of the ghetto until Mordecai Maisel's time. Maisel's name as a builder appeared for the first time in municipal books in 1567 (the inscription contains the name Marcus Maysl) when with his first wife he purchased a house from Isaac the physician and in the same year bought other parts of the house from other owners. Jews were able to arrange business contracts quite freely among themselves in the framework of the ghetto, Registrations and transfers were also recorded at the Town Hall of the Old Town, but it was the original document drawn up in Hebrew in the ghetto that was binding. Land registers were later apparently also kept at the Jewish Town Hall, but nothing has been preserved of them. In the case of civil disputes official decisions were taken by the so-called Council of Elders (in most cases the authority of the rabbi sufficed) composed of esteemed Jewish inhabitants of the ghetto. Criminal cases were the concern of the Old Town council.

At the time when Maisel began to build his private school or synagogue the ban placed on similar buildings was still valid. The Emperor Rudolph II had to issue a special permit, signed in August 1591, for the construction of the building. One year later, on the SIMHAAT-TORAH holiday, Maisel's synagogue was consecrated.The names of the designers of the synagogue are known – Judah Goldsmith de Herz and chief superviser Josef Wahl. The original building was destroyed by fire on 21 June, 1689.

Through his extensive building activity Mordecai Maisel lent the ghetto the appearance we know today. After the construction of some small public buildings and the modification of the streets (some of them were paved at that time and communications gained a certain character), he enlarged the area of the cemetery and helped to finance the construction of a smaller synagogue, where there was a school and also baths, on its boundary. Later it was called the Klausen Synagogue. He had the environs of the Old-New Synagogue newly laid out and in the years 1570 he had a public Town Hall and a new synagogue – the so-called High Synagogue – erected in its immediate neighbourhood. It is most likely that a building serving the community had already occupied the site of the Town Hall. It was destroyed by fire and a new Town Hall with its main entrance and portal facing former Rabínská Street was built on its enlarged area. The construction of the High Synagogue preceded the building of the Town Hall. The synagogue was completed in 1568.

It was Maisel's buildings that finally lent the ghetto a more compact urban character. Several more representative buildings also originated here whose individual character was emphasized by rich inner furnishings. Some of the synagogal drapes and other rare textiles have been preserved to the present.

Rabbi Judah Loew ben Bezalel (Der "hohe" Rabbi Loew-Maharal)

In the person of rabbi Loew of Prague we become acquainted with a personality known throughout the whole world. Rabbi Judah Loew ben Bezalel is the name of the miraculous rabbi Loew who is also known by the name of

MAHARAL, which expresses his esteemed wisdom and greatness. (MAHAR-AL, acronym for "most venerated teacher and rabbi"). Rabbi Loew's tombstone in the Old Jewish Cemetery is the most frequented place and visitors from the whole world still attribute miraculous power to him. Pilgrims who visit Maharal's grave trust in his great wisdom, enhanced by legends, and in silent meditation seek spiritual strength and hope for the realization of their most personal longings and expectations. Here visitors, regardless of their origin, mother tongue and world outlook, believers and atheists, young and old, the disappointed and the trusting – in brief, everyone with no exception – meditate on the possibilities of the fulfilment of their wishes which, written on a piece of paper, they place in a crack in the tomb.

Rabbi Loew's grave is covered with many small stones. Visitors to the cemetery often place them there without being aware of the original meaning of this small ceremony. Here we have an old Jewish custom from the times when the Jews were still nomads and buried their dead by covering them with stones to protect them from beasts of prey. It was usual for every member of the tribe to place a stone on the body of the deceased until it was wholly covered with a mound. This custom has been preserved to the present and so visitors to the Old Jewish Cemetery symbolically place a small stone on the grave. The question as to whether flowers may be placed on Jewish graves is often raised. According to tradition and custom it is permitted to place cut flowers on a grave, but not potted ones. However, flowers are not placed on graves at all in cemeteries traditionally characterized by the orthodox ritual.

Judah Bezalel's son was born in the rabbi's family in Poznan in 1512 (some researchers maintain that he was born at Worms in the Rhine valley). He lived in Prague from 1573 to 1584, from 1588 to 1592 and from 1597 until his death on 22 August, 1609. From 1597 he was the chief provincial rabbi in the Czech kingdom. For twenty years, from 1553 to 1573, he served as the rabbi at Mikulov and from 1592 to 1597 he was the chief rabbi in Poznan.

During his sojourn in Prague rabbi Loew wrote several works and founded and headed a Talmudistic school in the building which once stood on the site of the present Klausen Synagogue. His personal characteristics gained him renown during his lifetime and apart from this he was known throughout the whole then Jewish world as the greatest Talmudistic scholar. He was outstanding for his learning and his exceptional rhetorical talent. He was a firm authority in the Prague ghetto and not only from the religious aspect. He laid the firm organizational foundations of numerous charity societies such as the Burial Society and the society for study of the Mishnah. The former director of the State Jewish Museum in Prague, Dr. Hana Volavková, characterizes rabbi Loew with the following words: "Rabbi Loew belonged among the so-called religious philosophers who defended their faith with arguments formed according to philosophical systems. In his works he appears as an exceptionally logical philosopher well-versed in Neo-Platonic philosophy.

As a judge and arbitrator he held the opinion that the law requires unbiased application even though in his heart a judge may be on the side of the accused. He wants the law to be strictly applied, but he also has an understand-

The title page of "A Fine Sermon for the Great Sabbath" by Yehuda ben Bezalel, Rabbi Loew. Bezalel Kohen's printing shop, Prague 1589.

ing for the guilty person. Through his formulations he attacks the feelings of the reader rather than their intellect. He is an excellent narrator and makes successful use of contrasts. He is fond of mutually confronting speculative learning, whose aim is learning, and wisdom leading to a good deed."

Rabbi Loew concerned himself with pedagogical problems and studied natural history, particularly astronomy and astrology. No proof exists of his having personal contacts with the Emperor Rudolph II (even though myths and legends maintain just the opposite), but it can be presumed that he was in contact with the astronomer Tycho Brahe (1546–1601), who lived in Prague from 1599 to 1601 and who is also buried in Týn Church in the Old Town. His personal connections with other leading Czech representatives of Rudolphian Renaissance science and culture are also an unknown factor, because no historical proof of their existence is known to us.

In his book "Faust et le Maharal de Prague. Le mythe et le reél" André Neher questions statements maintaining that rabbi Loew had no personal contacts with the Emperor Rudolph II. In this work, published in Paris in 1987, the author maintains that on his own initiative the Emperor Rudolph II invited rabbi Loew to his palace on 23 February, 1592. This audience was also attended by his son-in-law and the rabbi's closest fellow-worker rabbi Isaac Cohen and his friend the scholar David Gans. David Gans left a somewhat mysterious report about this audience. In it he says that the emperor's conversation with rabbi Loew concerned Earth and the universe and that the emperor expressed the wish that the contents of the conversation remain a secret. And so the conversation has remained a secret to the present . . .

39

AFTER
THE BATTLE
OF THE WHITE
MOUNTAIN

A struggle was waged between two forces outside the boundaries of Prague's ghetto: the absolute power of the Catholic ruler against the opposition formed by the Protestant Estates. Both forces were merely waiting for a pretext to get at each other. Before the storm broke out the Estates demanded and received from Rudolph (in 1609) a so-called Imperial Charter of Re-

Jan Willenberg, Prague Castle and the Lesser Town, 1601.

ligious Freedoms, but neither Rudolph nor his successor Matthias were able to assert religious freedoms in practice. Incident followed incident and the final act which brought the patience of the non-Catholic Estates (noblemen and burghers) to an end was the forcible closing of two Protestant churches at the end of 1617, which opposed Rudolph's Imperial Charter.

When in 1618 the new king, Matthias (1611–1619), opposed the dealings of

40

the Estates' Diet and threatened to punish the originators, it was decided to start an open conflict.

The signal for the uprising was the defenestration of the royal governors (on 23 May, 1618) Vilém Slavata and Jaroslav Bořita of Martinicz, from the windows of the Czech Court Chancellery at Prague Castle. Real battle broke out two years later, on 8 November, 1620, in the Battle of the White Mountain near Prague. In the course of this armed conflict at the Hvězda (Star) enclosure the army of the Bohemian and Moravian Estates was driven back and defeated by the allied troops of the Emperor Ferdinand II and the Catholic League.

The battle had tragic consequences for the Czech nation. In spite of all the Emperor's promises and obligations Prague was plundered. The imperial governor Karel of Liechtenstein took over the rule of the town and started a systematic wave of persecution and punishment of the rebels. On 21 June, 1621 27 leading representatives of the resistance movement of the Estates were executed in Old Town Square and on 29 March, 1624 an imperial letters patent was issued according to which the Catholic religion was proclaimed the only permitted one in Bohemia and all others as heretic and inadmissible.

The vast majority of the non-Catholic nobility, rid of its property through confiscation, did not submit to the forcible pressure of Catholization and preferred to leave the country, whereupon its place was taken by members of the home and foreign Catholic aristocracy. The victory of the Hapsburgs was crowned politically in 1627 by the drawing up of a new constitution, the so-called Renewed Provincial Constitution, whose basic principle was that the Czech nation was to lose all its rights and freedoms in consequence of its "outrageous rebellion". The Czech royal throne was pronounced hereditary in the Hapsburg dynasty. Apart from the Czech language, German became an equal official language and all governmental power of the Czech Lands was transferred to Vienna.

What position fell to the Jews in the conflict between the opposition represented by the Estates and the ruling Catholic force? "Prague and Czech Jews were on that occasion delivered from the great blows prepared for them by the fact that the Christians fought among themselves. A period of oppression set in for the Protestants and events were set in motion by the government which led to the Battle of the White Mountain. There was no time to think about the banishment of the Jews."

It is most likely that the Jews distanced themselves from the conflict, but nevertheless they inclined rather towards the side represented by the counter-reformation. After the Battle of the White Mountain Ferdinand II even ordered that the army refrain from plundering the ghetto. However, the Jews had to pay dearly for this. It is alleged that after the battle they lent the emperor 240,000 gold coins!

Jacob Bassevi

The leading Jewish personality of that time was Jacob Bassevi (1580–1630). Of Italian origin, he settled in Prague and acquired enormous property. Con-

Opět Král powolaw k sobě Swětských y Duchownjch Rad/ rozta
Ziduw tolikéž při Saudech přjsahy wydáwali yako y Křestianůw
stáňa na tom/aby Zidé gestliby byli w čem narčenj a wywesti se z tc
oblj7 přjsahu činili/tu kteráž gest napsaná w Knihách práwnjch
ydna Cýsaře/genž slowe dwognásobnj/spůsobem timto :

Zid přjsahati má sám druhý/ stogjc Bosýma Nohami na Swinjé
owě odřené /tolito w Kossili/a druhý Zid má státi proti němu na
orditi geho přjsahu/přjsahagicý pak má mluwiti takto ;

Rakož gsem narčen od N. že gsem Statek geho totiž Klinoty ta
kowé/Ssaty takowé a takowé / tak yakž gest od toho mluweno a pr
edeno, k sobě přigal/ ge mám a o nich wjni/R přjsahám Pánu Bol
jž stwořil Nebe a Zemi / y wssecky wěcy které w nich gsau/přjsah
ssecky gména geho Swatá/kteráž napsal Mogžjšo sluzebnjk geho
hám skrz Patery Knihy Mogžjssowy/ w nichžto napsáno gest Desate

Jews taking oath before a Christian court,
Prague, the 16th century.

trary to Mordecai Maisel, Bassevi represented a higher order of Jewish capital, we can say financial capital. His name is inscribed in the history of the ghetto also because in 1622 Ferdinand raised him to the nobility (with the right to add the attribute "of Treuenburg" to his name) for his services, yet another reason being that he was the first Jew to receive this honour. The signatures on the respective document are those of Chancellor Popel of Lobkowitz and Fabricius of Hohenfall and in his coat-of-arm he had a blue lion and eight red stars. He also had other privileges. In 1599 he was appointed a "court Jew" – Hofjude – and was not obliged to wear the humiliating mark of Jewish origin. He was also allowed to move freely, etc.

It was not until about 1610 that Jacob Bassevi appeared in Prague. His enormous wealth most likely came from financial transactions connected with the arming and financing of the imperial army. His chief source of income lay in his participation in complicated deals connected with minting. He was a member of the society to which all mints in Bohemia, Moravia and Austria were leased in 1622 for a period of two years. Leading representatives of then political and public life – above all the administrator of the Czech kingdom Count Liechtenstein himself, the noblemen Albrecht of Wallenstein and Pavel Michna of Vacínov, the burgher Jan de Witte and others – also played a role in business deals connected with the minting of coins. Before long a whole lot of intrigues, scandals, tricks and curruption broke out round coin-minting. The new, so-called light coins contained less silver than the specified amount and confiscated properties were purchased for such devalued coins. On 1 April, 1623 the mints fell under state administration again and a letters patent issued on 14 December of the same year decreed that devalued "light coins" be obligatorily exchanged for new coins. The loss involved amounted to over 85% of the value.

The enormous fraud could not remain a secret for long, but the power of the participants in it and their connections with the imperial court made it impossible for the special committee set up and convened for the purpose to adopt the necessary resolutions. Not until after the death of Count Karel Liechtenstein did the committee fully renew its investigation. In 1631 (on 22 February) an order for Bassevis' arrest was issued. However, Bassevi was warned of this in time and escaped to Jičín, to his protector Albrecht of Wallenstein. From Jičín he made his way to Mladá Boleslav, where he died on 2 May, 1634.

Bassevi was married twice. He had four sons and a daughter Freidl. All of them are buried in the Old Jewish Cemetery. Apart from great financial wealth, Jacob Bassevi and his family owned several houses in the ghetto. In 1622 Bassevi even acquired two Christian houses free of charge and, along with his son, he purchased another four similar houses. All these immovables were later removed from the administration of the Old Town and incorporated in the ghetto. Jacob Bassevis' house was one of the most ostentatious in Prague's ghetto. It was of a really aristocratic character and featured the same architectural details as the houses of Czech noblemen after the Battle of the

The Old Jewish Cemetery in Prague, tombs of Hendl Bassevi and Katz Fanta (with the Cohens' symbol – the hands), 1628.

White Mountain. We know only one of the public buildings which Jacob Bassevi financed, namely the so-called Velkodvorská Synagogue which, until 1906 stood on the boundary of Pařížská Street of the present. It was demolished during the clearance of the ghetto.

The Velkodvorská Synagogue, which was used by the orthodox religious community, also had a moving destiny. Bassevi had it built in 1627 on the site called Velký dvůr (Grand Court). The synagogue fell victim to fire several times, the first occasion being in 1689.

In 1708 it was newly built and after the fire of 1754 it was restored to its original appearance. This final form of the synagogue has been preserved in drawings and it can also be seen in Langweil's model of Prague of 1826–1834. In 1905 the western façade of the building was photographed by J. Eckertand; a picture of its interior is afforded by the photographs of J. Štenc and Z. Reach, all taken in 1905 and 1906. The synagogue was rectangular in shape and it had a barrel vault with lunettes. The women's gallery was situated on the southern side. In 1854 and 1883 the building was provided with a new façade in Moorish style and its interior was decorated in the manner typical of the Neo-Renaissance.

We know of several synagogues dating from the Baroque period. One of them, the Klausen Synagogue, has been preserved to the present and mention will be made of it in the guide part of this book.

The "Cikán" Synagogue (Zigeuner Synagogue) got its name after its founder Solomon Salkid-"Cikán". It was built about 1613 on the north-eastern boundary of the ghetto in the place now occupied by Bílkova Street. During the great fire which occurred in the ghetto on 21 June, 1689 over 300 dwelling-houses and most of the synagogues, including the "Cikán" Synagogue, built again in 1701, were destroyed. Shortly after the fire of 1754 the synagogue was renovated and later supplemented with a women's gallery in its modernized interior. Contemporary photographs of the synagogue show the rich stucco decoration of its vault. The "Cikán" Synagogue, which served the neological part of the religious community, was destroyed in 1906 in the framework of the clearance of the Jewish Town.

The third of the Baroque synagogues which have not been preserved was the so-called Nová (New) Synagogue, founded before 1595 as a private place of prayer. It stood in former Josefská Street, on the corner of Pařížská Street and Široká Street. As Langweil's model of Prague shows, it was a modest building forming a part of the dwelling-houses in the street. The tabernacle proper was situated on the first floor of the building. The synagogue was destroyed along with the neighbouring house, which housed a ritual bath – mikveh – in 1898.

Apart from these most important synagogues of the Baroque period, several other private houses of prayer belonging mainly to wealthy and esteemed representatives of the religious community originated in the ghetto, particularly in the 18th and 19th centuries.

* * *

Let us narrate another unusual tale about Jewish Prague after the Battle of the White Mountain.

The rabbi of Prague's Jewish community was an extremely interesting personality. **Yom Tov Lipmann ha Levi Heller** was born in 1578 and at the age of eighteen he became head of the Talmudistic school in Prague, a post which he held for a whole 28 years.

He had four sons and five daughters. In 1632 the daughter named Dobrisch married Bassevi's son Samuel.

We can learn the details of his moving life from the autobiography which rabbi Heller wrote for his descendants.

After a short period of work in Vienna, Heller returned to Prague in 1627 in order to take up the rabbi's office. His numerous critics (in the ranks of the Jews) accused him of mocking Christianity in his statements and books. On the basis of these accusations he was summoned to Vienna, where he was imprisoned and finally sentenced to death or to a fine of 12,000 thalers. Moreover, all his writings were to be burned.

Heller was not able to pay such an enormous sum and so he turned for help to Jacob Bassevi, who lent him money to pay a part of the fine.

On being released from prison the crushed Heller was obliged to give up the post of Prague's rabbi. His writings were partly saved, but he was compelled to delete certain problematic formulations from them.

Thanks to his invincible spiritual strength and life optimism rabbi Heller recovered in Prague from the blows rained on him by fate and, furthermore, continued to work on his writings. On the day on which he paid the last instalment of his fine he left his beloved town and went to Namir in Lithuania, where he once again fulfilled the duties of the local rabbi.

He died in Cracow in 1654 as the chief rabbi.

✳ ✳ ✳

In contradistinction to the rest of Prague, especially the Little Quarter and Hradčany, the Baroque period did not leave any striking marks on the life of Prague's ghetto. While Prague, which after the Battle of the White Mountain was not a very important town from the political aspect, became in the course of just a few decades a town characterized by unprecedented building activity, the Jews took advantage of the situation to extend the boundaries of their ghetto. Jewish property owners acquired further Christian houses, shifted the ghetto limits and built new gates. The Prague ghetto was the destination of many emigrants, Jews who were forced to leave their original homes in Poland, Germany and Tsarist Russia.

An important event which, after a long period, once again codified the legal status of the Jewish minority was the privilege granted by Ferdinand II in 1623. By means of this document the king, supported by Chancellor Zdeněk of Lobkowitz himself, not only confirmed the old laws, but also considerably widened them. The new privilege extended the authority of Jewish courts and the mayor of the ghetto in regard to civil and penal law. A number of points of the new privilege concerned the economic sphere and more liberal modifications were realized in the sphere of duty tariffs and of the pawnbroking system, which was a Jewish monopoly. In 1627 the original privilege was supplemented with a royal favour according to which Jews could freely attend all fairs. Finally, they were even permitted to learn certain crafts.

Every year the ghetto celebrated the tenth of November as the day on which Ferdinand's troops entered Prague, this being its way of showing its gratitude to the king.

The Thirty Years War affected the ghetto only marginally. On one hand war events substantially restricted trade with foreign countries and on the other hand the Jews were not exempt from paying various home penalties and taxes. They were obliged to contribute not only to the war costs, but also to the upkeep of the imperial court. In 1645 it was decreed that the ghetto make several hundred military uniforms for the needs of the army. Shortly before the Thirty Years War came to an end in 1648, Prague was attacked by Swedish troops. They succeeded in conquering only the Castle and the Little Quarter, but in doing so they gained enormous wealth. The greater part of the Rudolphian art collections found its way to Sweden as war booty. The Swedes did not succeed in conquering the Old Town and the New Town. Considerable merit for this was due to the Jews in the ghetto, who later received a document from the military commander in Prague, Count Colloredo, certifying that the Jews conducted themselves well during the Swedish siege and even lent money for the defence of the town.

$$* \quad * \quad *$$

Unceasing attempts were made to convert the Jews to the Christian faith. In 1630 Ferdinand II ordered that all Jews should regularly attend divine service in the Church of Our Lady on the Pool. The Benedictine abbot Zdislav Berka of Dubá, who resided near St. Nicholas's Church near the ghetto, "got the old idea of chasing the Jews to Catholic sermons. The Jews attended them, but they stuffed their ears with cotton wool and wax."

The Story of Simon Abeles

The case of the Jewish boy Simon Abeles, who as a Christian is buried in Týn Church, near the tomb of Tycho Brahe, was recorded throughout practically the whole of Europe. This case, which took place in February 1694, was handed down as follows: When he was twelve years old Simon Abeles wanted, on his own will and with the help of the Jesuits, to become a Christian. When his father got to know about it and when Simon refused to give up his intention, his own father tortured him for several weeks and finally killed him with the assistance of his friend, a Jewish religious fanatic by the name of Löbl Kurtzhandl. The boy's corpse was secretly buried in the Old Jewish Cemetery. When his father was arrested and imprisoned in the Old Town jail,

Michael Stoeritz, Illustrated Story of Simon Abeles, 1694.

he hung himself with his prayer straps. In spite of this the decision of the court was such that the gruesome execution was carried out on the corpse. With the attendance of the high clergy and the highest nobility the bodily remains of the poor boy Simon Abeles were taken from the Jewish Cemetery and, with great splendour and to the sound of the bells of all Prague's churches, laid to rest in Týn Church, where we can still read the following Latin inscription below an idealized portrait of the Jewish boy: "Hic gloriose sepultus est Simon Abeles Catechumenus, ex dio fidei Christianae a proprio parente Hebraeo occisus." ("Solemnly buried here is Simon Abeles, a catechumen, killed in hatred for the Christian faith by his own father, a Jew".

The other murderer, Löbl Kurtzhandl, was sentenced to death and while being tortured on the wheel "became a Christian out of pain".

A brief narration of the story of Simon Abeles can be seen below the marble slab:

"Simon Abeles, a twelve-year-old Jew, followed God and fled to the Collegium Clementine of the Society of Jesus in September 1693 out of love for holy baptism; after several days he was dragged treacherously from this place of refuge and, cajoled by compliments, threats, beatings, hunger and outrageous imprisonment, proved stronger than all this and died at the hand of his father and his friend on 21 February, 1694. His secretly buried corpse was exhumed on the sixth day, officially examined and remained with no offensive odour and with its natural colour, unrigid, pleasant to behold and with pink blood spurting from it until it was sealed in a coffin. It was carried from the Old Town Hall with magnificent funereal ostentatiousness, accompanied by a unique crowd and the stirring sympathy of the people and buried here on the last day of March 1694".

Egon Erwin Kisch was among those who sought the truth of this story. He summarized the results of his investigation in a reportage entiteld "Ex odio fidei . . .", which was published in his book "Pražský pitaval" (The Prague Pitaval). Kisch arrived at the conclusion that the "fanatical murderers", the boy's father Lazar Abeles and Löbl Kurtzhandl, were the victims of judicial murder, – ex odio fidei –, on the basis of religious hatred. The original information maintaining that Lazar Abeles had murdered his son undoubtedly came from the Jesuits and Kisch proved that no legal representative was allowed to defend him. Lazar Abeles's suicide in jail, where he was "secured by both legs and one arm" was more than strange and although he was sentenced to death by torture not a shadow of suspicion was found against Löbl Kurtzhandl.

✳ ✳ ✳

In the 17th century the ghetto formed one ninth of the Old Town. It was the smallest quarter of Prague with zig-zagging little streets and an endless number of small courtyards with galleries. Sometimes as many as five persons

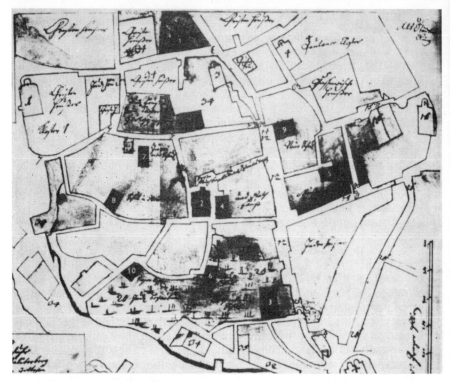

*Plan of the Jewish Town (the ghetto after the
fire in 1689) with the synagogues.*

crowded into one room and in all about two thousand people lived here.
There was one synagogue or house of prayer to every ten houses. The population of the ghetto had to cope not only with external elements, floods and
fires, but also unceasing persecution.

Two years after the termination of the war, in 1650, another disaster befell
them – the Czech Estates adopted the resolution that Jews who had moved to
the ghetto from 1618 were to leave Prague. In the end, however, not a single
Jew was expelled from Prague. Once again it was only a manoeuvre intended
to force an increase in the taxes paid to the Czech Chamber.

The ghetto of the Old Town was not the only territory in Prague occupied
by Jews. They had other small communities on the edge of the town, the biggest of them being situated on the territory of present-day Libeň. In 1656 the
Jews who had settled in Libeň gained the privilege of establishing their own
special quarter here – the Libeň ghetto. However, the Old Town ghetto always remained the spiritual and administrative centre of the Jews. The Libeň
ghetto often afforded refuge to Jews who were banished from the Old Town.
Reports exist to the effect that the Jews had a synagogue in Libeň already
from the mid-16th century. In 1770 it was rebuilt and in the years 1846 to

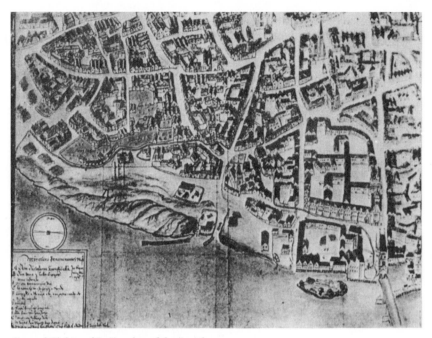

*Samuel Globitz of Bučín, plan of the Jewish
Town with environs, mid-17th century.*

1857 a new synagogue was built here (in Koželužská Street of the present) only to be abolished in the course of the Second World War.

The end of the 17th century was marked by two disasters which affected
the ghetto. In 1680 the towns of Prague and especially the ghetto were caught
in the grip of a plague epidemic during which approximately 3,000 persons
died. In the same year an imperial order was passed according to which the
Jews were to be compelled to move from the ghetto to Libeň. This did not
come about, however. The enormous fire which raged on 21 and 22 June,
1689, allegedly ignited by arsonists in the services of the French, was an even
greater blow of fate. It destroyed 749 houses in the Old Town, the New Town
and the ghetto and dozens of other buildings were gravely damaged. The Jewish Town, in which at that time there were 318 houses, mostly built of wood,
and several stone synagogues, was burned out. The inhabitants of the ghetto,
who saved their bare lives only, found refuge with certain Christian families,
but most of them moved to the suburb then called Špitálsko (now Karlín) and
Libeň.

With the substantial assistance of their fellow-believers – even abroad – the
Jews succeeded in rebuilding the ghetto in an unbelievably short time. In the

course of the reconstruction work it was ordered that only six synagogues should be built or restored instead of the former twelve. In spite of this order, however, more than six were built. By 1694 the new building of the Klausen Synagogue had been completed and the Old School restored. The Gipsy, Popper and Velkodvorská Synagogues were also built. In 1699 gates and gate-houses were newly erected in the ghetto in such a way that the Jewish Town was completely separated from the Old Town. In 1702 a court order decreed that the gates, which were closed at night, should have four keys which should be held by the district administrator, the local magistrate, the municipal magistrate and the Jewish representative on the Council of Elders.

In 1718 there were nine big synagogues and twelve smaller prayer houses, located in several private homes, in the ghetto.

It is quite amazing that not even the reconstruction of the ghetto after the great fire changed the character of this quarter. The houses were once again built of wood and the Baroque building activity which characterized Prague after the Battle of the White Mountain widely avoided the ghetto.

THE THERESIAN
EXPULSION
AND THE JOSEPHIAN
REFORMS

In the early 18th century the ghetto reached its highest number of inhabitants (approximately 12,000). Economic activity was not limited solely to credit monetary trade on the territory of the ghetto. Small workshops and later also bigger manufactories were founded not only in the ghetto, but also outside its boundaries and those of the Old Town.

Friedrich Bernard Werner, Prague 1742.

In the years 1712 to 1714 Prague was afflicted by the last big plague epidemic. Over 10,000 people died, among them many inhabitants of the ghetto.

In 1740 the Emperor Charles VI (b. 1685) died without leaving any male offspring. War broke out over his inheritance. In November 1741 the allied armies of Bavaria, Saxony and France occupied Prague and the Jews were obliged once again, as on every occasion, to pay "great contributions" to them. It is alleged that they paid the French general Charles de Belle-Isle over 300,000 gold coins for protection of the ghetto!

At the end of December 1742 the greater part of the French army retreated from Prague and shortly aftewards – on 12 May, 1743 – the coronation of Maria Theresa took place in Prague. However, this did not bring the war over the Hapsburg inheritance to an end. From 1 September, 1744 the Prussian army besieged Prague. It is recorded that on that occasion the Jews offered their assistance and took part in the fortification works. The town was finally plundered, however, and a heavy fine was imposed on the population.

Shortly before the occupation of Prague by Prussian troops the rabble of Prague tried to penetrate into the ghetto and make off with whatever they could grab. In spite of the fact that General Harsch along with fifty grenadiers summoned from Vyšehrad succeeded in preventing bloodshed in the ghetto, it is not surprising that the Jews also sought the protection of the Prussians. This did not pay off, however.

The Prussian occupation of Prague came to an end on 26 November, 1744. Not long afterwards the ghetto was plundered in return for the alleged collaboration of Prague's Jews with the Prussians. It was said that the Jews supported the Prussian king, "that the Prussian king took 15,000 ducats from the Jews", that during Prussian artillery fire not one single cannon ball fell on the territory of the ghetto and that the Jews purchased things stolen from the houses of the nobility from Prussian soldiers.

Zikmund Winter wrote the following about the pogrom: "Cries of despair inside the ghetto. The Jews locked themselves in their houses, scrambled on to their roofs, pulling the stairs behind them, and slept on these roofs with the women and children in mortal fear. Meanwhile for a whole half a day, throughout the night and part of the following day – i.e. for thirty full hours – the market and the ghetto were plundered house by house, shop by shop and the spoils taken away. More than one Jew into whose house the frenzied robbers forced their way was burned under the arms to make him confess where he had hidden his treasures."

✳ ✳ ✳

Maria Theresa (1740–1780) was not fond of either the Czechs or Prague, not to mention Jews. As though the pogroms were not enough, she issued an imperial rescript on 18 December, 1744 which laid down that the Jews be driven from Prague for their disloyal behaviour during the Prussian occupation. In future there was not to be one single Jew in Prague. Interventions, pleas for mercy were of no avail even though the Jews had a strong supporter in one of the governors, namely in Count Kolovrat. The Jews proved that they had lived in Prague since time immemorial, that they had always fulfilled their duties and paid their taxes and that it was impossible to move with their women and children, with old and sick people in winter without injuring their health. The only thing the Jewish representatives succeeded in

Detail of the engraving of the celebration procession of Prague Jews on the occasion of the birth of the subsequent Emperor Joseph II on April 24, 1741.

achieving was the postponement of the time fixed for the moving of the Jews from the ghetto to the end of February 1745. By that time, or perhaps by one month later, practically the whole of the population of the ghetto had moved out. In view of the severe winter the moving date was extended from the end of February to the end of March. Specially chosen commissioners, who also took over the keys of the synagogues, which they locked, presided over the moving-out of the Jews. In a state of despair the mayor of the ghetto Frankl allegedly committed suicide (he may even have been murdered), because he was accused of playing the greatest role in the collaboration of the Jews with the Prussians, the pretence under which they were forced to move. For the first time since its foundation the ghetto was deserted, only children and women in childbed remaining in it.

The Jews did not move far. They made their way to the nearest environs, mostly to Libeň and other villages. They lived in large numbers with farmers, in their rooms and barns, and during the daytime they went to the town on business and even visited the ghetto, where, it is true, they were not allowed to live, but where they had their businesses and shops.

In the meantime greater pressure was exerted and more interventions were made to get permission for the Jews to return to the ghetto. Not only the governor of Prague and the nobility (the absence of the Jews left a strong mark on their business interests), but also foreign governments placed re-

The eviction of the Jews from Prague, 1745.

quests with the imperial court in Vienna in which they asked that the Jews be allowed to return to Prague.

Maria Theresa gave way and, on the basis of a decree of May 1745, permitted the Jews to remain in Bohemia. As many Jews took this decree to mean that they could return to the ghetto, the empress issued a clear order on 20 June, 1746 which forbade Jews to live in the ghetto and the environs of Prague. A Jew was allowed to live neither in the ghetto nor "within a two hours journey round Prague". Another decree followed in August of the same year according to which Jews were to move out of the whole of Bohemia in the course of the following six years. A part of the Prague garrison was to be located in the empty ghetto.

However, once again everything turned out differently. The absence of the Jews in the commercial sphere was so strongly felt and the consequential harm suffered by the Czech kingdom so irreparable that Maria Theresa finally succumbed to the arguments of the Supreme Chancellor Filip Kinský, the rich, influential Jewish baron Diego de Aquilar and a deputation of Prague Jews. They acquainted the empress with what was happening in Prague's

The Prague ghetto in flames, 1754.

ghetto, with the fact that everything had been stolen and that the houses were just about to fall down. They also told her that if the ghetto was not speedily inhabited again it would be destroyed for ever and that what pogroms, fires and floods had not succeeded in doing in the past centuries was now being done by the rabble, by people who "climbed over the wall into the closed ghetto and, piece by piece, carried away everything that could be stolen, torn, taken and broken from Jewish houses: they were carrying away windows, glass, locks, doors, every piece of iron and every plank."

Most of Prague's merchants and craftsmen were in favour of the return of the Jews to the town.

On 5 August, 1748 Maria Theresa permitted the Jews to return to the ghetto. Their return was simultaneously accompanied by the renewal of the legal authority of the Jewish community. Furthermore, Prague's Jews regained their so-called "tandlmarkt" near St. Gall's Church. They were now also allowed to realize trade and crafts outside the boundaries of the ghetto. It was laid down that from then on the Jews would pay an annual tax of 204,000 gold coins which, after the elapse of five years, would be annually increased

Joseph Daniel Huber, Orthographic Sketch of the Old Town of Prague with the Boundaries of Extended Jewish Town, ink drawing, 1769.

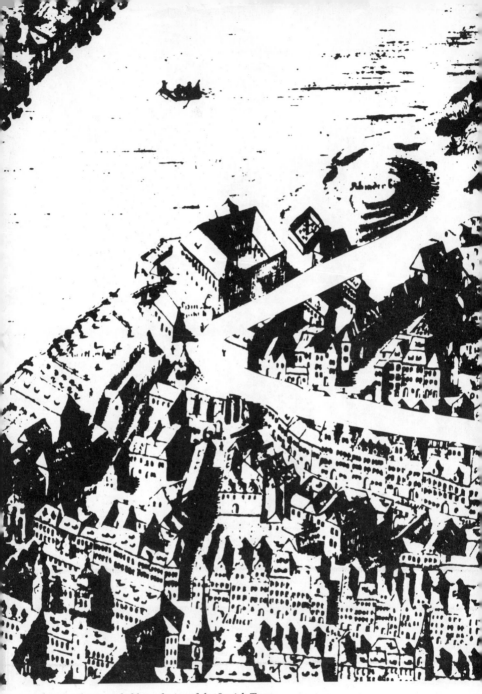

Detail – the extended boundaries of the Jewish Town.

by 1,000 gold coins. Hardly had the houses in the ghetto been made inhabitable again than another fire broke out in 1754 and destroyed about 190 houses. The Maisel, New and Velkodvorská Synagogues and a substantial part of the "Cikán" Synagogue were burnt out similarly as the Town Hall and, of the other public buildings, the hospital and the orphanage.

* * *

In 1780 Joseph II (1780–1790) succeeded to the Czech throne. This ruler differed in everything from his mother, the Empress Maria Theresa. Joseph II was aware that progress could not be halted in front of the gates of either Prague or the ghetto. He ruled in a tough, absolutistic, but enlightened way. His period of reign culminated with radical political enlightenment marked by staunch centralization, a relatively progressive church policy and measures which created conditions for economic prosperity.

The first manufactories, works for the printing of materials, cotton spinning and weaving mills, a sugar factory and chemical production originated in Prague. The Josephian reforms had a profound influence on the life of Prague and the country as a whole. One year after Joseph II's succession to the throne (on 20 October, 1781) a tolerance patent was issued affording limited religious freedoms to Protestants of the Augsburg and Helvetian faiths and an imperial letters patent of the same year liquidated serfdom. At the same time several men's and women's convents in Prague were gradually abolished. The Josephian government also manifested itself conspicuously in the cultural sphere. The state realized basic school reforms and in consequence of the abolishment of the Jesuit Order (which came about already during the reign of Maria Theresa, in 1773) the Church lost control over other non-Catholic religions as well. The penetration of the ideas of Enlightenment was accompanied by the development of modern scientific institutions in Prague.

On the other hand, Joseph II degraded Prague to a provincial town and a bad feature of his period was also the strong process of Germanization, which led to the Germanization of the municipal administration, justice and the greater part of the educational system and strengthened the German component of the population. Until the reign of Joseph II Prague had consisted of four separate towns – the Old Town, the New Town, the Little Quarter and Hradčany. On 2 June, 1783 Joseph II issued a court decree concerning the joining of Prague's four towns to form one single city. It was decided that the Old Town Hall should be the seat of the Prague magistrate's office. These changes necessarily involved the realization of a number of administrative measures, some of which directly concerned the ghetto. In the year in which the four towns were joined Prague had about 80,000 inhabitants, approximately 25,000 falling to the Old Town and precisely 8,532 to the ghetto.

* * *

Famous rabbis of Prague: Ezekiel Landau
(1713–1793)

Salomon Juda Rapoport (1790–1867).

The Josephian reforms had an influence also on the life and administration of the ghetto. They meant the beginning of the emancipation process, but only the beginning. A number of the decrees issued by Joseph II loosened the bonds under which the Jews had been obliged to live till then. They were no longer compelled to wear the humiliating piece of yellow cloth cut in a circle, access to public schools was opened to them, even to the university (in 1788 the first two Jews from Prague's ghetto graduated as doctors of medicine), and they were now free to learn crafts. The economic relief measures were also far-reaching. Apart from other things, Jews could now acquire immovables and other property outside the ghetto.

The tolerance patent of 1781 did not mean that the Jews and their religion gained equal rights and even its modification, the so-called systemal patent of 1797, was based on the principle that Jews were not subjects with equal rights, but merely a suffered minority. In spite of the advent of Englightenment all the orders restricting their dwelling rights continued to apply similarly as decrees concerning numerous discriminating tax and other measures. Charles VI's decree of 1727, according to which an institution of so-called "familiants", heads of families with the right to dwell in the country, was still valid. In practice this institution meant that only the eldest son could marry, because the number of "familiants" was fixed and could not be exceeded. In 1729 the number of "familiants" was 5,400 and by 1801 it had risen to 8,600. Not until 1847 was the "familiant" institution abolished.)

The gradually more tolerant policy towards the Jews is witnessed by the fact that in 1796 Jews were allowed to live in 66 Old Town houses outside the

Antisemitic pamphlets. *An antisemitic pamphlet of 1782.*

ghetto. In 1811 this number grew by 23 and by 1846 Jews were residing in 243 houses beyond the ghetto boundaries.

Data concerning one of the main streets of the ghetto, Josefská (now Široká) Street, also called Židovská Street, and, in its western part, Pinkasova and later also Dlouhá Street testify to the overcrowding of the Jewish community.

The said data tell us that in 1817 there were 273 Jewish houses here, mostly built of wood. Each one of them had several owners. For example, house No. 21 still had 14 owners in 1900 and house No. 30 even 33. In 90 houses the flats on the individual floors were mutually connected in such a way that it was not neccesary to cross the street when passing from house to house, use being made instead of the different mutually connected passages. In 1900 one Jewish flat was occupied by 6 – 7 persons.

(Some data concerning the total number of inhabitants of the ghetto: in 1783 8,532 Jews and 9 Christians inhabited it and in 1837 Jews accounted for

Illustration from the ERUV prayer, Prague, 18th century..

80%, in 1857 72%, in 1880 28% and in 1900 only 24% of the population. While in 1890 the former ghetto, now Josefov, had 11,535 inhabitants, by 1900 (the clearance of the ghetto) this number had fallen to about 9,000 only.)

The tax regulation established by Maria Theresa, according to which the Jews were obliged to hand over 200,000 gold coins every year, continued to apply during the reign of Joseph II. Furthermore, there was a property, a family and a so-called food tax. The property tax was payable not only on

Langweil's model of Prague, detail of the Old Town Square.

ready cash and valuables, but also on houses and plots of land. The family tax had to be paid by every husband. At the same time only the first-born son was permitted to marry and even this depended on whether he could prove that his existence was secure and that he owned a certain amount of property. If a bride brought a dowry with her, she was also obliged to pay this tax. The food tax was paid on all basic kinds of food and in fact Jews paid this tax twice – firstly as a general tax paid by every citizen and secondly as a food charge which only a Jew had to pay when purchasing victuals in the ghetto. A special chapter of the Josephian policy was formed by the endeavour to secure the total Germanization of public administration and life. It can be presumed that the Jews in the ghetto spoke several languages and up to the time of the succession of the Hapsburgs to the Czech throne Czech was also a generally used language for conversing. In the course of Joseph II's reign the Germanization process proceeded to such an extent that Czech became a secondary language. Subject matter was taught in German in schools and every public document had to be drawn up in German. And at this time Jews were given a German surname.

The concentration of the municipal administration at the Old Town Hall, headed by the first burgrave, Dr. B. A. Zahořanský of Vorlík, also meant that

Langweil's model of Prague, streets of the Old Town.

the council took over political, civil and penal law authority for the whole town – and also for the ghetto. He was also responsible for the police and security agenda in the whole of Prague.

After long centuries civil, administrative and penal matters in the ghetto were governed by special laws based on common law, on the Bible and, last but not least, on the mood or good graces of the sovereign. The rabbi and his collegium – a council of elders – represented the greatest authority. The council of elders was competent to deal with more serious court cases and also functioned as an institution of appeal for more complicated matters originating in the other Jewish communities on the territory of Bohemia. Simpler cases were dealt with, sometimes also with the presence of the rabbi, by a lower instance.

If a Jewish citizen was not satisfied with the decision of the council of elders he could appeal to the Royal Court of Appeal at the Castle. Public and administrative matters connected with the autonomy of the ghetto were handled at the Town Hall by the mayor of the community along with five councillors, six local elders and twelve associated elders. (This system of division applied from the time of Ferdinand II.) The autonomous representatives of the community were elected at different intervals under different rulers. During the reign of Joseph II the twelve-member council of the ghetto was degraded to a kind of auxiliary organ of the chief council of the Old Town. The function of mayor was a rotary one and changed every month. The rabbi's court and the council of elders were also abolished. Even though the council of elders continued to have only limited competence in matters exclusively of a church and marital nature, it often remained the only decisive authority even in the post-Josephian period. Henceforward the right to judge penal cases belonged solely to the Old Town court. (The chapter entitled "The Jewish Community" contains a description of the administration of the ghetto during the Thirty Years War.) The law forbidding further burials in the Old Jewish Cemetery was a significant measure in the life of the ghetto. The last burial took place in its grounds in 1787.

* * *

We have a unique testimony to the appearance of the ghetto in the Theresian and Josephian periods in the cardboard model of Prague created by Antonín Langweil. The fact that the model is, in its way, unique in the world, makes it worth narrating the story of the origin of the model. Antonín Langweil was employed as a servant in the University Library. This post patently guaranteed him plenty of free time and also free movement in the town, which he exploited by making sketches. Later he set to work on something that has no like anywhere. In the course of eight years (1826–1834) he produced a plastic model of Baroque Prague – the Old Town, the Jewish Town, the Little Quarter and Hradčany – on the basis of his own sketches and Jüttner's plan of Prague of 1815. On an area of 20 sq. metres he modelled 2,228 buildings with the maximum precision and care. Antonín Langweil also noticed small details: he provided houses with numbers, sketched irregularities in the paving and portrayed towers, spires, chimneys and statues.

Antonín Langweil's model affords us an idea of the ghetto of about 1830. It creates the impression that the Jewish Town formed an organic part of the Old Town. Its houses do not differ in any way from those around it and it is not yet the disintegrating municipal organism, the overcrowded quarter of Prague's poor that showed itself to visitors to Prague in the following century.

Antonín Langweil's model of Prague is exhibited in the Prague Museum.

* * *

ASSIMILATION

The first half of the 19th century brought about a radical change also in the appearance and character of the Jewish Town. In essence the liberalizing Josephian reforms meant the liquidation of the greatest barriers isolating the Jewish population from the Christian population. The Jews began in large numbers to take advantage of the possibility of moving from the ghetto to the whole of Prague. Perceptible differentiation began to occur inside the Jewish community. A group of orthodoxically thinking Jews headed by the rabbi adhered to the old traditions and found it hard to reconcile themselves to the assimilation endeavours of the young generation. It is paradoxical that a great part of the poorer Jews did not want to leave the ghetto and when its walls had already been demolished the Jews protested by replacing them with wire. This explains why the Jewish enclave gained the popular attribute "behind the wire".

While the surrounding town was marked by various architectural styles and while Gothic and Baroque churches and palaces sprung up in its immediate vicinity, the ghetto preserved its medieval ground-plan. The population of the ghetto had grown continously practically from the late 17th century, but its area had grown to a negligible extent only. It is not surprising that people sought the first opportunity to escape from the ghetto's zigzagging blind alleys and passageways.

It was those who took advantage of the economic freedoms that were offering themselves who succeeded in leaving the ghetto. A new stratum of Jewish merchants and beginning industrialists came into being. They moved into burghers' and noblemen's houses in the Old Town and the New Town, the Little Quarter and Hradčany remaining inaccessible to them for the time being. The generation of wealthy Jews such as Mordecai Maisel and the first Jewish aristocrat Bassevi made way for a new generation and, similarly, the type of medieval Talmudistic scholar who gained his education at synagogal schools was replaced by the student who attended German elementary and secondary schools. University education still remained inaccessible to the majority of people and the number of Jews able to gain it was limited by special regulations. Young people anxious to gain scientific knowledge also had to fight against the disfavour of the rabbi and the opinions of orthodox circles.

The new Jewish intelligentsia asserted itself particularly in the spheres of medicine and law and later also in those of philosophy and the humanities. The restrictions imposed on the rights of Jewish university graduates included one which prohibited them from being employed as civil servants. An important place among the well-known intellectual personalites of the first half of the 19th century included the physician Jonas Jeiteles and, later, also one of the first Jewish professors to lecture at Charles University, Eliáš Altschul. The ranks of the first of the large number of renowned Jewish lawyers included Wolfgang Wessely, a professor at the law faculty. The development of industry made it possible for Jewish entrepreneurs to purchase plots of

land and houses in the places where their factories were situated. This initial era of the industrial revolution, characterized by textile production in the case of Jewish entrepreneurs, especially by the printing of cottons, led to the growth of Prague's suburbs, particularly of Smíchov, and to the founding of new ones – Karlín, Holešovice and Libeň. In Prague the printing of cotton was the privilege of Jews and the biggest enterprises engaged in this activity included those of L. Epstein, the brothers Porges, A. B. Przibram and L. Dormitzer. The big strike movement of Prague cotton-printers against low wages which broke out on 17 June, 1844 and led to the plundering of the brother Porges' factory in Smíchov soon grew into an anti-Jewish demonstration. Prague's poor and rabble joined the ranks of the workers. The demonstrators penetrated to the "tandlmarkt" where they plundered Jewish shops and killed their owners.

The life stories of the brother Porges are quite remarkable. Less than fifteen years sufficed for them to rise from the anonymity of the ghetto to the then highest possible social summit. They built their cotton-printing factory opposite Dientzenhofer's summer palace in Smíchov. And it was in this factory that a steam-driven machine was put into operation for the first time in this country. When Ferdinand V visited the Porges' factory during his visit to Prague in 1841 he was so taken with the brothers' activity that he raised them to the ranks of the nobility and endowed them with the privilege of using the name von Portheim. The younger of the brothers, Juda Leopold, later left the Smíchov factory and founded a world-renowed china works at Chodov near Karlovy Vary. Apart from other things, Mojžíš of Portheim also owned a large palace in Národní Street. He was known as a patron of the Jewish community, in·which he founded and financed a home for 120 Jewish children.

Big Jewish capital still rooted in the ghetto was represented by the names of Israel Hoenig of Hoenigsberg, Simon Lämel and his son Leopold Lämel, Moritz Zdekauer and his son Friedrich of Treuenkron. The life course of these personalities was also characterized by a rapid ascent to the nobility. Israel Hoenig was a wandering fair stallkeeper in Bavaria, where he by chance became acquainted with the method of processing tobacco. After returning to Prague in 1752 he gained the tobacco monopoly and became the supplier to the army. In 1789 he was made a nobleman.

In 1787 Simon Lämel began to trade with wool and became an army supplier during the Napoleonic Wars. He was made a nobleman in 1812. His son Leopold was an outstanding personality also in Czecho-Jewish relations. He was the director of the Czech Savings Bank and a member of several educational and cultural institutions. In 1848 he was even elected to the Czech Diet. He founded many charity institutions whose number also included a Jewish home for the poor, situated in Dušní Street. The family's intensive connections with the Czech revival movement are also witnessed by the fact that Leopold Lämel's daughter Elisa was taught the Czech language by Václav Hanka and that her daughter married the Czech poet Karel Drahotín, Count Villani de Pillonico, who in 1848 was in command of the Svornost armed corps.

Leopold Lämel, was known for his liberal ideas and opinions and applied a more moderate and more modern trend as regards reforms. It was he who succeeded in getting the composer František Škroup appointed to the post of director of the choir of the Old Shul Synagogue.

The wholesale merchant, financier and benefactor Moritz Zdekauer became the owner of the once renowned Canal Garden, which he purchased from the heirs of their original owner, Count Josef Emil Canal of Malabaila. It is alleged that this count had the inscription "Juden und Hunden ist der Eintritt verboten" executed on the gate leading to the garden.

"Great, however, was the joy among Prague's Israelites when one of their tribe purchased their garden", wrote Karolina Světlá in her memoirs. Later the garden was named Zdekauer's Garden.

∗ ∗ ∗

The times when the Jew concept was a synonym of the ghetto or the image of a small tradesmen offering his shabby goods at a "tandlmarkt" now belonged in the past. Sharp-minded Jewish intellectuals seeking a rapid path to assimilation began to penetrate into Prague society. They were all supporters of liberal and democratic principles, but society more than hesitated to accept them. Even though most of them spoke German, they still had no access to German society. Their attempts to join the Czech Enlightenment movement can be said to be unique. The young František Ladislav Rieger was a frequent guest in the house of the nobleman Leopold Lämel in Celetná Street, but ties of this kind were exceptional. The endeavours of the poet, historian and journalist Václav Bolemír Nebeský to bring the Czechs and Jews together aroused a strong negative reaction on the part of Karel Havlíček Bo-

The Bridge Tower with the barricade in 1848.

rovský: "And how can Israelites belong to the Czech nation when they are of Semitic origin? . . . Thus it must not be said that Jews living in Bohemia or Moravia are Czechs of a mosaic religion. We must regard them as a special nation, a Semite one living in this country merely by chance and sometimes understanding and speaking our language. For the Jews, regardless of what country and what part of the world they live in, regard themselves as one nation, as brothers and not only as fellow-believers; and this tie, which binds them together, is much stronger than the one by which they are bound to their country (the one in which they live). And it is also impossible to have two countries, two nations and serve two masters. Thus he who wishes to be a Czech must cease to be a Jew."

In 1850, when passionate disputes were waged for and against giving equal rights to Jews, Karel Havlíček acted in their favour: "Let us also contribute to the reform of Jewry, let us behave towards our Israelite fellow-citizens as we do towards those with equal rights, let us not be apathetic towards them, let us not bother them in any way". And directly addressing the Czechs he added: "If we are really such a wretched and contemptible nation that we allow several thousand Jews to overtake and outdo us in all deals, etc. we are indeed not even worthy of pity".

✳ ✳ ✳

The revolutionary year 1848, the proclamation of the first Austrian constitution, brought the Jews equal rights. The millennium of history of the Prague ghetto came to an end.

In 1850 the separate Jewish Town spreading out in the Old Town between Old Town Square, present-day Kaprova Street, the River Vltava and present-day Pařížská Street, was joined to Prague as its fifth quarter. And at the same time the Jewish Town was renamed Josefov in honour of Joseph II.

The greatest obstacle preventing the Czech side from accepting the Jewish assimilation endeavours lay in the fact that Prague's Jews, representing a strong economic and intellectual potential, mostly spoke German and avowed German nationality. In the pointed Czech-German nationality climate of Prague the Jews represented a group which neither side welcomed.

This "split" situation, the constant search for a way out and the fight for recognition found expression in the literary phenomenon of the so-called Prague circle of Jewish writers writing in German. This group will be dealt with in the second part of this book.

✳ ✳ ✳

The activity of the physician and writer Siegfried Kapper (1820–1879), who is rightly regarded as the pioneer, the founder of the Czech-Jewish movement, also falls in this period. (Kapper was born in house No. 13 in Nádražní Street in the Smíchov quarter of Prague) Siegfried Kapper supported the circle of Jewish writers who tried to achieve not only an intellectual, but also factual Czech-Jewish synthesis already during his Prague studies. In his

Siegfried Kapper (1821–1879), poet and pioneer of the Czech-Jewish concept.

youth he was chiefly influenced by his later brother-in-law, the German-Jewish Prague poet Moritz Hartmann (1821–1872), who attended the Slavonic Congress in Prague in 1848. The group surrounding Siegried Kapper tried to gain full spiritual freedom for the Jews and to secure their assimilation in and merging with the Czech environment in the real sense of the word.

When Kapper published his collection of poems entitled "České listy" (Czech Letters), in which he also dealt with the principles of freedom and equal rights of Jews, in 1846, the response to it was not univocal. It gained both a positive (Jan Neruda') and negative reception, represented by Karel Havlíček Borovský.

Siegfried Kapper's ideas and deeds intended to bring the Czechs and the Jews closer together are of greater interest to us than his literary activity (Kapper was a connoisseur of South Slavonic literature and he also translated from Czech into German).

In 1848 and again in 1860 Siegfried Kapper took part on the Czech side in the revolutionary and nationality struggles and in 1864 he became a member of the town council at Mladá Boleslav.

His importance lies in the fact that at the time when most of Prague's Jewish intellectuals inclined towards the German language he headed a small group (shamefully called "Tschechojuden" (Czech-Jew) which endeavoured to bring the Czechs and the Jews close together. His time was far from being ripe for the realization of such ideas. Kapper remained alone in his endeavours. In recognition of his merits and priorities in the Czech-Jewish field the later organized Czech-Jewish assimilation movement avowed his heritage also by naming it the "Kapper Academic Society" in 1920.

THE TURN
OF THE 19TH AND 20TH
CENTURIES

Let us leave the territory of the former ghetto and take a look at how the latter half of the 19th century manifested itself in the life of Prague, which was marked at the time of Bach's absolutism and the strong process of Germanization not only by the greatest growth of the population (from 157,000 inhabitants in 1850 it rose to 314,000 in 1880), but simultaneously also by the fact that Prague was one of the most industrialized towns in the monarchy.

From the nationality aspect the whole of the latter half of the 19th century was characterized by the question of the mutual relations between the Czechs and the Germans and the sharpening of their mutual variances.

The more rapacious Czech middle class, which stood at the origin of and later at the realization of the national revival process, culminating in the laying of the foundations of Czech scientific life and the building of the National Theatre, began to assert itself to an ever greater extent in Prague's social and cultural life.

What position did Prague's Jews occupy at that time and what was their number in comparison with the Czech and German population?

Let us recall that still in the 18th century very many Jews moved from Prague to the countryside. Apart from others, a reason for this, as has already been said, were the so-called "family laws", which fixed the number of Jewish families for Bohemia and Moravia, permitted only the eldest son of a family to marry and prohibited Jews from moving to other areas than those occupied by them in 1724. Some Jews, especially in Prague, replied to this by marrying secretly or setting up a "household in a household", while others sought a way of escaping from the watchful eyes of the country lords or even fled abroad – to Hungary and southern Poland.

However, this period came to an end and in the mid-19th century they were able to move about freely. Moreover, new possibilities arose for them to participate in economic life and Prague's Jewish community once again began to increase in number. And so in 1880 there were already over twenty thousand Jews in Prague, i.e. over 20% per cent of the total number of Jews in Bohemia. In the course of the following twenty years another seven thousand set up their home in Prague, bringing the 20% up to 30%. And in 1921 40% of the total Jewish population resided in Prague.

From the demographic viewpoint this meant that throughout the whole 19th century the history of the Czech (and especially the Prague) Jewry was strongly marked by the changing relations between town and country and inside towns between their centre and their suburbs. At the end of enlightened absolutism Prague was, apart from Frankfurt am Main, perhaps the only town which did not banish its Jewish population. A different situation prevailed in Germany, where only small groups remained in the countryside,

JUDR. Alois Zucker (1842–1906), Professor of criminal law, Court Counsellor, Deputy of the Imperial Council, Dean of the Faculty of Law, exponent of the Czech Jewish movement.

and things were different in Moravia and Poland and again in Hungary – the survival of the Jews in Prague thus gave a unique demographic configuration.

A surprising number of Prague's Jewish inhabitants chose to be of Czech nationality. Approximately at the beginning of the 20th century 92% of them did so! However, the majority of them spoke German and this outwardly distorted the whole situation.

In spite of this, endeavours to secure the peaceful coexistence of Prague's Jews and Czechs were repeatedly thwarted, sometimes by those Jews (they were few in number) who not only spoke German, but also preferred to have German nationality. However, it was often Czech circles, which traditionally reproached Jews for being "Germanized", that obstructed the said endeavours. The fact that many people maintained that Jews would never be either Germans or Czechs for the simple reason that they were Jews did nothing to change the situation. Amidst these attacks, sometimes from the left and sometimes from the right, the Jews felt the need to associate themselves in some kind of organization, this applying particularly in the case of university students, among whom nationality questions were always the most pressing.

Thus in March 1876 the Society of Czech Academicians-Jews originated. (Spolek českých akademiků-židů) The ranks of its founding members included several former university graduates, three students of the law faculty, two medical students and one engineer as well as three factory owners, journalists, a member of the National Theatre in Prague and the conductor of the Czech Symphony Orchestra.

During the first year of its activity the society had 82 members, 28 of whom

JUDr. Jakub Scharf (1857–1922), editor,
Deputy of the Land Diet for Josefov,
exponent of the Czech Jewish movement.,

JUDr. Augustin Stein (1854–1937), head of
the clearance department, the first Czech
president of the Jewish Religious
Community in Prague.

were students. The first "protector" was Alois Zucker (1842–1906), a professor of law. Another important and leading member was Jakub Scharf (1857–1922), a lawyer and publicist who was also the founder of the Czech-Jewish National Union (Národní jednota českožidovská). (This was later renamed the Academic "Kapper" Society). From the very beginning the aim of the Society of Czech Academicians-Jews was to unite Jewish families whose members spoke Czech, but also to gain for the Czech national culture also those families which still mainly spoke German. The founders of the society were aware that the use of the German language was an obstacle preventing fluent communication with the Czech environment and also the gaining of a place in Czech society. It was chiefly young people that wanted to break down the barriers of the intellectual and cultural ghetto. One of the practical steps taken to secure the realization of this aim was the publication of the Czech-Jewish Calendar (Českožidovský kalendář) in 1881. This was preceded by the publication of Breuer's Textbook of Religion for secondary schools and Stein's Prayer Book for ordinary days and holidays. The society decided to publish the calendar with the aim of propagating the idea of assimilation, of reacting to all then contemporary problems and of concentrating in particular on problems of antisemitism and Zionism.

With its pocket size the Czech-Jewish Calendar resembled the German calendar and its contents were divided into three parts. The first contained the ritual cycle of the Jewish calendar written in Hebrew, but the second part contained the Christian calendar with popular names and a complete list of all the fairs and markets held in Bohemia, Moravia and Silesia. The third part of the calendar was devoted to belles-lettres, containing, in addition to several poems and short stories, also popular articles dealing with Jewish themes. The first editor of the calendar was Augustin Stein (1854–1937, he edited the first three volumes), the first Czech-Jewish mayor of Prague's Jewish community and chairman of the Supreme Council of Jewish Religious Communities in Bohemia.

At first the pages of the calendar contained only contributions by Jewish authors representing the Czech-Jewish intellectual environment (A. Zucker, J. Scharf, K. Fischer, J. Penížek). The first non-Jewish author to show his sympathy with the Czech-Jewish movement in his contribution was the dramatist and prosaist Ladislav Stroupežnický, the first dramaturgist of the National Theatre. He was followed by the journalist, writer and theatre critic Jakub Arbes. During the editorship of Karel Fischer (who edited 22 volumes of the calendar) the poet Jaroslav Vrchlický also contributed to the calendar by writing a poem called "BAR-KOCHBA" based on the heroic tale of the Jewish uprising against the Romans in 2 B.C.

The first real Czech-Jewish writer Vojtěch Rakous also published his short stories regularly in the calendar, doing so from the time of the seventh volume.

(Let us present several more data about this periodical, which played such an important role in bringing the Czech and the Jewish population closer together: the calendar was published regularly every year from 1881 to 1938 and the ranks of its editors in the course of its 58 volumes included, apart from A. Stein and K. Fischer, O. Guth, V. Teytz, M. Pleschner, E. Lederer and A. Fuchs. The editor of the calendar in the post-war period, when it was by then published by the Academic "Kapper" Society", was V. Markus, the 51st up to the 56th volumes being edited by the well-known Jewish writer Egon Hostovský. The last edition of the calendar bore the year 1938–1939 and its editor was Hanuš Bonn. One of its contributors was for the first and, unfortunately, the last time the poet Jiří Orten.)

✽ ✽ ✽

The assimilation movement had a direct influence on religious life. Most of the smaller Jewish communities, particularly in the countryside, gladly accepted the idea that religious rites be conducted in the Czech language. It was the most influential of them, i.e. the Prague community, that most strongly opposed this idea, but finally a shrewd solution was found and asserted by the OR-TAMID (Eternal Light) organization. It was based on the compromise conception that "it did not want to Czechisize religious rites conducted in Hebrew, but that it was concerned with Czechisizing what had so far been delivered in German such as sermons, public announcements, certain prayers, etc. . . ."

With the assistance of the OR-TAMID organization and the Society of

ČÍSLO 9.   V PRAZE, ve středu, dne 1. května 1901.   ROČNÍK VII.

ČESKOŽIDOVSKÉ LISTY.

Vycházejí dne 1. a 15. každého měsíce.

Adresa pro dopisy: Redakce „Českožidovských Listů" v Praze. — Administrace v Praze, ve Smečkách číslo 30. n. — Předplatné splatné a žalovatelné v Praze poštou pololetně 4 K celoročně 8 K Jednotlivá čísla po 40 h. Inseráty účtují se levně. Reklamace se nefrankují a nepočetí. — Rukopisů nevracíme, nevyplacených dopisů a nepodepsaných zpráv nepřijímáme.

OBSAH: Naše otázka školská. (Pracovnímu sjezdu Národní Jednoty českožidovské napsal Dr Ignát Arnstein.) Semitismus a jesuitismus. (Odpověď od V. Teytze.) — Národní Jednota českožidovská v Praze. — Různé zprávy. — Inserty. Belletristická příloha má tento obsah: Hry židovských dětí. — Pohádka o chudém králi. (Vypravuje Jos. Leda. Příteli Václavu Řihovi.) — Činoherní bilance Národního divadla. — Literatura.

Naše otázka školská.

Pracovnímu sjezdu Národní Jednoty českožidovské napsal Dr. Ignát Arnstein.

Z otázky školské se zrodila Národní Jednota českožidovská a odstranění německých škol židovských po českém venkově rozsetých, byla jednou z hlavních snah, která nás vedla při založení Národní Jednoty českožidovské.

Důvody k tomu byly přečetné.

Školy ty vrážely svévolně docela zbytečný a provokativní klín mezi mládež židovskou a křesťanskou a pomáhaly rozšiřovati propast mezi dorůstajícími generacemi.

Připravovaly dítky židovské ne-li pro germanisaci, tož aspoň pro úplný národní indiferentismus a činily je slepými pro jich okolí i pro kulturní ovzduší české, a byly-li následky ty u značného zlomku odchovanců těchto škol zamezeny, stalo se to jen šťastnou korrekturou, kterou proti vlivu jejich prováděly výchova na českých vyšších školách, prakticky život a pilná četba literatury a žurnálů českých.

Školy ty zkracovaly dítky židovské také ve vzdělání věcném i jazykovém. Poznatky ethické a praktické, přírodopisné, zeměpisné, dějepisné, počtářské, jež mají dítky ve škole do sebe ssáti, byly jim podávány jazykem cizím a byly jim tak učiněny ne-li úplně nechutnými a nepřístupnými, tož aspoň těžko srozumitelnými a mlhavými. Mimo to vyučovány dítky různého stáří a různého pohlaví současně v jedné nebo ve dvou třídách a byl tím, nehledě k ohledům mravnosti, jež také trpěly, řádný paedagogický postup namnoze vyloučen. K tomu přistupovaly u porovnání s řádně dotovanými veřejnými školám obecným nedostatečné pomocné prostředky těchto malých škol soukromých a mimo některé velmi čestné výjimky, které školy takových škol mírnití dovedly, také nedostatek paedagogicky vycvičených sil učitelských.

Se stanoviska politického pak bylo přímo absurdním, že židé, kteří tak ohnivě bojují proti zavedení škol konfessijních, sami pro sebe školy takové vydržovali, vydržujíce tak kadr, ku kterému by se snáze mohla připojiti důsledně provedená síť jinověrných škol konfessijních.

Školy ty vzbuzovaly také důvodné pohoršení právě v těch nejvážnějších vrstvách české veřejnosti a byly a jsou posud pramenem mnohých trpkostí. V tom nás nesmí klamati apatické mnohdy chování místních činitelů, kteří z osobních ohledů mlčeli, nebo kteří si následkem vlivů klerikálních neb i z obav před zvýšením nákladů na školní obec spadajících ani nepřáli, aby židovské dítky ze svého samovolného ghetta školského přešly do veřejné školy obecné.

Uvedu jen tři ukázky, jak o věci smýšlejí čelní representanti české veřejnosti.

Známa jsou přátelská varovná slova, která v tom směru promluvil roku 1894 vysoce vážený příznivec našich snah p. Dr. Engel na ustavující schůzi benešovského odboru. Ještě důtklivěji a se zřejmým steskem vyslovil se v době nedávné ředitel zemské banky p. Dr. Matuš o nezrušené posud škole mladoboleslavské a princ Dr. Bedřich Švarcenberk sám osobně se staral o zrušení jedné německé náboženské školy židovské svého okresu.

Nevhodnost separatistických škol židovských dosvědčuje také častěji již citovaný úsudek, který ohledně škol takových v Polsku existujících vyslovil r. 1893 sám náš císař, dav vůči přemýšlivému starostovi náboženské obce Jaroslavu Strisovrovi potěšení svému výraz nad tím, že tamější dítky židovské navštěvují spolu s dítkami jiných vyznání společnou veřejnou školu obecnou.

Z tábora židovského pak pro škodlivost a pro provokativní ráz německých náboženských škol židovských mohu citovati jako velké nesmazatelné veřejné svědectví provolání k českým židům, vydané po schválení zákona o upravení poměrů náboženských obcí židovských dne 20. dubna 1890 a podepsané vedle přímých pracovníků českožidovských uznávanými representanty židů ze všech končin království Českého. Ještě lapidárnější svědectví, o kterém ale stydno se zmíniti, vydaly o tom mimodék obce táborská, milevská a jičínská, které na dlouholeté přátelské důvody naše neslyšely, ale při hanebných bouřích roku 1897, jakoby instinktivně dav se svých německých školních náboženských na své straně cítili vinníka, podle rady známého biblického vypravování rázem hodily školy ty v oběť rozbouřeným vlnám.

The title page of the "Českožidovské listy" (Czech-Jewish Newspaper), vol. VII, May 1, 1901.

Czech Academicians-Jews a Czecho-Hebrew prayer book was published in 1884 which was intended above all to serve Czech-speaking Jews. On the other hand, however, it was also meant to acquaint the Czech public, which often had only a hazy or even wholly distorted idea of them, with the principles of the Jewish religion.

* * *

The Czech-Jewish movement had to fight against Czech and German nationalism, antisemitism and also the growing tendency of the Zionist movement on "several fronts" in its endeavours to secure complete assimilation. A more important shift to the benefit of these assimilation tendencies proclaimed by the Society of Academicians–Jews and published in the Calendar came about before the end of the century after the founding of the so-called National Czech-Jewish Union (1893), (Národní Jednota česko-židovská), followed by the publication of the first Czecho-Jewish weekly – The Czech-Jewish Newspaper (1894) (Českožidovské listy).

The very first number of this publication contained a proclamation in the form of the following basic ideological credo: "We want every Czech Jew to be a real Czech, to feel, to think and to behave like every loyal Czech!"

Later the Czech-Jewish Newspaper carried articles oriented in particular against German Jewish schools. This pressure was so strong that in 1906 the National Czech-Jewish Union was able to state that since the time of its foundation it had succeeded in contributing to the abolition of 52 German Jewish schools in Czech-speaking regions. The Jewish children involved were naturally transferred to Czech schools.

In spite of the efforts of Prague's Jews to merge themselves with the Czech environment to the greatest possible extent, antisemitic tendencies always manifested themselves which accused the Jews of insincere conduct and an inborn inability to assimilate themselves with any part of the Czech population.

A dramatic threat to Jewish certainties, freedoms and property, indeed, even to their very lives occurred in 1897 when the fall of Badeni's government came about and the Jews suddenly found themselves in the focus of Czech-German national disputes. After being elected to the Imperical Council, Badeni decided to at least partially fulfil the requirements of the Czech nationalists and make the use of both Czech and German legal, especially in official proceedings. This move was unpopular with German chauvinistic, national circles and this led to mass anti-Czech demonstrations in Vienna and later also in Prague. German students marched through Prague to the accompaniment of patriotic songs and shouted threatening slogans. The Czech population defended itself by throwing stones at the German theatre and other buildings. Attacks were also made on German shops and coffee-houses. The show-windows of more than one Jewish firm in the street Na Příkopě and Václavské náměstí (Wenceslas Square) were broken in the course of street uproars. The anger of the crowd was directed in particular against Jewish shops and no one was interested in whether or not their owners avowed Czech or German nationality. True, at that time Jews formed nearly 40% of the German population. The support of the press, which would back the Jews and thus lessen the anti-Jewish moods and demonstrations, was not forthcoming. On the contrary, "The National Newspaper" (Národní listy) incited the anger of the crowd still further by stating that the whole incident had been evoked by German and Jewish provocations.

Allegedly the coffee-houses from which German students affronted Praguers were usually full of Jews and "Semite" faces could be seen in the doorways during the incident proper. Such at least was the account carried by "The National Newspaper".

Not only show-windows, but also all hopes that Czech Jews in Prague had of solving all their problems and living peacefully and fearlessly in Prague found themselves in ruins.

The endeavours of the Czech-Jewish movement to secure full assimilation remained at freezing point. Were, then, the Zionist circles which believed that assimilation was impossible right?

* * *

Hardly had the Jews recovered from the shocks of the end of 1897 than another affair broke out. The so-called Hilsner affair agitated public opinion even far beyond the boundaries of the country. Once again anti-Semite flames flared up! On 1 April, 1899, at the time when the Jewish Easter holiday was approaching, the body of a murdered young Christian girl by the name of Anežka Hrůzová was found in the small East Bohemian community of Polná. Suspicion fell on a local Jewish footwear journeyman of the name of Leopold Hilsner. In view of the fact that the young girl met her violent death at the time of the Jewish holiday, with which an ancient medieval legend connected with the use of Christian blood was linked, the murder evoked the impression that it was the question of a ritual act.

Anti-Jewish hunts and attacks broke out throughout the whole country, unfortunately also with the participation of certain members of intellectual circles. (Karel Baxa, later to become the mayor of Prague, voluntarily offered to defend the interests of the mother of the murdered girl and directed the whole proceedings on an anti-Jewish basis with the aim of gaining political capital for himself.)

In the conditions of the general anti-Jewish atmosphere, which bordered on mass hysteria, Leopold Hilsner was found guilty. This patently represented a miscarriage of justice motivated by and tributary to then contemporary public opinion.

Heard in this tense social atmosphere was the voice of T. G. Masaryk who with the weight of his personality and scientific authority defied in particular the truth of the legend concerning a ritual murder. Similarly as in the case of

Antisemitic caricatures from the period of the
Hilsner affair, Prague 1899–1901.

Dreyfus, the wrongly convicted French officer, in the course of which the writer Émile Zola became the target of French anti-Jewish attacks, Masaryk also became the victim of fanatical attacks waged on behalf of nationalistic and clerical interests. Demonstrations took place against his person and against his lectures at the university.

At that time T. G. Masaryk wrote the following in defence of the Jews: "In the course of my work it has continuously become clearer and clearer to me that the ritual legend is a direct incrimination against the Czech people. The Jews in Bohemia and in the Czech Lands in general (this is confirmed for me by learned and critical connoisseurs of Jewry) belong among the elite not only of Austrian Jewry, but of Jewry in general – so how can a ritual murder be attributed to them!" (Note: L. Hilsner was sentenced to death during court proceedings at Kutná Hora. After the publication of Masaryk's article "The Necessity of Revising the Polná Process" a new trial was ordered which took place in October 1900 at Písek. L. Hilsner was again sentenced to death, but this was changed to life imprisonment. In 1918 he was pardoned and released from prison. Later he changed his name to Heller and lived in freedom until 1928.)

* * *

Antisemitism, nourished by the Hilsner affair and now also officially avowed by the politician Lueger of Vienna, was manifested not ony in attacks

in the press, but also in the clear discrimination of Jewish citizens and by the boycotting of Jewish shops in the sphere of economic life. In particular the editors Eduard Lederer (1857–1944) and Viktor Vohryzek (1864–1918) devoted attention to this problem on the pages of the Jewish press. They believed in the strengthening of progressive forces and the fight against obscurantism. "We must not fall flat in front of every newspaper bandit", wrote V. Vohryzek boldly. However, to their surprise their approach seemed too radical to the editors of The Czech-Jewish Newspaper. A dispute arose whose result was that the few "radicals" headed by Viktor Vohryzek founded a new organization in Pardubice in 1904 under the name of Progressive Jewry (Pokrokové židovstvo) (from 1907 it bore the name The Union of Czech Progressive Jews) and also the weekly called ROZVOJ (Development) – the only Czech publication to fight against antisemitism. The Czech-Jewish Newspaper ceased to exist from 1907 and the journal Development became (up to 1939, when its publication was stopped) the most important speaker of Czech-Jewish rapprochement.

✳ ✳ ✳

Jewish students who inclined rather to German ethnics followed a different path. Their participation in various "Burschenschafts" and in societies such as Lese- und Redehalle der deutschen Studenten in Prag was undesirable. In 1893 a small group of Jewish students formed a society called Maccabäa (Maccabea) which in 1896 was changed into the Union of Jewish University

MUDr. Viktor Vohryzek (1864–1918), physician and exponent of the Czech Jewish movement, founder and editor of the weekly periodical "Rozvoj" (Development) and writer.

Students (Verein der jüdischen Hochschüler). The programme of these societies was not univocal. It neither avowed the Jewish religion nor fully supported the assimilation endeavours.

* * *

A picture of Jewish Prague and its rich life as regards societies would not be complete without a mention of the international **B'nai B'rith** lodge whose members came from wealthy Jewish circles regardless of whether they belonged in the Jewish community or were of Czech or German nationality. In the period between 1892 and 1898 lodges were founded, apart from the Prague lodge (lodge Praga), at Plzeň, Karlovy Vary, Liberec, Brno and Opava. Apart from Jewish solidarity, the **B'nai B'rith** lodge laid emphasis on the realization of a cultural programme and charitable activity.

* * *

In 1896 the Austrian Jewish journalist Theodor Herzl published his work entitled The Jewish State and one year later the 1st Zionist Congress took place in Basle at which the World Zionist Organization was founded.

The ideology of Zionism, based on consolidation of the consciousness of the Jewish national identity and endeavours to secure the return of the Jews to their original historical country, offered a univocal solution also to Jews in the Czech Lands. This solution, expressed also by T. Herzl when, in his arti-

ROZVOJ

Vychází každý pátek.
Předplácí se ročně K 12·—.
Půlletně K 6·—.
Jednotlivá čísla po 24 h.
Redakce a administr. v Praze-II. Mariánská ul. 6.
Administrace úřaduje od 8—12 a 2—6 hod. Redakční návštěvy od 10—12 hodin vítány.
Účet poštovní spoř. čís. 91647.
Telefon čís. 505|VIII.

ROČNÍK IX. V PRAZE, dne 22. ledna 1915. ČÍSLO 2.

Dr. Otakar Guth:

Poznámky k židovské otázce.

I.

Ve dnech, kdy odehrává se na zemi, ve vzduchu a na moři válka, jak ji ani fantasie H. G. Wellse nevymyslila větší, může se zdát absurdní psát poznámky k židovské otázce. Válka rozbila víru ve slova, v programy, v potištěný papír. Svět chce fakta, ne slova. Přes to bylo by chybou udělat kříž nad dosavadní prací a věřit, že po válce nastanou z brusu nové poměry. Válka může opravit leckteré dosavadní názory, může politicky a hospodářsky přivodit nové konstelace, ale nepřetvoří povahy člověka ze základů. Komu na př. kniha, obraz a kultura vůbec byla nutností před válkou, ani válečné události neučiní nekulturním. Bylo by také chybou myslit, že je nyní všechno theoretisování zbytečným a že jen suchá fakta mají smysl. Ne. Theorie bude i na dále připravovat půdu praxi.

Co zde všeobecně uvedeno, platí také o židovské otázce. Jsou, kdo věří, že židovská otázka bude rozřešena mluvou děl na pláních východního bojiště. Nemyslím. Pravda je, že důsledky války vtisknou stranám a hnutím v židovstvu, na př. sionismu, nový ráz. Změní snad mezinárodní všesvětovou základnu sionismu a ukáží jasně praktickou nemožnost zřídit židovský stát v Palestýně. Nebo rozbijí zdi ghetta, v nichž se tísnilo tisíce židů v Haliči a v Ruském Polsku. Náboženský a kulturní život východních židů bude se asi brát jiným řečištěm. Právní a politické poměry největší části židů budou pravděpodobně po válce jiné. Vždyť ze 13 milionů židů žije jich na válečné scéně

v Rusku	6,000.000
v Haliči a v Bukovině	1,000.000
v Uhrách	900.000
v Rumunsku	270.000
v evrop. Turecku	200.000
	8,370.000

nebo-li okrouhle 8 a půl milionu.

Ale bylo ukvapeností čekat, že po válce rázem a náhle bude židovská otázka rozřešena. Tomu jistě tak nebude. Kdyby i na př. dostalo se židům na Rusi svobod nyní jim slibovaných, assimilovali by se teprve během mnoha desítiletí a jen znenáhla by klesl odliv jich do Ameriky.

II.

V říjnu 1914, takřka uprostřed válečných událostí vyšla v Německu kniha, jež svým autorem a svým obsahem zasluhuje, aby na ni bylo zvláště důrazně upozorněno. Napsal ji Karel Kautský*) — dnes vedle F. Mehringa a Bernsteina nejpřednější theoretik říšsko-německé strany sociálně demokratické.

Není to poprvé, že theoretikové socialismu zabývají se obšírněji židovskou otázkou. Byl to především Karel Marx, jenž ve spisku „Zur Judenfrage" obíral se problémem a vyslovil názor, že židé přizpůsobují se prostředí, poněvadž toto okolí je proniknuto podstatou židovství. Židé byli nositeli peněžního hospodářství a peněžní hospodářství proniklo celý svět. „Die Juden haben sich insoweit emanzipiert, als die Christen zu Juden geworden sind." Žid se přizpůsobí ostatní společnosti, „weil das reale Wesen des Juden in der bürgerlichen Gesellschaft sich allgemein verwirklicht, verweltlicht hat". Také Otto Bauer věnoval v knize Die Nationalitätenfrage und die Sozialdemokratie kapitolu o národní autonomii židů a dovozoval zde, že jako přestali býti národem židé západní, přestanou býti národem i židé východní a splynou s ostatními národy.

Studie Kautského je zajímavá hlavně ve dvou směrech: že dobíjí rasovní theorii, hlásanou H. St. Chamberlainem nebo docentem Dr. Zollschanem a dále, že bezohledně účtuje s sionismem. Nebude snad nemístno upozornit, že Kautský dospívá v otázce rasovní k týmž důsledkům, jež od let byly v č.-ž. hnutí mnou i jinými na základě stejných pramenů jako prof. Luschana, Ratzla, Fhischberga a Hertze hlásány. Moderní věda o člověku (anthropologie) nezná příkrého rozdílu mezi rasami. Všechny lidské rasy mají týž původ; během doby se měnily a prostupovaly, takže není dnes rasy, jež by nebyla krevně promísena s jinými. Není vyšších a nižších ras, není panujících a poddaných ras. Na počátku byla jednota. Nejrůznějšími vlivy se stalo, že se lidstvo rozestoupilo v různé vrstvy. Ale vývoj směřuje opět k jednotě. Typy zanikají, individuality rostou. V ohromném kotli stmelují se skupiny a roste nové jednotné pokolení lidstva.

Hlavní zásluha studie Kautského, pokud jedná o otázce rasovní, je v tom, že výsledky dosavadních zkoumání přehledně shrnul a že velmi přesvědčivě vyvrátil „esthetiky rázu Wernera Sombarta". Se Sombartem, Zollschanem a Lamprechtem zachází Kautský — velmi nemilosrdně.

Neobyčejně ostře odmítá Kautský sionism. Také zde kryjí se celkem názory Kautského se stanoviskem č.-ž. hnutí. „Literárně vznikl sionism v západní Evropě, avšak jen u židů ruských a rumunských je skutečnou potřebou…" „Ve snaze oddělit židy od nežidů setkává se sionism s antisemitismem a dále také v tom, aby všichni židé byli odstraněni z dosavadních států." „Sionism je neproveditelnou utopií"*) atd.

Názory Kautského o sionismu jsou významny.

*) Rasse und Judentum. Nákladem knihkupectví Vorwärts v Berlíně.

*) Výňatek z díla Kautského o sionismu bude uveřejněn v některém z příštích čísel Rozvoje.

M. Schoenbaum:

Assimilace, či — sionismus?

Příspěvek historický.

(Pokračování.)

II.

Není divu, že za známých rakouských poměrů dnes, počítajíce patrně s krátkou pamětí rychle žijící, sensacemi přesycované generace novinářských čtenářů svých, reklamují pro sebe Fischhofa dokonce titíž Němci,

Beseda.

Ticho vládne v zástupu. Poslední dobou kolikrát již stejný zástup putoval na nádraží, aby se loučil s odjíždějícími vojíny, aby pohostil válečné transporty odjíždějící na bojiště a provolal jim „s bohem", jež mnohému z odjíždějících asi bude posledním, aby politoval raněné a nemocné, přijíždějící z bojiště, aby pokusil se zahlédnouti pochmurné vozy se zajatými. A vždy bylo v zástupu plno ruchu, hovoru, šumu. Dnes vládne ticho, nejisté očekávání něčeho neznámého. „Uprchlíci přijedou," rozlétlo se po městě, a „jsou to polští židé", doplnilo zprávu prvou. Soucit, zvědavost, odpor, nejistota, milosrdenství, strach, všecky tyto city pronikají duši zástupu, ano mísí se v divoké směsici i v srdci jednotlivcově. Vědí, že to, co přijde, je kus hrůzy válečné, hrůzy nejhroznější, neboť postihla lidi vlastního bojování úplně vzdálené, vědí, že je to kus bídy, bídy nejbídnější, neboť úpí již ti, kteří už za normálních poměrů patří mezi největší chudáky lidstva. Ale je zde nepříjemný pocit cizoty, neznámého, nevalného.

Polský žid! Kus instinktivně nenáviděného světa, světa odlišné národnosti, náboženství, zevnějšku, tělesným i duševním uspořádáním. Ten, kdo zabloudil do Haliče, vypravoval vždy s hrůzou a posměchem o nečistotě, hrabivosti a ortodoxnosti polských židů, s nimiž se stýkal, a třeba to byla spodina jich — kramář, faktor, lichvář — znaky jejich se generalisovaly během času na polské židy vůbec. Ti z nich, kteří k nám přišli — šnorerové, obchodníci nejnižšího druhu — nepřispěli k zlepšení utvořené představy. A teď jich přijde 300, tři sta do našeho města a okolí, tři sta mezi nás, aby žili snad měsíc, dva, snad i šest, sedm měsíců mezi námi, s námi. A duše se instinktivně brání. Ale přijdou zničení, zbavení všeho, hladoví, sešlí. Přijdou jako prozatímní oběti války, jež vede se pro nás, za nás. Půjdou, nemajíce na mnoze nic, než svou bídu, i ti nejbohatší z nich, bídnější než žebráci, bez peněz, bez domova, ano namnoze i sobě ztraceni, otcové bez dětí, děti bez rodičů.

Temným nočním pozadím prorazila dvě bílá světla. Pomalu blížil se vlak, jakoby vezl mrtvoly. — Na plošině prvého vozu stojí starý žid; bělovlasý, s vlajícími pejzy, upřená zoufalý pohled do rozjasňující se tmy. Symbol té celé bídy, zoufající a doufající, proklínající a lkající, a při tom všem se modlící. Ortodoxnost nesmyslná, neživá proniká vším, prostupuje celou tu bídu. Lidskost zvítězila v obecenstvu: ve velkých kotlích přináší se čaj, v ošatkách chleba. Jako vlci vrhají se na chleba, perou se oň, trhají si ho z ruky. Neviděl jsi nikdy hroznějšího obrazu než tyto lidi, kteří se rvali o suchý chléb. Ale čaj snášejí pouze pro děti, vychladlí, vyhladovělí muž. i ženy odpírají si ho. Není prý košer. Matka s šesti dětmi a kojencem u prázdných prsou odmítá mléko, neví, není-li v trefe nádobě. Dva světy se srážejí, úplně cizí. Konflikt opět vystupuje. Chudáci, kteří snesli zdarma mléko, nechápou, jak lze jím opovrhovati. Konečně na domluvy domorodých židů část ortodoxních povoluje, ale část se jich ještě brání. Spokojují se chlebem. Kolik dní již nejedli nic teplého, nejen z bídy, nouze, ale vzdalováni pěněním nesmyslnou, zde úplně zbytečnou, jistě ne bohumilou pobožností. Přes noc zůstali ve vagonech, přechází podle vozu. U jednoho okna stojí hezký chlapec, v polské gymnasijní uniformě, vedle něho jeho sestra, krásné děvče s černými vlasy a očima. Hledí do černé noci a hledají. Co? Rodiče své, domov svůj, sny své. A vedle nich konejší matka svých šest dětí. Křičí jedno přes druhé a chtějí ještě chleba. Posíláme pro chleba. Je půlnoc.

Za ohrouhlým stolem sedí komisař hejtmanství. Vedle něho zástupci obce a židovské náboženské obce. Před nimi houf bídy. Je to první rodina, jež má být umístěna. Rodina: otec, matka, 10 dětí, tchán a sestra matčina, 14 osob, jedna rodina. Nezvyklé u nás požeh-

The weekly periodical "Rozvoj" (Development). Vol. IX, Nos. 2 and 14 of 1915.

cle "Die Jagd in Böhmen" carried by the journal DIE WELT, appealed to Jews in the Czech Lands not to identify themselves in the Czech-German nationality conflict.

It is interesting that the first founders, pioneers of the Zionist movement, came from the Czech (and not the German) Jewish environment.

In 1899 Filip Lebenhart and Karl Rezekemper founded the Zionist society "Zion". Shortly afterwards they also merged the Union of Jewish University Students (Verein der jüdischen Hochschüler in Prag) and the Society of Jewish Academicians in Prague to form a single society with the new name BAR KOCHBA. Filip Lebenhart in particular was responsible for this as one of the leading representatives of the Zionist movement in Prague. He was a friend of Jaroslav Vrchlický, with whom he waged long discussions on the essence of the Zionist movement.

After 1900 the Zionist ideas spread to other Czech and Moravian towns. Intellectual groups, students, in particular supported the Zionists. This conditioned the programme of the movement, which by now was mainly of a cultural character.

From 1901 to 1905 the BAR KOCHBA society was headed by the philosopher Hugo Bergmann (1883–1975), a fellow-pupil and friend of Franz Kafka. During this period great emphasis was laid on "living Judaism" which was based on the principle that "in the first place Zionism is a return to the Jewish faith and only then a return to the Jewish land." In 1903 the religious philosopher and pedagogue Martin Buber (1878–1965) delivered a speech at the BAR KOCHBA ceremony (the famous "Three Speeches about the Jewish Faith"). Similarly as his speeches in the coming years, this one was also of fundamental importance for the future destiny of Prague's Jewry.

Martin Buber spoke about a "new" Jew who, true enough, no longer adhered to rigid regulations, but sought his own path, endeavoured to find creative approaches and sought an answer according to his own judgement and feeling. It was a mistake when a part of the Jewish nation "instead of creating and accepting new, spiritual values itself adopted a great deal from the nations where it lived as guests. These foreign values were adopted at the cost of their own soul ..."

It is worth mentioning the fact that Prague Zionists were aware that both the nationality friction betwen the Czechs and Germans and the ideas of certain leading personalities in the Czech camp, in particular of T. G. Masaryk, whose emphasis on the spiritual and moral aspects of nationalism found response and approval among the Zionist-members of BAR KOCHBA, were factors which contributed to the crystallization of their feeling of independence and the finding of their identity.

(At that time members of BAR KOCHBA also attended T. G. Masaryk's lectures organized for Czech workers. Afterwards they enthusiastically related how many parallels they found between the words expressed by Masaryk and Buber on nationality problems.)

Many of the tendencies determined at BAR KOCHBA by the intellectual personality Hugo Germann and oriented mainly to the cultural and spiritual spheres were not accepted by all members. For this and also other reasons a split came about followed by the origin of another Zionist organization called **"BARISSIA"**, which inclined more towards the political orientation propagated by T. Herzl.The new organization was neither anti-Czech nor anti-intellectual, its chief aim being to assert itself politically to a greater extent.

In 1907 the members of BARISSIA founded a new weekly called **"SELBSTWEHR"** (Self-defence). From the very beginning its purpose was to portray everything that happened in the life of Czech Jews and to help build up a stronger base for the fragile relations between the Czechs and the Jews. In the course of time the publication passed from the defence of the honour of the European Jewry and the criticism of anti-semitism and German-Jewish assimilation to "a positive programme and active support of all the modern forces of Judaism."

Another important publicistic act was the anthology published annually by BAR KOCHBA. It contained deliberations, articles and essays written by leading Zionist writers and scientists (Martin Buber, Hugo Bergmann, Kurt Singer, Gustav Landauer) on the idea that "Zionism is not knowledge, it is a kind of fight, it is life itself."

✳ ✳ ✳

Apart from polemics, the Zionists also waged disputes with the Jewish religious community which did not concern solely the question of their representation in official Jewish institutions.

The fact that they also founded their own Jewish school society (1907), which, however, practically functioned until 1917, when it organized courses of history and Hebrew, can be ranked among their successes. (Jewish national schools were opened after the outbreak of the First World War.)

✳ ✳ ✳

In the period preceding the First World War Prague's Zionists made only a negligible contribution to the Jewish idea of the 20th century. The consequence of their individual cultivation of the spirit in the manner described above all in Buber's interpretations of Judaism was certainly an unmeditated paradox. For Zionists Judaism was what they created themselves through freedom of the spirit and because they had only a hazy idea of what traditional Judaism had formerly been like they actually moved in a cultural desert without any historical ties.

Otherwise the Czech-Jewish movement as a whole (as well as writings) differed substantially in those pre-war years from the method of writing and argumentation of the former editors Lederer and Vohryzek. Its attitude towards the Czechs was more self-assured and it showed greater tolerance towards others. Moreover, it became calmer and less agitated. Assimilation questions were less burning, the aim being rather to find optimum social relations and paths.

Redaktion,
Administration und Expedition:
Poříč 7.

Telephon 2226.

Poštsparkassakonto 50.120

Anonyme Einsendungen werden
nicht berücksichtigt.

Manuscripte
werden nicht zurückgegeben.

Unverlangte
Zeitungs-Reklamationen sind
portofrei.

Erscheint jeden Freitag.

Abonnement mit Zustellung ins
Haus oder Expedition:
Ganzjähr., K 6.—
für Deutschland Mk. 6.—
für das übrige Ausland 10 Frcs.
oder 10 sh.
Einzelne Nummer 12 h

Insertionspreis:
für die fünfmal gespaltene
Petitzeile 20 h.
Kleiner Anzeiger 16 h

Inserate können direkt oder in
den Annoncen-Bureaux aller
Länder aufgegeben werden.

Selbstwehr
Unabhängige jüdische Wochenschrift.

Nr. 42.   **Prag, den 13. Dezember 1907.**   **1. Jahrgang.**

Die Parlaments-Rede Dr. Arthur Mahlers

bei den Verhandlungen über den Antrag Masaryks hat einen starken Eindruck gemacht. Nicht nur im Parlament, sondern auch in allen jüdischen Kreisen, wo man über die moderne Form einer Abwehr auf jüdische Interessen überrascht und erfreut war. Der Redner hat es verschmäht, seine Argumente etwa aus dem theologischen Arsenal zu holen oder etwa mit Gegenangriffen auf die Luegerpartei zu antworten, wie es an Frauzenring so lange liberale Sitte war, sondern er blieb immer politisch und schete sich als gleichberechtigter Staatsbürger durchaus nicht, gegen den Klerikalismus eine Lanze einzulegen, wenn er auch einen Zusammenstoß mit der Kirche gescheit und taktvoll auswich. Der jüdische Klub im Reichsrat hat mit dem Auftreten Dr. Mahlers sicherlich Ehre eingelegt, der einen hohen Standpunkt mit geistreichen Argumenten verteidigte und die Aufmerksamkeit des Hauses besaß, welchem er das fortschrittliche, demokratische Programm seiner Partei als Berichtigung gegen ihren klerikalen Beruf entwickelte. Die Wirkung war eine ausgezeichnete, nicht nur für die Partei des Redners sondern auch für alle Juden. Mehrere Redner von gegnerischer Seite kamen darauf zurück und wieder einmal, wie sonst fast selten, hörte man die Juden von den Antisemiten ohne Schmähung, ja sogar mit einem höflichen Ausdruck der Anerkennung für Selbstbewußtsein und Ehrlichkeit nennen. Das werden der jüdischnationalen Partei gewiß einige perverse liberale Politiker zum Vorwurf machen. Es gilt ja als Verbrechen von den Antisemiten gelobt zu werden. Sicherlich ist es niemals einem Juden um Luegers oder Syl-vesters Beifall gegangen. Aber ebenso gewiß ist es, daß der jüdische Klub auch in Zukunft kann durch seine Kopfzahl wird wirksam sein können. Er ist auf eine moralische Stärke angewiesen, deren erste Voraussetzung wohl die Achtung des Gegners ist.

Feuilleton.

Aus dem Bukowinaer Gebirge.

Unsere Zeit hat große, bedeutende Männer geschaffen und kann wohl mit Recht im Pilgerfahrt von Künstlern genannt werden. Und wird es ... sein.

Dr. Mahler konnte keinen Widerspruch haben, denn er brachte als ein Mann des Geistes nicht seine persönlichen Ansichten über Ereignisse des Tages vor, wie das etwa Lueger tut, sondern die Philosophie der Freiheit, ihre unzerstörbaren, unwiderleglichen Grundsätze, die höchstens einer Vergewaltigung unterliegen, wie er sich ausdrückt. Im Kampfe zwischen Religion und Wissenschaft muß sich der Glaube an die Wahrheit halten. Ausgezeichnet war die Wendung gegen die Beschuldigung umstürzlerischen Geistes an den Universitäten. Wenn da Aufklärung Revolution bedeutet, wenn die Belehrung eines Menschen über seine Interessen und Notwendigkeiten Aufruhr ist, dann wäre dieser Vorwurf gerechtfertigt. Die Universität hat nur den Fortschritt des Wissens zu dienen ohne Rücksicht auf die Interessen der Besitzenden.

Bei der Besprechung des Themas von der praktischen Seite zeigte Dr. Mahler, daß jemand der Gerechtigkeit verlangt, auch Gerechtigkeit zu üben versteht. Wiewohl die Ereignisse der letzten Zeit einen Angriff oder einen Unterstützung des Luegerschen Angriffs auf einen Teil der Juden-Studenten feindliches Studentenschaft gerechtfertigt hätten, stellte der Redner den einen großen Vorzug, den stürmischen Irealismus der studierenden Jugend mit Worten höchsten Lobes vor alle Lautigenten, wobei er natürlich mit besonderem Stolz auf die Studenten der eigenen Partei hinwies, die in jeder Beziehung die erste Schlachtreihe ihres von allen Seiten bedrängten Volkes stund.

Das war der Übergang zu einer näheren Charakterisierung des eigenen Parteiprogrammes dessen drei Schlagworte lauten: Nation, Demokratie, Fortschritt. Den Abstand von einen jüdischen Klerikalismus kann man an der Feindschaft aller wirklichen jüdischen Klerikalen gegen die Partei des Redners messen. Für letztere kommt die jüdische Religion als solche nur insoweit in Frage, als sie eine Rolle in der jüdischen Gleichberechtigung spielt. Ihre Hauptaufgabe ist

sie streuen den Samen ihres Könnens nur in großen Städten aus. Die toten Buchstaben der Zeitungen dringen zwar bis zu uns, aber wir wollen die sehen, jene Männer, wir wollen ihre Rede hören um ihnen zurufen mit jugendlicher Begeisterung: "Wir sind eins mit Euch, auch wir wollen nach unseren Kräften mitarbeiten an der Verwirklichung der großen Pläne, welche das Judentum bewegen.

Aber immer der Großen besaßt sich mit dem Leben und Treiben des Bukowinaer Gebirgsbewohners, der in Massen in Dörfern und Städten wohnt. Von Hatna bis Bistryj mit dem Kimpolung wieder die Bugzig von großer Höhe, wie reich ist dieses Land! Hohe Berge umkränzen die Gegend und filberhell schlängelt sich ein Bach durchs Tal. Doch jene Berge, für jedermann ein erhabener Anblick, sie lasten wie ein Alp auf dem Herzen des jüdischen Bewohners. Er kann sich der Schönheit seines Landes nicht freuen, die lästigen Schikanen der Regierung und der anstrengende Existenzkampf rauben ihm die rechte Lebensfreude. Obwohl den Rumänen von Natur aus mißtrauend, zwingt ihn die Regierung, seine Kinder in rumänische Schulen zu schicken. Der Bergjude bekleidet kein Amt, er ist immer in der Minorität. Seine ideale Veranlagung läßt ihn doch nie in

vor allem die Politik als Staatsbürger. Als Vertreter der jüdischen Bürgerrechte wendet sich Redner energisch gegen die Übergriffe des klerikalen Antisemitismus, der es nicht einmal dulden wolle, daß um die Wissenschaft hochverdiente jüdische Dozenten den Titel ohne Mittel eines außerordentlichen Professors bekommen und der den Juden nur das Recht zuerkennen wolle als Patrioten zu sterben, nicht aber als Patrioten zu leben. Man schädige schließlich nur, dem Staat dadurch, welcher der geheime Protektor des Antisemitismus sei, obwohl eine lange Ehrentafel jüdischer Berühmtheiten aus allen Zweigen des öffentlichen Lebens besser als alle Argumente für Vernunft und Gerechtigkeit spreche.

Für seine Ausführungen wurde der Redner vielfach beglückwünscht, nachträglich sicher auch im Geiste von den breiten Schichten des jüdischen Publikums. Vieler Augen ruhten an ihm, als er sich zu Reden anschickte. Diese Neugierde und die Spannung des selbst Beteiligten gaben gespannt darauf acht, wie Dr. Mahler die heikle Stellung eines jüdischen Abgeordneten ausfüllen werde, wie groß sein Mut und sein Geschick, wie hoch sein Geist sein werde. Unter dem erschwerenden Umstand des ersten Auftretens hat der Redner einen glänzenden Befähigungsnachweis eines jüdischen Politikers erbracht, seine stolzen und freien Ausführungen gereichen jedem modernen Juden zur Genugtuung, ihm selbst zur Ehre.

Die Affäre Hilsner.

Die Hilsnersache ist wieder ein bißchen in Rollen. An Beratungen und Bemühungen gewisser Korporationen hat es wohl nie gefehlt, von ihnen kam aber wenig ans Tageslicht. Nun hat der bekannte Wiener Advokat Dr. Friedrich Elbogen sein journalistisches Geschick in einem Majestätsgesuch betätigt, das er als Anwalt der Mutter Hilsners, Maria Himmelreich, verfaßte und auf Grund jemandes Kosten (Kultusgemeinde) einer ganzen Auflage den "N. Fr. Presse" beilegen ließ.

Das Extrem des Fanatismus verfallen. Das alte, patriarchalische Gastrecht wird von dem Gebirgsjuden besonders gepflegt, wiewohl er des gesellschaftlichen Lebens fast vollständig ermangelt.

Nicht einmal vom Hörensagen wissen Viele etwas von der gegenwärtigen politischen Bewegung, die ganze Denkkraft ist nur darauf gerichtet, den andauernden in der Konkurrenz zu überbieten. Dreißig Meilen entlang reihen Haus an Haus von jüdischen Bewohnern und jüdischen Geschäften. Wohl sieht der Gast, der nach Dorna kommt, die prunkenden Häuser und die feinen Villen, jedoch nicht den Kampf und das Elend des jüdischen Inwohners, der für seine Kinder das Brot sucht und ihnen keine geistige Nahrung bieten kann. Kein Wort tönt herüber aus der weiten Ferne, daß sich dem armen Gebirgsjuden annehmen würde. Totgeschwiegen von den Fremden, unbeachtet von den eigenen Brüdern! Niemand hört seinen Schmerzensruf nach Erlösung und Trost. Kein Golusprophet findet es der Mühe wert, auch hier seine Stimme erschallen zu lassen und doch würde es eine Freude sie so schön widerhallen.

Hermann Margules, Dorna-Kandreny.

JUDr. Bohdan Klineberger (1859–1928), barrister and exponent of the Czech Jewish movement, writer, author of scientific studies on law and sociology.

Such was the situation in which Prague's Jews entered the First World War. The Czech-Jewish institutions lost the greater part of their member-writers; editors and activists were called up into the army and those who remained were unable to write or speak freely, because the blue pencil of the censors had to be borne in mind.

A special situation arose with regard to the journal **ROZVOJ** (Development) where Lederer, Vohryzek and Klineberger took over the reins again after the departure of the younger generation. They exerted considerable efforts to keep the magazine in circulation, but even so it did not appear regularly and quite often it contained large blank spaces bearing witness to strict censorship. After 1915 it ceased to be published.

The fate of the magazine **SELBSTWEHR** (Self-defence) was somewhat better. In 1917 it was able to celebrate the tenth anniversary of its foundation even though the ranks of the celebrators were thinner. A modest, but nevertheless dignified anthology entitled "Jewish Prague" was even published thanks to the editor Siegmund Kaznelson, who succeeded in gaining contributions from forty-five writers. This good friend of Franz Kafka and Max Brod also included numerous works by non-Jewish writers of well-known names such as Otakar Březina, J. S. Machar and others in the anthology.

Similarly as the Czech-Jewish movement as a whole, Prague Zionism experienced a hard trial and material crisis during the First World War. For both movements the war meant a traumatic confrontation with incomparable cultural aspirations and added to this a loss of confidence just at the time when the Jewry could conclude a firm bond with Czech nationalism.

The disappointment of Czech Zionists was not so profound. The cultural renascence had, after all, been realized to a great extent and all that remained was to improve the political (but also social) conditions in which the majority of Jews lived.

THE CLEARANCE
OF THE JEWISH
TOWN

The Jewish Town, the most densely populated part of Prague, where 1,822 persons were crowded together on one hectare of built-up space, had, apart from dwelling-houses, sixteen public buildings in 1850: nine synagogues, a tax office, a Town Hall, two schools, a hospital, a slaughter-house and a mortuary. Burials no longer took place in the Old Jewish Cemetery. The

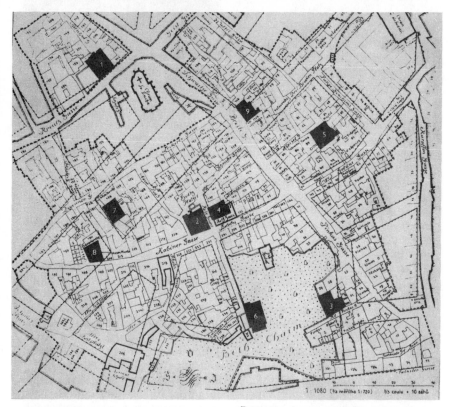

Plan of the Jewish Town (state of 1843, with the clearance plan of 1895) with the synagogues:

1 – *The Old Shul – The Spanish Synagogue*
2 – *The Old-New Synagogue*
3 – *The Pinkas Synagogue*
4 – *The High Synagogue*
5 – *The Maisel Synagogue*
6 – *The Klausen Synagogue*
7 – *The Cikán Synagogue*
8 – *The Great-Court Synagogue*
9 – *The New Synagogue*

Houses and alleys of the Old (Jewish) Town
intended for clearance.

poorest of the poor moved into the half-ruined little houses deserted by the Jews when they took up residence in other quarters of Prague. Only the poorest Jews remained here along with the most desolate strata and orthodox fanatics who did not wish to leave the Jewish Town. During the next three decades the former ghetto became, as described by Gustav Meyrink, the site of a "demonic underworld, a place of anguish, a beggarly and phantasmic quarter whose eeriness seemed to have spread and led to enervation; it could be said that the ghetto was an expression of the weakened state of Europe at the beginning of the new century".

The state of the ghetto bore witness to its absolute decline: the paving was full of revolting rubbish, a suitable sewerage system was lacking and thousands of rats nested in the narrow streets. In this period the ghetto became the refuge of human wrecks, tricksters and prostitutes. It was a quarter of grey buildings where the shop windows were "full of second-hand clothes, old iron and all kinds of things it would be difficult to name", a quarter where the night hours were enlivened by the red light of the lanterns of brothels and the sounds of accordions from dance-halls and ale-houses named, for example, The General, The Old Lady, The Three Carps and the famous "Morning Star".

M. Reach's second-hand clothes shop in Pinkas Street, 1890.

Members of the clearance commission inspecting one of the houses. ▶

The Jewish Town Hall and the Old-New Synagogue, unmolested by the clearance.

The writer Ignát Herrmann tells us about the bad reputation enjoyed by Josefov: "Whenever a murder or a big robbery took place in Prague, the culprits could regularly be traced to a dark corner of the ghetto. He who committed a fraud or embezzlement, he who commited robbery or murdered with the intention of committing a robbery and grew rich in a criminal way, where did he hurry to in order to hide or change his spoils for money --- his destination was regularly the Jewish Town".

✳ ✳ ✳

In the late 19th century the territory of the former Jewish Town reached a real state of collapse. Its social, sanitary and hygienical conditions were on the edge of a catastrophe. At that time Josefov was only a source of infection, a high death rate and moral and physical decline. It was unthinkable that the sick organism of the former ghetto should remain – and in its very centre – in Prague, a town of Baroque churches and palaces, a town with magnificent Neo-Renaissance architectural waves of buildings of the type of the National Theatre, the National Museum and the Rudolphinum. The architects who were called upon to draw up plans to restore this quarter to health had a source of inspiration. In the history of architecture similar activities involving the liquidation of old and no longer adequate environments always preceded new, modern building needs. This was the case in Paris, Budapest and Vienna.

With the substantial support of home building speculators and entrepreneurs plans began to crystallize concerning the future "recuperating" process, the scene of their origin being the governmental circles of the Austrian building bourgeoisie. In particular (if not exclusively) this process applied to the Josefov district, i. e. to the historical territory of the Jewish Town, which had long since ceased to be Jewish, because the number of Jews living here had dropped from the former 80% in 1850 to 20% in 1890.

From 1885 the draft of a slum clearance law went from one institution to another until it was finally approved by the Imperial Council and the Czech Provincial Diet on 11 February, 1893. This slum clearance law did not concern the territory of the former ghetto only. The area on which clearance activity was to take place included other unsuitable parts of the town, especially in the Old Town, the northern side of Old Town Square, the embankment called Na Františku and the environs of St. Castulus's Church. As regards the New Town, the Vojtěšská and Podskalí quarters were subject to the slum clearance law.

The slum clearance law afforded the expropriation right mainly to Prague communities and in the case of new buildings slum clearance districts were freed from paying taxes and building charges for twenty years. The whole of Josefov was included in the slum clearance area. This meant 288 houses in 31 streets and lanes with two small squares. The owners of all immovables had the possibility of modifying them or building new ones within the space of one year, i. e. up to 1896. The expropriation right was applied in negative cases. A certain paradox lay in the fact that the realization of the whole slum clearance project was entrusted to an official on the town council of Prague, Dr. Augustin Stein, a Jew who came from a country rabbi's family which had contacts in Prague with the family of František Ladislav Rieger, whose child he had taught privately in his youth. The role played by Dr. Stein in the slum clearance operation cannot be overestimated and it also cannot be presumed that he influenced it either positively or negatively. He was a very zealous and, as recorded, honest official who did not act for his own benefit. And this was the only positive aspect of his activity.

By the time the Czech public got to know what was being prepared and what was happening it was too late. The demolition of the first houses had started when the intellectual elite of the nation joined Vilém Mrštík, Jaroslav Kamper and Václav Hladík with a manifesto bearing the title Bestia triumphans. It was published on 5 April, 1896. The open letter written by Ignát Herrmann to the mayor of Prague, Dr. Jan Podlipný, had no effect either.

Apart from the decaying houses, many others which were supposed to be preserved for the next generation also became victims of the slum clearance movement. Furthermore, no one succeeded in documenting the demolished houses at least for the needs of conservation evidence. The slum clearance works proceeded at an exceptional rate and by the end of 1897 the town council took note with full satisfaction that the slum clearance programme had been fulfilled to the extent of nearly 100%. This programme was not

 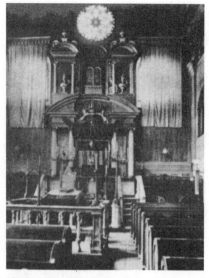

The interior of the Cikán Synagogue, torn down during the clearance on May 1906.

The interior of the Great Court Synagogue, torn down during the clearance on May 20, 1906.

based solely on the demolition of no longer adequate houses. For the purpose of further works it was chiefly necessary to raise the level of the whole territory in order to eliminate the threat of damage by floods, which had already threatened the ghetto in the past. It was necessary to build a sewerage, which the locality lacked, and to secure the realization of all technical matters so that the construction of new buildings, of a new quarter intended to meet not only residential purposes, but also those of trade and social life, could be started.

According to the plan of the builders the centre of this new quarter was to be Old Town Square, which then opened into newly built Pařížská Street. The radially planned streets of the reconstructed town were to run into the square. Apart from reconstructed Kaprova Street and newly built Pařížská Street, the reconstruction of other streets in Na Františku direction remained a plan only. The only more important public building erected on the cleared area practically on the very edge of the Old Jewish Cemetery in the years 1897 to 1901 was the one housing the Arts and Crafts Museum. This building, which was supposed to determine the architectural style applied in other realizations, was the work of the architect Josef Schulz, a leading personality in the sphere of Czech Neo-Renaissance historicism. The museum building is not incorporated organically in the old quarter, but stands with its back to it.

Construction work was started on the cleared area about 1900 and by 1914, by the outbreak of the First World War, the majority of the new houses had

*Art Nouveau houses in Pařížská Street built
after the clearance in 1906.*

been built. The winning design in the competition for the master plan of the
future reconstruction of the Jewish Town was the one entered by the surveyor
Alfréd Hurtig (in cooperation with A. Štrunc and F. Hejda). This was confirmed on 13 November, 1889. In February 1893 a slum clearance law was
passed according to which about 300 houses were demolished in the follow-

ing years. By the beginning of the 20th century a new quarter had been built on the cleared site.

Alfréd Hurtig's plan simplified the street network of Josefov. He made the chief axis of the territory newly built Pařížská Street (then called Mikulášská Street) of a width of 24 metres, running northwards from Old Town Square. Kaprova, Maiselova, Josefovská (now Široká) and Dušní Streets were widened according to the master plan, but otherwise the direction in which they ran remained unchanged. Of the old buildings only the former Town Hall, six synagogues and the Old Jewish Cemetery were preserved.

A deficiency of the plan lay in the fact that the blocks of houses projected in it were of relatively small dimensions, which resulted in the origin of only small, cramped courtyards inside the blocks due to the depths of the comfortable apartment houses. Park greenery was limited to a small park near the Old-New Synagogue.

In the early 20th century construction work was started on the corner of Old Town Square after the carrying out of slum clearance works. A corner appartment house was built here after a plan by Professor R. Křiženecký and opposite it, next to St. Nicholas's Church, a house designed by Professor J. Koula was erected. Both buildings featured the Neo-Baroque style. Other Neo-Baroque houses designed by architect Dlabač and Art Nouveau buildings designed by architects Koula, Budra and others originated in Mikulášská Street.

Big corner houses built after a design by the architect J. Vejrych in the style of the Czech Renaissance with Art Nouveau decorative elements were erected on the corner of Jáchymova and Salvátorská Streets. The result is represented by present-day Pařížská Street, to where Prague's promenade was to move and where the counterpart of Wenceslas Square, a modernly conceived metropolitan boulevard, was supposed to originate. The new quarter was meant to be full of life and ostentatiousness. This aim was not fulfilled just as the planned building of the metropolitan "Monte Carlo" coffee-house was never realized (in Nos. 56, 57 and 58 in present-day Maiselova Street).

The houses in Pařížská Street, one like another, full of decorative ornaments, "present the most widespread historical motifs, Baroque motifs" of the architects Jan Vejrych, Jan Koula and Knight Klenk of Vlastimily in the sphere of Art Nouveau themes. Gothic and Renaissance details were used on the façades of the houses. A large number of gables, turrets and other embellishments can be seen here. The houses in the environs of the Old Jewish Cemetery are more moderate in appearance. Rather than making use of rich ornamentation, the architects Antonín Engel and Bohumil Hypšman tried to respect tradition. The building No. 36 and 37 in present-day Široká Street, housing the premises of the Jewish Burial Society, is also an example of the moderate, elegant Art Nouveau style. As one of the few local houses (another one is, for example, house No. 40 in Břehová Street, the work of Antonín Engel), it was placed on the list of immovable cultural monuments in this district.

THE FIRST REPUBLIC

The origin of the independent Czechoslovak Republic in 1918 brought about the return of Prague, after a verv long period, to its former residential position. The city was predetermined for unwonted development. It became the seat of central offices, diplomatic and trade representations and social structures representing all spheres of life and yet it preserved its character of a developed industrial town.

What role did the Jews play here?

Let us read what the rabbi Dr. Richard Feder wrote in his book "The Jewish Tragedy":

"We, the Jews, lived peacefully and sagely and therefore contentedly and happily in the first republic of Czechoslovakia, in Masaryk's republic. We were its citizens enjoying full rights, and not only on paper, but also in real life. We had the same duties, but also the same rights as other citizens, we could, without any risk, avow Czech, Slovak, German, Hungarian and even Jewish nationality and we could write with a small or capital J. We could settle anywhere and we could choose any kind of employment. The gates of all schools and training institutions were open to our children". Further on Dr. Feder writes: "We were everywhere and nowhere, because we were relatively few in number and we did not stand in anyone's way. The Jews accepted Bohemia and Bohemia took the Jews into its services. Various Jewish associations and institutions cared for our special cult and cultural needs and jews and Jews published newspapers, calendars, brochures and books. The Zionists waged a tough fight with the assimilants of which we were often ashamed even though it was waged in a decent way."

It is thus clear that the origin of the Czechoslovak Republic met with the great sympathies of the Jewish population of this country. Among other things, they resulted from the moral confidence which the Jews had in such personalities as the first president of the Czechoslovak Republic, T. G. Masaryk, whose involvement in the fight against anti-semitism in the former monarchy had become an inseparable part of his political activity.

✳ ✳ ✳

Thus it would seem that the ruling circles of the first republic deleted the word anti-semitism from their programme. In practice, however, things were somewhat different.

Shortly after the origin of the republic conditions remained unconsolidated and the atmosphere against the Jews was not particularly idyllic. Storms broke out in December of 1918 and again in May of the following year, in the latter case due to high prices. Worst of all, however, was the situation in November 1920, when masses of people even penetrated into the Jewish Town Hall and destroyed furnishings and furniture in it.

According to the newspaper "Neue Freie Presse" published in Vienna the

American consul was obliged to lend an American flag, which was hung on the Town Hall and was supposed, at least symbolically, to protect the Galicia Jews who had been temporarily accommodated within its walls. (In a letter addressed to Milena Jesenská Franz Kafka also referred to these tragic events.)

It is only natural that the new Zionist magazine ŽIDOVSKÉ ZPRÁVY ("Jewish Reports"), published alongside "SELBSTWEHR", devoted special attention to the whole matter. In the meantime the Zionists had achieved considerable success in their endeavours to set up their own Jewish school, at least on a modest scale, in Prague.

This Prague Jewish school with one class began its activity in 1920. In 1924 it had five classes. It is interesting to note that one of its teachers was Valli Pollaková, sister of Franz Kafka, who himself manisfested great interest in the school and attended its organizational meetings. A speciality of Prague Zionism lay in the fact that even though it endeavoured to secure its own cultural development and a kind of Jewish autonomy, it did not place any obstacles in the way of Czech-Jewish integration in political, economic and social matters.

This fact had a strong influence on the Czech-Jewish community between the two world wars.

Both movements, the Czech-speaking Jews who fully supported assimilation and their opponents trying to secure Jewish national identity, thus had in essence a positive influence on the general process of Jewish integration. The programme of the Czech-Jewish movement was also changed in this connection.

The Czech-speaking Jews no longer had to fight for the legal recognition of a national minority. This was expressed by the fact that Jewish nationality was officially recognized. The political aspirations of this group of Jews were now limited to Jewish support of the new state, cultural endeavours being oriented to even more intensive integration.

Within a year after the formation of the new state a new structure of Jewish institutions intended to reflect the social and political contexts of independent Czechoslovakia more faithfully originated. The Czech-Jewish Political Fraternity (Politická jednota českožidovská) and the Union of Progressive Czech Jews (Svaz českých pokrokových Židů), antagonistic organizations from the beginning of the century, even joined forces for a short time only to be separated again by their different opinions on an old problem: how to overcome anti-semitism in official Czech circles. Nevertheless, they made one more attempt to achieve unity (in 1919), when they adopted a common name – The Union of Czechs-Jews. At the same time the journal ROZHLED ("Outlook") was combined with the better-known magazine ROZVOJ ("Development").

The union changed its statutes to such an extent that now members of all religious groups were accepted. Jewish integration was now also supported by the society of students bearing the name, as stated previously, the "Academic Kapper Society (Akademický spolek Kapper)".

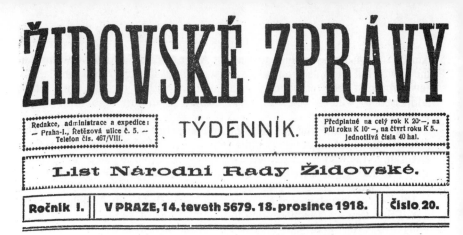

ŽIDOVSKÉ ZPRÁVY

Redakce, administrace a expedice:
— Praha-I., Řetězová ulice č. 5. —
Telefon čís. 467/VIII.

TÝDENNÍK.

Předplatné na celý rok K 20·—, na
půl roku K 10·—, na čtvrt roku K 5..
Jednotlivá čísla 40 hal.

List Národní Rady Židovské.

| Ročník I. | V PRAZE, 14. teveth 5679. 18. prosince 1918. | Číslo 20. |

Ben Jomtov:

Rabíni, čím byli a jakými by měli býti.

V době, kdy židovský národ, jako snad nikdy před tím za svých třítisíceletých dějin jest stavěn před otázku být či nebýt, jest třeba, aby všichni, komu vskutku záleží na obrození národa, také hledali jedině pravou cestu.

Snad nikdy před tím nebylo židovství ve svém základu a ve svých kořenech tak ohroženo jako nyní a nikdy nebyla nalehavěji nutna náprava.

Nikdy nebylo Židovstvo početnější než dnes a přece nikdy nebylo třeba mocnějšího napětí veškerých sil, aby bylo zachráněno před nutným zánikem.

Jest snad nejvznešenějším rysem našich dějin, že životní síla Židovstva nebyla založena na fysické moci, že jeho silou nebyli jeho vojáci, nýbrž jeho učitelé a jeho proroci.

Učitel židovský, rabi, byl v Israeli representantem nejvyššího mravního úsilí životního, byl ohniskem národního života.

Leč veliký rabi, jenž ve své duši nosil posvátný oheň Věčného života a jenž byl strážcem, hlasatelem a suverenním nositelem židovství, před nímž musil se peněžní žok skloniti, jenž dovedl hliněného golema oživiti jménem Věčného života, scvrkl se v malého rabína, sluhu golemova.

Ano, třeba sobě uvědomiti, že příčinou rozkladu Židovstva jest dekadence jeho representantů — naprostý nesoulad mezi učením a učiteli. Z proroka a učitele národního stal se napodobitel kněžský patetického kazatelství, které každou opravdovou duši židovskou, kte-

rá jest ještě schopna pravého zápalu, odpuzuje a od Židovství zahání.

Učitel národa stal se učitelem náboženského vyznání, jenž v nejlepším případě nemá dosti síly, aby slovům svým dodal náležité váhy a víry, zpravidla pravé víry sám nemá.

Vypravování o nejkrásnějších a nejnohutnějších událostech našich tisíciletých dějin stává se v jeho ústech únavným, vnitřního hřejivého ohně zbaveným povídáním o málo uvěřitelných zázracích, které se životem žákovým nemá nižádné spojitosti. Jak málo nás interesují z úst takového rabína dějiny doby makabejské. Jak může on hlasatel asimilantského, stuchlým olejem prosáklého konfesionalismu vůbec i jen vycítiti velikost a jásající krásu onoho hrdinského vzepětí národní duše židovské, vtělené v rekovskou postavu Judy Makabejského proti všemu polovičatému, prolhanému asimilantství judských helenčíků. Vždyť on sám byl by prvním, který by byl obětoval na oltáři cizích model. Jej samého by byl prvního sklál meč Matatáše hasmonejského. Jak může duše bez vnitřního ohně židovského pochopiti význam velikého vidění syna Amocova?

Rabín ten musí každé slovo hebrejských proroků, jež jest planoucí výzvou k obrození Sionu, ke vzkříšení národa, jenž na sebe vzal závazek Věčného života, nového, opravdového života v zemi otců, prohlašovati jedním dechem za svatou víru otců a v debatě se sionisty za klam a šalbu i přízrak.

Jeho modlitbě o nové vzkříšení Sionu schází vnitřní pravdivost a přesvědčení. Jeho náboženství jest v nejlepším případě sbírka suchopárných mravních poučení, které z jeho sobě samému nevěřících úst ani jeho žáci věřiti nemohou a není nic přirozenějšího,

The title page of the weekly "Židovské zprávy" (Jewish News), the paper of the National Jewish Council, No. 20 of 1918 and No. 31 of 1919.

Cena tohoto čísla 1 K.

ŽIDOVSKÉ ZPRÁVY

Redakce, administrace a expedice:
— Praha-I., Celetná ulice č. 22. —
Telefon čís. 467/VIII.

TÝDENNÍK.

Předplatné na celý rok K 20·—, na
půl roku K 10·—, na čtvrt roku K 5..
Jednotlivá čísla 40 hal.

List Národní Rady Židovské.

| Ročník I. | V PRAZE, 5. veadar 5679, 7. března 1919. | Číslo 31. |

. . . Jestliže však odtud budete hledati Pána věčného Života, Boka svého, naleznete Jej: Jestliže Jej budete hledati z celého srdce svého a z celé duše své.

Budeš-li v bídě, a až tě potkají všechny ty věci na konec dnů, pak se navrátíš k Věčně Jsoucimu, Bohu svému a poslouchati budeš hlasu Jeho.

Neboť Pán Věčného Života, tvůj Bůh jest milosrdný; nezanechá tebe a nezkazí tebe a nezapomene smlouvy otcův tvých, kterou jim byl přisahal.

Sionistické požadavky mirovou konferenci jednohlasně přijaty.

Těsně před redakční uzávěrkou dochází nás zpráva: „Stockholm, 5. března. Židovská tisková kancelář telegrafuje Pražské židovské tisk. kanceláři: Anglický ministr vnějších záležitostí, Balfour, poslal sionistické delegaci v Paříži blahopřání, ve kterém oznamuje, že mírová konference přijala jednohlasně sionistické návrhy." Bližší v listě (rubr. „Z celého světa").

Dr. Ludvík Singer:

Úroveň českožidovské argumentace

Před několika dny konala se v Kolíně veřejná schůze, na níž promluvil tajemník Národní rady židovské, dr. Angelo Goldstein „o podstatě a cílech hnutí sionistického a národně-židovského". Českožidovští asimilanti zavolali si na schůzi p. dra Ottu Bondyho z Kutné Hory, jednoho z předáků českožidovských, organisovaného jinak ve straně sociálně demokratické. Po zkuše-

nosti z Pardubic nutno Kolínským připsati k dobrému, že vyslechli vůbec referát řečníka národně-židovského. V Pardubicích ovšem jsou republikáni a demokrati sui generis, tam sionistického referenta ukřičeli hned při prvních slovech, takže bylo nutno schůzi ukončiti. Zajisté pádný argument proti sionismu a pro asimilaci. Avšak slyšíme-li to, co vykládal pan dr. Otto Bondy v Kolíně oproti věcným a vážným vývodům referentovým, nemůžeme se diviti, že si čeští Židé debaty raději nepřejí. Dra Bondyho znám přes dvacet let a poněvadž jsem nikdy nepochyboval o jeho osobní poctivosti, mám za to, že ho politika úplně zaslepila, anebo že mu hluboké a přesvědčivé vývody dra Goldsteina popletly koncept. Nechci se o tom šířiti, že se nachází v rozporu s vlastní stranou, která hnutí národně židovské plně uznává, nechci se také rozepisovati o pozvání socialistické strany židovské „Poale Zion" na konferenci bernskou socialistickou internacionálou a o jejím významném působení tamtéž, jest nám již dávno známo, že jsou to ve všech politických stranách jen Židé, kteří naše snahy potírají, především příslušníci židovští ve stranách socialistických, německých i českých, neboť v ostatních politických stranách buď vůbec nejsou anebo hrají nevalnou úlohu. Slyšme tedy pana dra Bondyho! Když jakýsi antisemitský sociální revolucionář prohlásil slavnostně, že každému Židu dá facku, jenž by promluvil na ulici německy, pochvaloval p. dr. Bondy jeho vývody a podotkl, že to nemusí býti zrovna facka, že stačí nějaký ten . . . . . . a naznačil rukou, že stačí „štulec". O sionistech řekl, že chtějí býti otroky a že by se jim měly podle zákona Mojžíšova propíchnouti uši. Avšak vrcholem všeho jest argumentace následovní: Anglie přeje sionistickému hnutí

VĚSTNÍK

ŽIDOVSKÉ OBCE NÁBOŽENSKÉ V PRAZE

ROČNÍK II.   V Praze, dne 31. října 1935.   ČÍSLO 9.

28. říjen.

Sedmnácte let života v samostatném, svobodném státě a mraky, zahalující evropský horizont, působí, že se letošní oslava výročí politického osvobození československého stala intimnější a lze-li, i ještě hřejivější. Není to jen pocit zadostiučinění a radosti, nýbrž i vědomí, pronikající všemi vrstvami obyvatelstva, že je tu i velký mravní závazek a úkol, dobytou svobodu státní i politickou také tak upevniti, aby se jakékoliv ohrožení zvenčí nebo vnitřní muselo předem považovati za neúčinné a nutně muselo ztroskotati.

Věrna vysokým ideám, jimž vděčí za vítězství své pravdy, hájí mladá Republika v moři běsnících násilností, brutálního utlačování a pěstního práva zásadu demokracie politické i státní. Nestalo se zajisté náhodou, že předseda Národní rady československé, representující dnes všechny vrstvy československého národa, končil svůj projev na letošní oslavě u presidenta státu projevem důvěry, že u nás budou příslušníci našeho státu ochráněni před národnostním a rasovým záštím.

Poměr silnějšího k slabšímu jest svůdný a láká k použití násilí, ale jen krátkozraký, nebo svůdce, potřebující nutně okamžitých úspěchů, nechá se svésti. Obezřetný, pravý vůdce ví, že nejen lze utiskovati slabšího, ale že nikdo není sám tak silný, aby zde zase proti němu nebylo silnějšího, který by mohl tu použíti téže metody. Není možno volit metodu podle síly nebo slabosti. Lze voliti jen zásady: buď demokracii, s právem na požadavek také sám zase mezi většími a silnějšími

býti slyšenu v demokratické spolupráci a souhře světové, nebo násilí a diktát s risikem, že najde se někdo silnější, jehož diktát pak rovněž bude třeba přijati bez odporu. Oživené svědomí států hlásících se k spolupráci ve Svazu národů za cestou míru jest nám dokladem, že cesta demokracie a spolupráce jest a byla jedinou správnou cestou a současně jest nám i nadějí, že tvoří se tu tak silná moc kolektivní, že vždy bude silnější než kterýkoliv jedinec státní a že zaručen bude onen poslední kategorický imperativ, o který se musí definitivně roztříštit každý násilník, ohrožující světový mír a pokoj.

Židovstvo našeho státu spolu s ostatními spoluobčany raduje se z výročí velikého dne, který se stal symbolem státní jednoty a myšlenky a jest si vědomo své povinnosti, jež vyplývá z jeho srdcí jako milá samozřejmost.

O loyalitě se mluví tam, kde se někdo neidentifikuje, kde se distancuje a kde právě touto distancí vzniká poměr, který může být loyální, kladný nebo záporný, a — také se může měnit.

Proto u nás jen o loyalitě mluviti nelze. Slova nejsou přípustna tam, kde rozhodují jen činy. Těší nás, že naši zodpovědní spoluobčané z našich činů chápou, že v tomto směru není rozdílu mezi námi, že jednotně stojíme v sjednoceném šiku za svým státem a jeho demokratickým zřízením. — Každé výročí pak těší nás dvojnásob, neboť každým novým rokem sílí a mohutní jich základy.

drfr

The title page of the Věstník Židovské obce náboženské v Praze (Gazette of the Jewish Religious Community in Prague), Nos. 3 and 9 of 1935.

VĚSTNÍK

ŽIDOVSKÉ OBCE NÁBOŽENSKÉ V PRAZE

ROČNÍK II.   V Praze, dne 22. března 1935.   ČÍSLO 3.

Dr. František Friedmann:

1135—1935
Mojžíš ben Maimun.

Ve Španělsku, v této zemi, kde před staletími tak vysoko plál plamen židovské kultury, že k jeho jasu vzhlížel s úctou celý tehdejší svět, aby náhle byl hrubým násilím zdeptán a ráj změněn v žhavé peklo, v této zemi později tak strašného zvuku pro štvaný Izrael, že na své bludné pouti světem mijel po staletí ony břehy nasáklé krví tisíců obětí inkvisice, chystají se ohromné státní oslavy za účasti vlády a presidenta Republiky na počest Žida Mojžíše ben Maimuna.

. Stačí jen uvážiti z mnohých pověstí, pojících se k tomuto židovskému velikánu, uctívanému po staletí nejen židovským ale především i arabským světem onu o poslední jeho cestě, kdy prý průvod pohřební byl přepaden loupeživými beduiny, kteří však nemohli hnouti s místa rakví tohoto božího muže, takže ohromeni vyprovázeli jej pokorně až k místu jeho posledního odpočinku, abychom vytušili, čím byl své době, když jej lid opřádal takovými zkazkami.

Jestliže však na jeho hrob neznámá ruka napsala v zanícení: „Zde leží člověk a přece nikoliv člověk. Jestliže's byl člověkem, pak Tvou matku zastínili tvorové nebeští", a tento nápis v pozdější době smazán byl nahražen slovy: „Zde leží Mojžíš Maimun, v klatbu daný kacíř", pak chápeme jak hluboce svými myšlenkami rozvířil duševní život židovský.

Nejen jeho dílo, i jeho dráha životní poskytuje nám hluboký pohled do osudů židovských.

Mojžíš ben Maimun, Maimonides, arabským jménem Abu-Amran Musa ibn Maimun ibn Abdallah, všemu Židovstvu známý pod jménem RaM BaM narodil se v předvečer pesachového svátku (30. březen) 1135, tedy před osmi sty léty v Cordově z rodiny po osm generací proslulé studiem talmudu a rabínské literatury.

Jeho otec nebyl jen učencem Písma, ale i matematikem a astronomem a autorem učených děl těchto oborů.

Mladý Maimun neužil klidu slunného mládí. Když byl 13 let stár, padla Cordova do rukou fanatických Almohadů a rodina jeho spolu s většinou židovského obyvatelstva volila vyhnanství, nechtějíc setrvati za cenu zrady víry, byť bylo i vynutí přijetím mohamedánského vyznání na oko. Ale jen tři léta žijí v Almerii a i toto přístavní město upadá v ruce Almohadů a rodina snažíc uchovati víru svých otců bloudí léta cizinou. Tato věrnost duchovní, přesvědčení tak těžkými obětmi vykupovaná ocelí jeho vážnost, sílu vůle a smysl pro reálnost. Kolem r. 1160 nalézá rodina Maimonova konečně útulek v africkém Fezu, kde však jsou Židé rovněž nuceni ke konfesi mohamedánské, byť se tak dělo jen slovy, že Mohamed je prorok. V tuto dobu spadá první veřejné vystoupení Maimonidovo. Píše „Iggereth há šemad", list o odpadlictví jako repliku na pastýřský list ortodoxního rabína africkým obcím židovským proti „anusim", tvrdící, že Žid, byť

In the economic sphere there appeared, apart from many other organizations, the "Union for Economic and Cultural Care" headed by the industrialist Leon Bondy. This Union organized lectures on the economic reconstruction of Czechoslovakia, contributed to several cultural projects and played a strong role also in the investment policy of the new state.

* * *

In 1919 the TRIBUNA newspaper began to appear (in the Czech language) for "Jews who need a Czech newspaper" and for the "Czech nation which needs an economic newspaper."

From 1921 the "Tribune" was headed by Arné Laurin with the cooperation of such personalities as Josef Kodíček, Alfred Fuchs, Jindřich Kohn and Karel Poláček. The Tribune ceased to be published in 1928.

* * *

The ŽIDOVSKÉ ZPRÁVY ("Jewish News") oriented to Zionism and headed from 1918 by Ludvík Singer, presented readers with the main principles of its programme, drafted by Max Brod and Felix Weltsch:

a) To establish a Jewish national centre in Palestine

b) To make it possible for Jews living outside Palestine to develop their own national culture

c) To secure equal rights for the Jewish community in all places where its members lived.

The next twenty-five years provided a tragic reply to the question of the extent to which the Czech-Jewish assimilation movement had succeeded in realizing its endeavours to secure the merging of Jews with the Czech nation.

The next twenty-five years also replied to the alternative of the Zionist movement.

* * *

Although Jews represented less than 2.5% of the population in the first republic (including Slovakia and Carpathian Ruthenia), they were an important factor particularly in the economic and cultural life of the country. For the first time since they had arrived on this territory they also had their own independent political representation. The Jewish party was represented in the highest governmental organs (in 1929 by Dr. Ludvik Singer and Dr. Julius Reisz and in 1935 by Dr. Angelo Goldstein and Dr. Chaim Kugel).

The number of Jews in the Czech Lands did not exceed 1% of the total number of the population (over 115,000 in all) and nearly one half of this number, about 50,000, lived in Prague. As already said, in view of its economic and cultural influence it was the most important of all the Jewish communities in the Czech and Slovak regions and districts. Their relationship with the local – Czech and German – population continued to be very complicated. The fact cannot be overlooked that just as in the past, a part of the Jews on the territory of the historical countries still inclined towards the German element and that certain barriers separating this part of the Jews from the Czech national forces were therefore historically created.

These complicated nationality frictions in the Czech-German-Jewish triangle manifested themselves especially sensitively in the situation of Prague's Jewish community, which in its search for its identity vacillated from the extreme pole of complete assimilation (the Czech-Jewish movement with the ROZVOJ (Development) magazine) to the opposite pole represented by the Zionist movement (with the ŽIDOVSKÉ ZPRÁVY Jewish News magazine).

Zionism and the Zionist movement did not find such a response or member base as in Slovakia or Carpathian Ruthenia. This is also witnessed by the fact that from 1924 to 1936 only some one hundred persons moved from Bohemia to Palestine.

Zionist societies and associations such as **HEHALUC, MAKABI, HASH-OMER-HACAIR** and **BETAR** did not arouse a mass response among young people. Popularity was enjoyed in particular by the **HAGIBOR HAMAKABI** sports society of Jewish youth whose members achieved outstanding results, comparable with the world's best, in certain branches of sport (specially in swimming). They rivalled the **BAR-KOCHBA** Jewish sports club in Bratislava whose members held, at their time, practically all Czechoslovak swimming records. (The ranks of outstanding Jewish sportsmen included, to mention at least two, the sprinter Andrej Engel and the tennis player Ladislav Hecht).

The **B 'NAI-B'RITH** lodge in Prague, the oldest Jewish world organization which owned house No. 5 in Růžová Street and whose activity was manifested in the cultural and social spheres, played an important role in the life of Prague's Jewish community. In 1928, on the initiative of this lodge, the Society of the History of Jews in Czechoslovakia was founded which from 1929 to 1938 published nine volumes of the annual "Jahrbuch der Gesellschaft für die Geschichte der Juden in der Tschechoslowakischen Republik." Its editor was Professor Samuel Steinherz. The Jewish Religious Community, which was rather of a neological (more modern) character, represented the part of the Jews which also formally avowed the Jewish religion. For its members it published The Journal of the Jewish Religious Community in Prague.

$$* * *$$

The Czechoslovak Republic gained recognition also in the international field. It was the scene of important international events which included, for example, the World MAKABI Congress held at Moravská Ostrava in 1929 and the World Zionist Congresses at Karlovy Vary in 1921 and 1923 and in Prague in 1933.

It would be outside the framework of this chapter to name at least the most

A drawing by František Gellner (1881–1914) –
Self-portrait.

renowned personalities of Jewish origin who played an active role in public life, whether in the economic, the political or the cultural sphere.

Let us devote our attention particularly to the literary sphere with a view to the writers who wrote in the Czech language.

The now world-recognized phenomenon of Prague-Jewish German literature deserves greater space and a separate chapter will thus be devoted to it in the second part of this publication.

The literary personalities working in the period preceding the First World War included **František Gellner** (1881–1914), who in his youth joined the ranks of poets in the anarchist group. They formed themselves round the poet Stanislav Kostka Neumann. František Gellner was an all-round personality. He studied painting in Munich and Paris. He published his poems mainly in the Popular Newspaper, but they also appeared in the repertoire of well-known Czech cabarets, especially at the Red Seven Cabaret at the Central Hotel in Hybernská Street. At the beginning of the First World War he served on the Galician front and in September 1914 he was reported missing.

The first writer of Jewish origin who really wrote in Czech was perhaps **Vojtěch Rakous** (real name Albert Österreicher, 1862–1935). His life story is also an interesting one. He gained experience as an assistant in a shop engaged in the sale of footwear and later opened his own shop in the Libeň quarter of Prague. He also worked in the Czech-Jewish movement. In his small, socially inclined humoristic prosaic works he described the destinies of the Jewish population of the central Elbe valley, their merging with the Czech environment and the minor differences between their way of life and their dogmatic religious rules. We can read his best-known stories in his novels en-

Karel Poláček (1892–1944)   *Vojtěch Rakous (1862–1935).*

titled "Vojkovičtí a přespolní" (The People of Vojkovice and Those from Somewhere Round About" and "Modche a Rézi" (Modche and Rézi).

In a certain sense of the word **Karel Poláček** (1892–1944) can be regarded as Rakous's follower. He also came from the bourgeois family of a Jewish merchant. From 1923 he worked as an editor on The Popular Newspaper. During the war he was transported to Terezín and soon afterwards died at the Oswieczim concentration camp. His literature also deals with Jewish strata and vacillates on the border between humour and tragedy.

The First World War also affected the life of Prague-born **František Langer** (1888–1965), who served on the eastern front as an army physician and rose to the rank of general. He established himself as an author of theatre plays and from 1935 to 1938 he was employed as a dramaturgist at the Vinohrady Theatre. During the Second World War he served as a medical officer in the Czechoslovak army abroad.

One of his best-known plays is the comedy "Velbloud uchem jehly" (A Camel Through the Eye of a Needle) and the drama "Periferie" (Outskirts).

As regards the approach of writers to Jewish themes, František Langer's brother **Jiří (also Georg) Mordecai Langer** (1894–1943), who inclined towards East-Jewish hasidism, is regarded as being exceptionally outstanding and important. In Prague he had contacts with Franz Kafka. He taught him Hebrew and acquainted him with eastern Jewish legends. Later he moved to Palestine. He wrote ethnical and philosophical prose based on the life of rabbis and their fellow-believers (Devět bran – Nine Gates).

Caricature by Adolf Hoffmeister: J. Kodíček,
J. Langer and K. Poláček.

An exclusive phenomenon in Czech literature, who is sometimes compared with Franz Kafka, was **Richard Weiner** (1884–1937), who from 1912 found his way to literature after previously working in the field of chemical engineering. He was employed as the Paris correspondent of a Czech newspaper. One of the decisive experiences which influenced his literary work was his knowledge of the cruelty and senselessness of the world war.

Two important Czech lyric poets, **Hanuš Bonn** (1913–1941) and **Jiří Orten** (real name Jiří Ohrenstein, 1919–1941), also came from the Jewish environment.

As a secondary school pupil Hanuš Bonn had already worked in the Czech-Jewish movement and after studying law he became an employee of the Jewish religious community. In October 1941 he was arrested and shortly afterwards he was most likely hung or shot at the Mauthausen concentration camp. His poems are mostly spiritually orientated. His inclination towards the spiritual sphere was also manifested in his translations of the poetry of primitive nations into German and English.

Jiří Orten also came from the family of a small Jewish merchant of Kutná Hora. From 1937 he studied in Prague at the Conservatory of Drama, from where he was expelled for racial reasons, however. On 30 August, 1941 he was knocked down in the street by a German ambulance and died two days later.He was a lyric poet and his complicated artistic development proceeded in an atmosphere of fear, the loss of life certainties and the direct danger of anti-semitism.

Alfréd Fuchs (1892–1941), whose complicated destiny was reflected in his works, also died during the Second World War.

Richard Wiener (1884–1937).　　　　　*MUDr. František Langer (1888–1965).*

Even as a student he worked in the Zionist movement and was involved in particular in the Czech-Jewish movement, which propagated the merging of the Jews with the Czech nation. In 1921 he converted to Catholicism and soon began to work for it. From 1925 he held the post of chief editor of the "Prager Abendzeitung" newspaper.

His literary activity was mostly of a publicistic character. He also published several collections of anecdotes and translated works by Heinrich Heine, J. W. Goethe and, in particular, Max Brod into Czech.

In 1940 he was arrested and deported first to Terezín and later to Dachau, where he was fatally ill-treated.

Another figure in the centre of Czech cultural life was the leading scholar of German studies, poet, translator and theatre expert **Otokar Fischer** (1883–1938). He became an associate professor and later professor of the history of German literature at Charles University in Prague. He also worked as a dramaturgist and later as chief of the drama ensemble of the National Theatre. He published monographs about the German poets Heinrich von Kleist and Heinrich Heine and the philosopher Friedrich Nietzsche.

Due to the breadth and depth of his cultural interests Otakar Fischer ranked among the most outstanding cultural personalities in the First Republic.

Pavel Eisner (1889–1958) was an intermediator between German and Czech literature. After completing his studies at the German university

Hanuš Bonn (1913–1941).

Jiří Orten (1919–1941).

Alfred Fuchs (1892–1941).

Pavel Eisner (1889–1958).

*Karel Čapek (centre) with Gerhard
Hauptmann and Otokar Fischer (1932).*

(1911–1916) in Prague, where he devoted his attention to Slavonic and German studies, he became a noteworthy translator of works by German classics into Czech. Apart from this, he was an untiring propagator of Czech culture in the German language environment. He wrote in verse. All his translations can be regarded as creative deeds.

Another person concerned with Czech literary reviews and the theory of literature was **Kurt Konrád** (real name Kurt Beer, 1908–1941). He came from a German Jewish family and studied medicine and history at the university in Prague from 1927 to 1933. He was active in the camping and communist movements from the time of his youth and later worked as an editor of communist newspapers and magazines. Apart from publicistic activity he was, as regards history, particularly interested in the Hussite period. He also devoted his attention to aesthetics and the writing of literary and theatre reviews.

In 1941 he was arrested by the Nazis, imprisoned in several places and died in Dresden.

Jiří Weil (1900–1959) studied at the philosophical faculty of Charles University in Prague, his subjects being philology and the comparative history of literature. From 1922 to 1931 he was employed at the Soviet embassy in Prague and afterwards worked mainly as a free-lance writer and journalist. During the war he went into hiding and afterwards worked as an editor.

Kurt Konrad (1908–1941).   *Norbert Frýd (1913–1976).*

From 1950 to 1958 he was employed as a scientific worker of the State Jewish Museum. His novels are based on the Jewish tragedy of the Second World War ("Život s hvězdou" – Life With a Star, "Na střeše je Mendelsohn" – Mendelsohn is in the Roof). "Harfeník" – The Harpist – affords a historical picture of Prague in the first third of the 19th century and presents a confrontation of the destinies of two Jews, a destitute wretch and a factory owner.

His experiences as a Jew during the Second World War also determined the character of the works of **Norbert Frýd** (1913–1976). During the war he was imprisoned in Terezín, Oswieczim and Dachau. From 1953 he engaged in writing. In his autobiographically orientated novel "Krabice Živých" (Box of the Living) he afforded an unpathetic picture of life in a concentration camp. In his three-part family chronicle ("Vzorek bez ceny" – Worthless Sample, "Hedvábné starosti " – Silken Worries – and Lahvová pošta – Bottle Post) he described in a plastic manner the Czech and the Jewish society from the mid-19th century to the end of the Second World War.

Arnošt Lusting (b. 1926) was also a victim of racial persecution. He was imprisoned in Terezín, Oswieczim and Buchenwald and from 1946 he worked in Prague as a reporter, a radio director, a film scenarist and a writer.

The heroes of his works are persons experiencing the horrors of prisons and concentration camps. His most outstanding works include "Démanty noci" (Diamonds of the Night), "Noc a naděje" (Night and Hope) and "Modlitba pro Kateřinu Horowitzovou" (Prayer for Kateřina Horowitzová).

112

Arnošt Lustig (b. 1926).

Egon Hostovský (1908–1973).

Ota Pavel (1930–1973).

Hugo Haas (1901–1968).

Otto Gutfreund (1889–1927).   *Arne Laurin (1889–1945).*

The ranks of notable Czech-Jewish writers also include **Egon Hostovský** (1908–1973), who spent a part of his life in the diplomatic service. From 1932 to 1937 he edited the Czech-Jewish calendar.

In his works he shifted the specific Jewish problem onto a pan-human plane and portrayed homeless individuals in the upturned world ("Ghetto v nich" – The Ghetto in Them, – "Listy z vyhnanství" – Letters from Exile, "Cizinec hledá byt" – A Stranger Seeks a Flat, "Osamělí buřiči" – Lonely Rebels).

The work of **Ota Pavel** (1930–1973) was best characterized by Jan Werich: "Its becoming a gem of Czech literature is gradually coming about. It is as equally valuable as, for instance, For Whom the Bell Tolls. If it were written in English the world would kneel at Pavel's feet." In his short stories concentrated in several volumes ("Jak jsem potkal ryby" – How I Encountered Fish, "Smrt krásných srnců" – The Death of Beautiful Roebucks, "Plná bedna šampaňského" – A Crate Full of Champagne, "Pohár od Pánaboha" – A Cup from God, "Syn celerového krále" – The Son of the Celery King) Ota Pavel did not show himself to be merely an individual sports reporter or original prosaist, but also and in particular a narrator with a sensitive soul whose childhood was marked by the trauma of the Jewish tragedy of the Second World War.

In his brilliantly written short story entitled "Běh Prahou" (A Run Through Prague) he drew attention, as one of the first to do so, to anti-semitism as an accompanying phenomenon of communist practice.

114

The parade of German students welcoming Adolf Hitler at Prague Castle on March 15, 1939.

Beginning with František Gellner and ending with Ota Pavel, the list of Jews in the literary life of the first Czechoslovak Republic is not and cannot be complete. (In this connection clarification of the Jew concept, covering Jewish origin and who was and who considered himself to be a Jew, is more than problematic. To add to the picture it can be said that in the census of 1921 in the Czech Lands (with Moravia) 13% avowed Jewish nationality, 46.7% Czechoslovak nationality, 32.7% per cent German nationality and others 6.8% Jews.

Let us hope that the prepared encyclopaedia about Jews and the Jewish faith in the cultural life of the Czech Lands, based on personal entries, will fill this gap.

If we wanted to name the best-known actors we should have to allot first place to Hugo Haas (1901–1968) and of the great pleiad of musicians-composers we should have to present just a few names chosen at random: Jaromír Weinberger (1896–1967), Ervín Schulhof (1894–1942), Hans Krása (1899–1944), Karel Reiner (1910–1979); conductors – Vilém Zemánek (1872–1922), Karel Ančerl (1908–1978), Walter Süsskind (1913–1980), Adolf Heller (1901–1954), Georg Singer (1906–1980).

The leading places among creative artists belong to the sculptor Otto Gutfreund (1889–1927), Hugo Steiner-Prag (1880–1943), Adolf Wiesner (1879–1934), Bedřich Feigl (1884-1965), Jiří Kars (1880–1945)and the naivist Robert Guttman.

The Deputy Reichsprotektor, SS Obergruppenführer R. Heydrich, with K. H. Frank in Prague Castle.

Without any exaggeration it can be said that Jewish journalists ranked among the élite in their branch in the First Republic. This applies whether we speak of such personalities as Arné Laurin (1889–1945), on the Prager Presse paper, Alfréd Fuchs on Lidové listy, Egon Erwin Kisch (1885–1948) on Prager Tagblatt, Jaroslav Stránský (1884–1973) on Lidové noviny, the popular sports reporter Josef Laufer at the Radio, or a whole number of journalists working for the communist press (Stanislav Budín, Kurt Konrád (Beer) and others).

✳ ✳ ✳

Home profascists and anti-semitic circles also began to show activity with the approach of the danger of German fascism. In spite of the official tolerant policy adopted by the government towards Jews, right-wing political parties existed during the First Republic which had an explicitly anti-Jewish programme. These were naturally headed by Henlein's Sudeten-German Party.

✳ ✳ ✳

15 March, 1939, the date of occupation and breaking of Czechoslovakia, meant the beginning of the end of the millennium of history of Prague's Jewry. At first Czech Jews refused to recognize the danger which really threatened them. The monstrosity and horror of the so-called final solution of the Jewish question still seemed to lie in the remote future and not even the first anti-Jewish regulations (the marking of Jewish shops, inscriptions reading "No entry for Jews", the fixing of special shopping hours for Jews, etc.) were sufficient indications of what was to follow.

The first step towards the later complete liquidation of the Jewish community in the Czech Lands was the setting-up of a special office which, under the name of "Zentralstelle für jüdische Auswanderung", had the tasks of merging all religious communities in Bohemia and Moravia to form one single whole with the aid of the Prague religious community and of concentrating and evacuating all Jewish families.

According to the already valid racial laws a list was drawn up of all members of the Jewish population. (Apart from other so-called purity of race criteria, every person who came from at least three Jewish grandparents was regarded as a Jew.) Let it be recalled that the number of families which succeeded in emigrating in that period was really negligible. And if we are to tell the truth, we must say that it was only the wealthiest that succeeded in getting away.

Restrictions against the Jews continued during the Protectorate. These included the liquidation of all Jewish shops and legal and medical practices, the expelling of pupils and students from all schools and later the closing of all synagogues and the prohibition of Jewish religious rites.

From September 1942, once again after two centuries, Jews were obliged to wear a humiliating badge in the form of a yellow star with the inscription JUDE! All Jewish societies and foundations were naturally abolished. After the dissolution of Prague's Jewish community the so-called Jewish Council of Elders was instituted.

THE TEREZÍN
GHETTO
(THERESIENSTADT)

The taking up of the function of deputy imperial protector by Reinhard Heydrich meant the beginning of the last phase of "the final solution" of the so-called Jewish question in the Czech Lands. The phase at whose end there were only the crematoria of the extermination camps at Oswieczim, Birkenau and elsewhere.

* * *

For Czech Jews the halt on this journey "to death" was the so-called ghetto at Terezín.

The Terezín concentration camp, called the Jewish ghetto, represents one of the most shocking historical anti-Jewish facts documenting the bestial criminality of Nazism. Terezín was intended above all to serve as a reception camp for Jews before they were definitely transported to concentration camps in the east.

* * *

Terezín, once a fortress built during the reign of Joseph II, from 1780 to 1790, lies about 60 kilometres north of Prague, in the Litoměřice district.

The interesting thing about this former fortress is the fact that although at its time it was ingeniously built as an inconquerable defence system it was never used for military purposes. Already in the 19th century the whole fortress complex showed itself to be quite senseless. It completely lost the military importance it was expected to enjoy and in 1882 it was abolished.

A military garrison was stationed here and a part of the fortress complex, the so-called Small Fortress, was used as a jail. The town as a whole, including the Small Fortress (proclaimed a national cultural monument in 1962), still creates a gloomy impression.

Today it is difficult to imagine the effect of this place in the years 1942 to 1945, when over one hundred thousand Jews and thousands of other prisoners from countries occupied by Hitlerite troops were continually crowded here until they were transported to the death camps. Persons from the whole of Europe – from Germany, Austria, Holland, Denmark and, later, also from Slovakia and Hungary – were imprisoned here.

What did Terezín look like and how did the town function at the time when the Jewish ghetto was founded in it?

In the centre of the town there is a big square along which six streets run lengthwise and eight crosswise. There were fourteen big military buildings, barracks, in the town which served as dwellings for the Jewish population of the ghetto.

At the beginning of 1942 (16 Feburary) the Terezín municipal community was abolished and the original population was obliged to move out by the end of June 1942. The whole town was transformed into a Jewish concentration camp.

The so-called **Small Fortress,** which during the war served as a special prison of the Gestapo, formed a special territory, a fortress within a fortress.

Before Jewish citizens were transported to Terezín they were concentrated in the Holešovice quarter of Prague, in the place now occupied by the Park Hotel and where the building of the Prague Sample Fairs used to stand.

The first transport of Jewish prisoners, the so-called "Aufbaukomando" consisting of 342 men, arrived at Terezín on 24 November, 1941. The persons who made up this transport were forced to establish mass cells in the empty barracks for further thousands of men, women and children marked as Jews in accordance with the Nuremberg racial laws. (This transport was not, however, the first transport of Jews from the territory of Bohemia. In the period of from 16 October to 20 November, 1941 about six thousand Jewish inhabitants were deported from Prague and Brno to ghettos in Lodz and Minsk. Only a negligible number of these persons survived.)

From the beginning of January 1942 the Terezín ghetto was the destination of Jewish transports from Bohemia and Moravia. Very often the Small Fortress at Terezín was the last abode of many political and racial prisoners from practically the whole of Europe.

Statistics tell us that from the end of November 1941 up to 16 March, 1945, i. e. in the course of 41 months, 69 transports passed first through the building of the provisionary pavilion of the Prague Sample Fairs and from there to Bubeneč Station in the company of gendarmes. From here they continued to Terezín or other places. In all 45,413 men, women and children were dragged away and 37,669 of them never returned.

With the exception of one transport (the so-called criminal transport of Jewish inhabitants of Prague which on 10 June, 1942 made its way directly to Majdanek and other extermination camps in revenge for the assassination of the imperial protector Heydrich by Czech patriots on 27 May, 1942 in consequence of which he died at the beginning of June) all transports headed exclusively for Terezín.

Prisoners of the ghetto of Terezín.

Terezín fulfilled the role of a stopping-place from where (from 26 October, 1942) transports went directly to extermination camps (Oswieczim II – Birhenau), where the greatest number of Terezín prisoners were murdered in gas chambers.

Of the total number of 86,900 prisoners deported from Terezín to various extermination and concentration camps hardly 3,000 returned after the war!

It would be hard to described the dreadful conditions which prevailed in the Terezín ghetto. In August 1942 over fifty thousand persons were crowded in twelve barracks and several houses. Every corner, every corridor, every house attic and even the casemates below the fortress itself were full of people. The per capita living space amounted to 0.6 sq. metres!

Over 30,000 prisoners died directly at Terezín as the result of hunger, epidemics, infectious diseases and the unbearable living and sanitary conditions, which meant that every fourth prisoner of those transported to Terezín died there.

About 15,000 children passed through Terezín. They were up to fifteen years of age and only approximately one hundred returned after the war.

Almost unbelievably an unexpectedly rich, almost hectic social life proceeded even in this atmosphere of anticipation of a death transport, of the "last but one station".

One of the furnaces of the Terezín crematorium
built in 1942.

A characteristic, individual culture was not only spontaneously maintained, but also created here. A large part of not only the Czech, but also the
German Jewish intelligentsia, artists, professionals as well as enthusiastic
amateurs organized recitation, theatrical and musical performances. Several
theatrical and vocal ensembles existed here. The exceptionally distressing situation caused by the unbearable conditions and the uncertainty of the future
were expressed in particular in the poetry, children's drawings and music
which originated in the ghetto. (These moving children's drawings, which
number about four thousand, and poems are deposited in the archives of the
Jewish Museum in Prague. They have been exhibited here and in 1959 they
were published in book form).

The ranks of those who passed through Terezín were not made up exclusively of renowned – often on the world scale – Czech scientists, university
professors, politicians, physicians, teachers and artists, but also included writers Norbert Frýd and Karel Poláček, painters Bedřich Fritta, Oto Ungar and
Lev Haas, architect František Zelenka, sculptor Rudolf Saudek and composers and conductors such as Jan Krása, Karel Ančerl, Karel Herman, Karel
Reiner and Rafael Schechter.

In spite of the constant threat of transports, life in the ghetto proceeded in
a regular rhythm.

The Jews here had their own autonomy. All adults had to work, the average working period being 80–100 hours per week. Children of from fourteen years of age had the same work duties as the adults.

There were locksmiths', metal-workers', cabinet-makers', box-makers' and fashion jewellery workshops at Terezín. Everything needed by the town and the Germans was manufactured here. Toy production was on a particularly high level.

Over 3,500 children lived at Terezín, about 2,000 of them being accommodated in children's homes. Although teaching was forbidden (there were no schools here), lessons were given in secret. Apart from tuition for children, courses and specialized lectures were often held for adults. After all, there were so many outstanding scholars, professors and scientists here – specialists who could have been the pride of any world university.

A Jewish health service also operated in the ghetto in spite of the catastrophic lack of medical remedies.

Jewish autonomy stretched so far that the ghetto had its own guard service (Ghettowache) and even its own Jewish court (Ghettogericht). In 1942 the ghetto got its own bank (Bank der jüdischen Selbstverwaltung), which issued special banknotes (Ghettokronen). This money could be used to purchase goods in special shops inside the ghetto which the Germans sometimes filled with stolen articles and the contents of confiscated luggage.

✳ ✳ ✳

The most terrible place at Terezín which existed wholly separatelly from the ghetto was, however, the so-called Small Fortress. (Kleine Festung). It was a fortified part of the former Terezín fortress, a place which had a special position in the town itself. Shortly after it had been built it began to serve as a prison for military persons. Apart from these, however, political prisoners in particular also served their sentences here.

From 1823 the Greek revolutionary Alexander Ypsilanti was imprisoned here and in 1856 Anna Rosická, who fought for the rights of the Polish population in Galicia, also died here. (The principal participants in the assassination of Archduke Franz Ferdinand in 1914, Principe, Gabrinovič and Grabeš, were also imprisoned in the Small Fortress, where all of them also died.

From 1940 the Small Fortress served as an auxiliary prison of the Prague Gestapo, chiefly in order to relieve the police prison in the Pankrác quarter of Prague.

The first prisoners arrived here on 14 June, 1940. The persons imprisoned here were mainly prisoners of the Gestapo who had not yet been placed under arrest before facing court proceedings. Originally the Small Fortress was also intended to be a transit station for prisoners, but in actual fact it became one of the worst concentration camps.

Tens of thousands of representatives of eighteen countries occupied by the Nazis passed through the walls of the Small Fortress.

Children's drawings from the stop on the way to death, Terezín, from 1942–1944, about which the author Jiří Weil wrote: "Let their drawings and poems speak to you, it is their voice which has been preserved, the voice of truth and hope . . ."

The large area in front of the Small Fortess is occupied by the National Cemetery containing the bodily remains of 26,000 victims of Nazi tyranny.

The Small Fortress was also a prison for many Jewish citizens. They were transported here directly from Gestapo prisons in the manner of other political prisoners, or were brought here from the Terezín ghetto for breaking the camp regulations.

On the direct order of the commander of the fortress, Jöckel, Jewish prisoners were inhumanly tyrannized, beaten and finally "liquidated".

✳ ✳ ✳

The cynicism of the Nazi management of the Terezín ghetto is also witnessed by a case in June 1944 when the Nazis granted permission for a commission of the International Red Cross Committee to visit the Terezín camp, which was supposed to be presented to the world public as an "exemplary German camp for the re-education of Jewish citizens."

The Germans put up a cruel show in front of the commission and thus also in front of the world and after so-called beautifying activity (Verschönerung) the members of the international commission saw only buildings which had been carefully prepared for inspection in advance, including a selected group of prisoners or individuals.

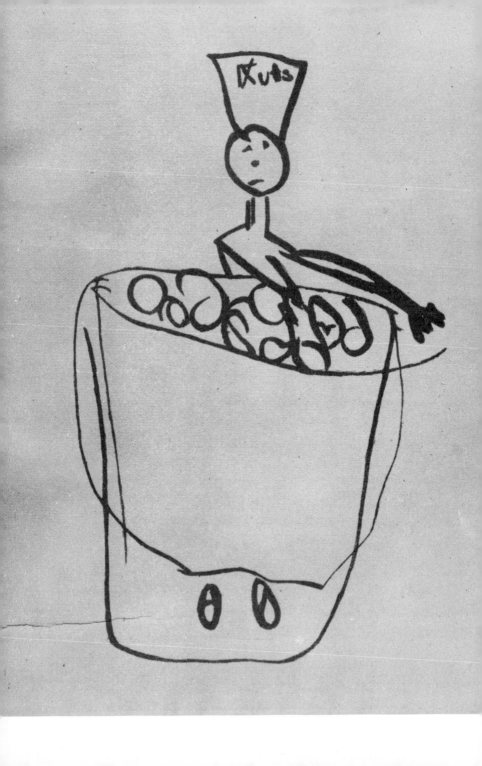

*The reverently maintained cemetery in front of
the Small Fortress at Terezín.*

It is a tragic fact that many members of the commission were successfully
convinced that everything was in order. The Nazis really succeeded in
camouflaging the mass murders and horrors of their concentration camps
from the eyes of commissions.

The last visit of a commission of the International Red Cross Committee
took place one month before the end of the war – on 6 April, 1945.

Now, when the defeat of the Nazi was secure, the members of the Terezín
commission pronounced Terezín to be what in actual fact it had been from
the very beginning – a concentration camp.

✳ ✳ ✳

The Terezín concentration camp was liberated on 8 May, 1945 in the late
afternoon hours in the framework of the so-called Prague Operation of the
3rd Guard Tank Army headed by General P. S. Rybalko.

. . . . .

The year 1945 meant the beginning of the new, by no means simple history
of the Jews living on the territory of Bohemia, Moravia and Slovakia.

The Jewish cemetery of victims of the Terezín concentration camp with a commemorative tablet.

II.

NOTES ON CULTURE

ORDINARY DAYS AND HOLIDAYS IN THE GHETTO

The history of the ghetto is a history of encounters and conflicts with the surrounding world. For many reasons – religious, social and rivalry ones – the surrounding society tried to isolate the Jews, to differentiate them. Their rights were always limited. (Already in the 16th century it applied that Jews were not allowed to leave their homes on Christian holidays and had to close their homes and windows when the host was carried, that Christians were forbidden to live side by side with Jews, etc.)

In 1215 the Lateran Council laid down that Jews were to distinguish themselves from their environs by their clothes and their colour. These regulations had different forms in different periods.

Dalimil's chronicle already speaks about "the Jewish hat", which was a funny yellow hat decorated with a ball. The decree according to which Jews were obliged to wear a hat was renewed during the reign of Charles IV. Later, in the Hussite period, they were made to wear a hood instead of a hat. From 1551 they were compelled to wear a ring and an order of 1748 and later of 1760 laid down that a Jew had to wear a beard and have a yellow cloth band on his left shoulder. A Jew was not permitted to carry a weapon and he had to count with the fact that if he left the ghetto he would be the object of abuse, insults and mockery and often even of physical assault.

Intimate relations between Jews and Christians were unthinkable. In Prague there is a record according to which a Jew was killed in 1536 for having "a love affair with a Christian girl".

* * *

The first numbers of Jews in the ghetto have been known to us from the mid-16th century, specifically from 1546. Approximately 1,000 persons lived in the two quarters known as the Stará škola and V Židech districts. In view of the fact that their number increased substantially (in 1655 1,492 Jews of over twenty years of age and about 500 between ten and twenty years of age lived here and in 1729 there were already about 10,000 of them in the ghetto), it was decreed before the emancipation process that only the first-born son of a family could marry. This decree was intended to radically limit the number of inhabitants of the ghetto.

* * *

Let it be added that although the Jewish Town of Prague was separated from the rest of the population of the town by real and symbolic walls, it was in constant contact not only with the other towns of Prague, but practically also with Jews in the whole of Europe if not in the whole world.

The population of the ghetto was of a cosmpolitan nature in the real sense of the word. Emigrants from various regions of Germany lived here and there were also enclaves of eastern Jews from Russia, Poland and the Balkans and at the time of the Inquisition also of Jews from Spain and Portugal. In quieter times Prague Jews travelled throughout Europe for trade purposes. On the other hand, Jews from various regions made their way to Prague in order to teach the Talmud in the renowned Prague rabbi school. Quite often Prague rabbis were active also in other well-known Polish or German religious communities.

The population of the ghetto changed continuously. It was in constant motion and huge emigration waves alternated with forced migration from the ghetto.

* * *

Nothing is further from the truth than the deeply rooted belief in the unity and social equality of the Jewish population in the ghetto. Poor strata lived here, but there was also a narrow stratum of wealthy persons, financiers (from the 16th century) who even lent money to sovereigns and noblemen.

It has previously been said that Jews represented a source of revenues for the ruler and the ruling power. Every year they paid (the sum in question changed) about 400 talents of silver and this was one of the reasons why they were tolerated in Bohemia. This was not the only tax they were called upon

Václav Jansa, The Jewish Town Hall and the Old-New Synagogue, drawing of 1896.

to pay, however. They were made to pay special taxes on the most varied occasions, to pay for permission to reside in Prague, etc. We know of a list of personages and dignitaries to whom the Jews were obliged six times a year to give presents and money on various holidays. The year of origin of this list was 1730. The ranks of those who received these gifts included the archbishop, the bishop, military and municipal dignitaries, the mayors and the burgomasters, magistrates and clerks.

The economic power of the Jews sprang from their financial deals which were realized in the shadow of the church ban on usury valid for Christians. The lending of money on an interest basis became a Jewish privilege and monopoly which in time led to an excessively high interest rate. This vacillated to a considerable extent and entries in municipal books of Prague confirm the fact that in some cases it fluctuated between the limits of 43%–290%. A complicated mechanism of loans, interests and securities, forfeited if a loan was not repaid in time, developed in the course of this business. Numerous middlemen, advisers and, naturally, a court of judges who resolved both simple and complicated cases connected with the forfeiting of the movable and immovable property of debtors participated in financial transactions. Forfeited immovables, which a Jew could not own (because he was not allowed to acquire any immovables without royal permission), were sold to Christians.

Zikmund Winter tells us: "Jews lent money also on the basis of simple receipts or I. O. U.'s, of notes and of debentures, even mortgage ones, reinforced with guarantors and books. Offences were committed on both sides

134

Jewish butchers and tailors.   *Jewish musicians.*

even in this lending business. In one case the debtor forged a seal, in another he completely denied the whole sum. Here a woman did not want to take on the debt of her husband even though an I. O. U. existed in respect of it, here again a Jew wanted more than he had lent, or he sold off a debenture to goodness knows how many people the last of whom finally charged the debtor an unexpected amount of interest which had been deliberately prolonged and dragged out. And there was always a lot of quarrels and court proceedings and the reputation of the Jews got continuously worse." And so things continued, often leading to anti-Jewish hatred, to anti-semitism on the part of the Christian population whose roots lay in Jewish usury, in the lending of money for interest, to which the Jews were, however, forced by their then public position.

However, the Jewish Town was also inhabited by unwealthy persons who did not concern themselves with usury, small craftsmen, because in spite of all prohibitions and restrictions material production had not disappeared from the ghetto. At first only things that were essential for life or that were too closely connected with a number of ritual or cult regulations were produced in the ghetto. Small tailors, shoemakers and butchers who adhered to the ritual regulations governing the slaughtering of animals and the preparation of their meat worked in the Jewish Town. Other branches also gradually began to appear here. It is interesting, for example, that Jewish musicians were hired to perform on various solemn occasions even outside the ghetto. In his Kronika Královské Prahy (Chronicle of Royal Prague) František Ruth writes that "at the wedding of lord Petr Vok of Rožmberk solemnized at Bechyně there were also Jewish musicians from Prague, who played very pleasingly for dancing."

Certain crafts were forbidden to Jews also in a later period, one of the rea-

Work of Jewish housewives.

sons for this being what could now be called "trade union discrimination". Jews were not accepted as members of guilds and neither were they allowed to practice a craft outside the ghetto. They were not allowed to own land and agricultural activity was also fobidden to them. Most of the buildings in the Prague ghetto were the work of Christian architects, builders and workers, although exceptions to this rule occurred later, in the Baroque period.

The Jews in the ghetto formed a compact whole differing from the surrounding world in practically everything. They lived in a closed community, married among themselves and had their own autonomy and courts. The supreme authority in the ghetto was the rabbi, whose word was law. Jews always gave priority to the verdict of their rabbi over that of secular courts. Public matters were the concern of the Jewish town council headed by a presidium with a primate. The status of primate had to be confirmed by the Royal Chamber. The seat of the community was the Town Hall, while the centre of the ghetto was the synagogue, where there was usually a school.

Life on ordinary days and holidays was subordinate to religious rules with numerous regulations. Apart from humiliating marks in the form of a tall hat or a strip of yellow cloth worn on the coat (this decree did not apply during the reign of every sovereign) the Jews themselves specified the way in which they were to dress. The more pious of them wore long coats – kaftans – and long hair, uncut at the temples and twisted into side-whiskers. Both at home and in the synagogue they wore a small cap on their head. This was usually black and it was called a "kipa" or "yarmulka". On the main holidays, YOM KIPUR and ROSH HA-SHANAH (New Year) they wore a "kitl" – a white linen shroud in which the body of a deceased person was also wound – in the synagogue. God's laws and commandments were brought to mind to pious Jews by CICIT, fringes worn under their chief garments. The life of every inhabitant of the ghetto was marked from the time of his birth to his death, on ordinary days and on the sabbath, by God's commandments. One of the most important duties of every father was to have his son circumcized at birth. This was the sign of the membership of a male offspring in the society of God's people, chosen by the Lord. Children attended school – CHEDER, – where they learned the word of God, from their earliest childhood, practically from four to five years of age. Attainment of the age of thirteen was an important event in the life of every young Jew, because he was proclaimed an adult during the BAR MITZVAH synagogal service. The carrying out of religious rites was conditioned by the presence of ten adult men over thirteen years of age.

The Cohens, considered to be descendants of the high priest Aaron, had a special position and certain privileges among the population of the ghetto. They were the first to be chosen to read the Torah. What might be called a function of honour was also fulfilled by members of the BURIAL SOCIETY – HEVRA KADDISHA – who carried out rites and organized burials. Another indispensable person in every community and synagogue was the synagogal servant SHAMES, the eternal subject of many Jewish anecdotes.

The week culminated with the celebration of the SABBATH, which began on Friday evening. White wheat bread of a long plaited shape – BARCHES – was baked before every Saturday and holiday. Every Jewess burned a Saturday light – NER-SABBATH – on the eve of the sabbath.

The ritual bath called MIKVE was intended for the purification of women.

The rhythm and monotony of every-day life were enlivened by holidays governed by religious rites. The feast of unleavened bread, PESACH, was celebrated to commemorate the exodus of the Jews from Egypt. Nothing containing yeast was allowed to be eaten for seven days and a number of other foodstuffs were also prohibited which were not even allowed to be in the home. MATZOH were eaten instead of bread. The superstition that the blood of Christians was necessary for the baking of these flat flour cakes prevailed for a long time, even surviving long after the issuing of the papal edict of the 13th century according to which Jews liberated themselves from the common saying that they needed Christian blood for their rite. A ban was also placed on the eating of Jewish unleavened bread.

The chief Jewish holiday was YOM KIPPUR, the day of atonement on which a day-long fast had to be kept. Former enemies became reconciled on this day. On the occasion of ROSH HA-SHANAN, the New Year holiday, believers carried out good deeds. In order to recall the fact that Mount Sinai

was full of blossoms when Moses received the Torah and the ten commandments they decorated their homes and synagogues with flowers at the SHAV-
UOT holiday. Meals made from cottage cheese had to be eaten on the occasion of this holiday. The PURIM holiday was of a merry nature. It was
celebrated in memory of Queen Esther, who saved all the Jews in the Persian
empire.

The Prague ghetto was a town of very mixed languages. Immigrants spoke
the tongue of their native land. German prevailed in the 14th and 15th centuries, but later Czech also began to be used for mutual communication. The
mixture of languages which characterized the ghetto is also reflected in the
names on the preserved tombstones in the Old Jewish Cemetery. Hebrew,
German and Czech names in particular can be seen here. The Hebrew names
which occurred most frequently in the ghetto were Abraham, Isaac, Michael,
Mayer, Moses, Solomon, David, Joseph, Nathan and Israel. In the first part
of his work Dějepis Prahy (The History of Prague) V. V. Tomek presents as of
1347 several Czech names such as Beneš, Jaroš, Trostlin, Ebruš, Muschlin.
Other Czech personal names such as Muňka, Muž, Mušátko and Viktor are
mentioned in the period of Charles IV's reign. From the late 15th century
Jews added a surname to their personal name. This was based on their individual characteristics (Šťastný – Happy, Vokatý – Goggle-eyed, Chromý –
Lame, Dlouhý – Tall, Krátký – Short). Very often they also used the name of
their place of origin or a community (Kolín – Cologne, Wiener – Vienna, Polák – Pole, Ungar – Hungarian, Sachs – Saxony). The extent to which the
Czech language influenced the life of the Jewish population of the ghetto is
witnessed by some 250 names on tombstones in whose case the name of the
Prague quarter Libeň (Lieben) served as a surname. Similarly, the name of
the town Roudnice occurs some 150 times, followed by surnames derived
from the names of the towns Sobotka, Kolín, Příbram, Náchod, Jičín and
others.

Use was also often made of the names of animals such as Lev (Lion), Kapr
(Carp) and Jelen (Stag). Many German names can still be encountered, for
example, Wolf, Taussig, Pinkas and Pick.

Although German was mainly spoken in the ghetto also later (in the 16th
and 17th centuries), the Czech language was used to a continuously greater
extent both colloquially and officially. Czech names appeared quite frequently in the official register "Liber albus Judeorum" in which property transfers
were recorded.

In 1627 the Jewish community submitted a request in the Czech language
concerning the possibility of organizing an election of its representatives. The
names of those concerned are presented in the Czech version – Lybrmon instead of Liebermann and Brandeysky instead of Brandeis.

✳ ✳ ✳

An idea of life in the ghetto during the Thirty Years War is afforded by
unique authentic materials preserved by chance to the present.

Forty-nine private letters written in the Prague ghetto in 1619 and addressed to relatives in Vienna were never delivered to their addressees and – two hundred years later – found themselves in the hands of researchers. Apart from information of a private nature, these letters contain a number of facts which supplement our picture of the ghetto.

The letters are written in German (also Yiddish) in Hebrew script with the frequent use of Czech words. Polish expressions also appear in them. It is touching to observe the prevalence of anxiety about spiritual and ethical matters in them. In spite of the fact that the writers of these letters lived in a period marked by war with its consequent material misery and want, optimism and an idealistic conception of life prevail.

We learn from these letters that at that time the ghetto was practically completely shut off from its environs. Strangers who came to it had to spend

The symbol of the Jewish butchers' guild (1620).

several days in quarantine in the cemetery only "to finally be told that access to the ghetto was prohibited to them."

* * *

More specialized branches and crafts gradually began to originate in the ghetto, for example, window-glazing and pottery. The Jews began to trade with wool and feathers and gained the monopoly in the import of furs and their working. Small workshops where not only Jews were employed originated in the ghetto.

The traditional branches included the butcher's trade, which was connected with religious, ritual regulations concerning the "kosher" preparation of meat. There were so many butchers that they had their own special little street with "meat shops" which were handed down from father to son. It is interesting that the customers of these Jewish meat shops were not only Jews. Meat was purchased at them specially during the period of Lent, when it was forbidden to sell meat in the Old Town. As Jews had no access to Christian guilds, they formed their own guild associations in the ghetto, one of the first being the association of butchers, who, just as Christian butchers, used the Czech lion in their emblem.

In the 16th and 17th centuries there were Jewish wheelwrights, tawers, hat-makers, locksmiths, potters, glaziers and, later, also goldsmiths in the ghetto. Tailoring was also a traditional craft. Records tell us that Jewish tailors maintained business relations with their Christian colleagues and even applied for membership in the tailors' guild.

Jewish firemen, who rendered assistance also outside the ghetto, enjoyed great renown. A record exists of a number of cases in which Jewish firemen extinguished fires. For example, in 1525 "when the mill in Poříčí Street caught fire the Jews made earnest endeavours to quench the flames while the Christians stole everything they could". In the accounts in the Hradčany book pertaining to 1607 we can read that "when a fire broke out at Michalovice, beer and rolls were given to the Jewish firemen".

On festive occasions and during big gatherings of citizens Jewish firemen stood in a state of readiness by all Prague's fountains in order to be able to act quickly if a fire broke out. In 1619, on the occasion of the coronation of Friedrich of the Palatinate, four hundred Jews were summoned to Prague's fountains.

From time immemorial a second-hand dealer added colour to the ghetto. This branch of trade involved a whole number of auxiliary activities. Rag-and-bone women went from house to house collecting old clothes, bones and glass articles. A second-hand dealer, a peddler, called a "handrlevi", purchased everything of which a household wanted to get rid. The variegated life of the ghetto was enriched by an organ-grinder, a wandering musician, a violinist and, of course, fortune-tellers.

There were also several taprooms in the ghetto. These were highly frequented by Christian craftsmen, a fact noticed even by the emperor who in 1650 drew the attention of the magistrate of the Old Town to the fact that "young labourers and craftsmen preferred to drink distilled liquor with the Jews instead of attending the church of the Lord on Sunday . . .".

* * *

The widespread trade activities in the ghetto included the pawning of goods. Numerous pawnshops existed here for the purpose. A pawned thing was forfeited if its owner did not pay for it or pay interest on it (6%) within a year and a day. The pawnbroker's trade was subjected to many other complicated rules and regulations.

Commercial (as well as non-commercial) activity ran up against rival interests. Records exist of long-drawn-out disputes led by Christian butchers who complained that Jewish butchers sold meat more cheaply and also that they sold their goods to Christians during Lent. Of a different nature was the dispute waged by Christian musicians, who complained that "Jewish musicians

The physician Issahar Beer Teller (about 1607).

The Old Jewish Cemetery, detail of the tombstone of the physician Beer Teller with the symbols of bear (Beer) and pincers (1688).

often performed on Christian holidays and at christenings and weddings." In 1641 the archbishop forbade Jewish musicians to play at Christian weddings and christenings, but he permitted them to play for Christians on ordinary and other festive days.

The long-term dispute waged by Christian manufacturers of military equipment and weapons resulted in Jews being forbidden to produce such goods. (With the substantial assistance of Christian competitor, however, a way was often found of getting round this prohibition. It is therefore characteristic that skilled Jewish craftsmen enjoyed a good reputation as manufacturers of pistols and carabines.) Christian journeymen or apprentices were not allowed to be employed in the ghetto for a long time either.

In 1633 the competition question had gone so far that the municipal authorities banned Jewish merchants from selling their goods on such traditional market-places as the "tandlmarkt" in the Old Town, where they had previously been able to trade with their merchandise since time immemorial. On the basis of an appeal this prohibition was finally withdrawn.

Later, from 1648, Jewish trade rights were extended. From then on they were allowed to trade with furs, wool and corn and also with animals and fish. They were also permitted to purchase wood from Podskalí.

Hebrew book-printing attained a high professional standard. In the early 16th century the first preserved Hebrew book with woodcuts was published in the ghetto. The printing house was under the management of several persons associated in a consortium where the printer Gershon Kohen also worked. Later he founded his own printing workshop which remained in the possession of the family up to the latter half of the 18th century. In view of their print and graphic design the first books published at this workshop rank among the foremost works of Hebrew Renaissance typography. All the specialized printing marks indicate connections and cooperation (block production) with then contemporary Czech typography. Works by Moses Isserles (1569), Jakob Polák (1594), Mordecai Jaffe (1609) and Jssarchar Ber ben Moshe Petachja (1611) were printed at the printing workshop founded by Gershon Kohen. The founder of the next printing house was Jakob Bak, whose descendants worked there until the end of the 18th century. Abraham Lemberk's printing house was in operation in the first half of the 17th century. About 250 works were printed at Jewish printing houses in Prague up to 1620.

In the years 1704 to 1736 David Oppenheim, the chief rabbi of Prague, owned a renowned collection of Hebrew books printed at printing houses in Prague before 1650. This library remained in the possession of the Oppenheim family in Hannover and Hamburg until 1830 from where it was allegedly sold to the Oxford library for 10,000 thalers.

The fact that the feeling of hatred for Jews was also oriented to their books is witnessed by the confiscation and burning in 1559, on the order of Pope Pius IV, of all books, including prayer books, owned by Jews also in Prague.

Medical practice was one of the most esteemed activities in the ghetto. Jewish physicians treated patients also outside the ghetto. Preserved among the documents housed in Prague's archives is the record of the special rights granted by King Václav IV in 1417 to his physician, a certain Teifl "a Jew from Jerusalem", as a reward for his successful medical treatment. In Part 9 of his work Dějepis Prahy (History of Prague), V. V. Tomek mentions the names of several Jewish physicians – Angelin, who worked at the court of King Vladislav (1589, resident in Malá Strana – the Little Quarter), May Žid physician (1499) and Juda Mojžíš (1522–1523). In the 17th century two outstanding physicians, a father and son by the name of Teller, worked in the ghetto.

* * *

Let us mention briefly some of the social aspects of life in the Jewish Town as recorded in 1902 by Zikmund Winter, Ignát Herrmann and Josef Teige in their attractive narration about the Prague ghetto. The life of Jewish families was governed by religious regulations. The rhythm of their every-day life was determined by centuries old traditions. Marriages were arranged between parents and were often based on financial and economic interests. The virginity of a bride was beyond all doubt and faithfulness to the husband was a law.

Women held a subordinate position in society, but they had the chief word in the home and with regard to the upbringing of children.

A Jewish funeral by an anonymous 18th century painter (section of a large painting).

Although Christian rulers and church circles tried (often with the use of force) to make Jews give up their faith and become Christians, cases of Jews being christened were rather an exception until the 18th century. Archives contain many cases of religious fanaticism leading to a forced christening. Tragic cases also occurred: their former society repudiated them and never took them back again. Still in 1765, during the reign of the Empress Maria Theresa, an order was issued according to which it was forbidden to christen a Jewish child until its seventh year of age, whereupon the ceremony could take place even against the will of the parents. A feeling for Jewish society and mutual solidarity were essential conditions of survival. The Jews always took great care of their old citizens and their poor (it was a benediction to invite a poor wayfarer to sit at the family table on the occasion of a Jewish holiday or to partake in the solemn evening meal on Friday, the eve of the sabbath). They also cared for those who were ashamed to beg in public. They placed money and gifts on the tombstones in the cemetery for them to pick up when it got dark.

* * *

The Burial Society, HEVRA KADDISHA, whose members enjoyed great respect, held a unique place in the ghetto.

Tablet of mourning days to commemorate the deceased (1893).

The original mission of this society was to care for the old, the sick and the deceased. Later its activity was extended and covered all spheres of charity.

According to the Jewish religion certain rules and regulations must be adhered to on the occasion of a death and burial and it was the task of the members of the Burial Society to see that this was done.

Membership in the Hevra Kaddisha was voluntary and honorary. It was a tradition of the ghetto that only educated and cultured God-fearing members of the community, well-acquainted with all its religious rites and regulations, could join the society.

A member of the society on whom exceptional ethical requirements were imposed (he had to lead an exemplary family and religious life) had to fulfil all the duties placed on him by the religious ritual. And these were by no means few in number. Strict regulations (connected with hygiene) stipulated that the body of a deceased person had to be buried on the day of his or her death. And the respective grave was allowed to be dug only on that day.

The Burial Society probably existed from the time of the beginnings of Prague's Jewish community. More precise reports of its activity date in 1564 similarly as the foundation charter which, along with the statutes and records of the society, represented an important source for study of life in the ghetto.

THE JEWISH COMMUNITY

In religious and judicial matters the Jewish community was entirely autonomous and, inside the ghetto, practically independent of the surrounding world. However, elected representatives of the community had to be approved by the Provincial Chamber. A representative of Prague's Jewish community was in actual fact a kind of unofficial speaker of the Jewish community as a whole in the Czech Lands.

The Jewish court, headed by a Jewish judge elected by the Jewish community (as a rule this function was held by the rabbi, because the law was based on old books of learning) and presided over by a representative of the community in the form of the "public elder primate", usually held its sessions on Sunday with the attendance of the public.

It had to resolve all internal disputes (apart from penal ones). In the first instance it also dealt with minor disputes between Jews and Christians. However, a Christian prosecutor could freely decide whether the venue of court proceedings should be the Old Town or the Jewish court. Whenever a Christian party was involved a Christian judge also had to be present, even when the given case was judged at the Jewish court.

The Jewish court could also sentence a guilty party to imprisonment in the prison available in the ghetto. Another punishment consisted of banishment for a period of eight days or perhaps even longer.

The Jewish court was later divided into two instances. The first (Beth Din Sutah) was headed solely by the rabbi, who dealt with lighter cases, while the second (Beth Din Rabbah) coped with more serious cases, judged by a collegiate of rabbis presided over by the provincial rabbi. A court of appeal was instituted for particularly serious and complicated cases. It consisted of the primate of the community, five judges, six elders of the community and twelve associate judges.

In 1630 the competence of Jewish courts was considerably restricted by an order according to which all more important and more general disputes concerning the Jewish community or even the most minor imperial interests were to be dealt with exclusively by municipal and not Jewish courts.

However, in 1633 Jewish courts regained several competences on the basis of an imperial privilege.

* * *

The community of the ghetto formed a diverse spectrum with individual interest groups often occupying mutually antagonistic positions. A conservative group (more frequently in power with regard to the administration of public and religious affairs) and opposition existed here.

As was usually the case (here we have in mind the conditions prevailing in the ghetto during the Thirty Years War in the years 1620 to 1650), a neutral middle group existed between these two poles. This suffered most, being dissolved in accordance with an imperial order. Following this, only two parties were allowed to be active inside the ghetto.

A disputation of Jewish and humanistic scholars.

The Gemara says: Rabbi Simon tells: A perfectly righteous man, who has been pious all his life and has become sinner in the last days of his life, loses all his merits, as it is confirmed by the verse: „The righteousness of the righteous shall not deliver him when he transgresses" (Ezekiel 33, 12).

A record exists of a case in which the existing parties were incapable of reaching an agreement on the question of the appointment of members of the corps responsible for law and order. This resulted in the intervention of the imperial bureau which, on the basis of its official power, appointed these members without the possibility of their election.

In former years the administrators of the Jewish community traditionally changed every year. Later (about 1635) the mandate was extended to a three-year period. After its elapse, however, no member of the old administration could be newly elected.

The voting right and the voting procedure itself were exceptionally complicated. To a certain extent everything depended on the solvency of the voters, their financial possibilities and, last but not least, the way in which they paid their taxes and the height of the sum with which they contributed to obligatory schemes.

The course of the election of members of the administration of the community was extremely complicated. Voting was carried out through the medium of a corps of voters with two hundred members who only then elected the administration of the community by secret vote. This administration was made up of twenty members. It is believed that only inhabitants of the Prague ghetto took part in the elections, technical and other reasons excluding the presence of Jews living outside Prague even though they were represented by the Prague primate.

* * *

One of the most delicate questions of life in the ghetto was the division of contribution charges, sums which the ghetto was obliged to hand over every year.

These special Jewish taxes or charges had to be paid precisely and regularly and if this were not the case, the threat of military executions and also high additional charges in respect of delayed payment hung over the ghetto.

As has already been said, the contribution that had to be paid by the ghetto amounted to 40,000 thalers; however, apart from this main tax, the Jews had to pay other different charges and taxes such as home, monthly, provincial and other rates.

* * *

Public "political" life inside the ghetto proceeded just as hectically as life outside the gates of the ghetto. One interest group replaced another. Individual groups fought among themselves and maligned their members in the manner common in public life.

If we trace the period of the Thirty Years' War and the conditions in the ghetto we shall have to say that great tension existed here and that the individual power groups lived in a constant state of controversy. This controversy often ended in mutual denouncements as in the case of rabbi Heller and later, in 1647, also in the case of the primate Moses Geisvogel against whom the Jews laid charges directly at the Czech Chamber.

In 1635 opposing parties became united for a short time and jointly proclaimed the extensive autonomy of the ghetto. The answer to this was the appointment of a kind of governmental "inspector of the Jewish Town" (originally he was to be marked as a royal magistrate, but in order to prevent this function from being confused with the function of the magistrate of the Old Town he continued to be called "inspector").

In 1636 the prosecutor Georg Willig was made the first governmental inspector. No detailed reports of his orders and regulations exist. It is only known that established at the same time as his function was the new office of "minister of finance" (held by Georg Albrecht Reich), who was supposed to cooperate with the administration of the community in contribution matters.

* * *

The year 1648, which brought the so greatly longed-for Westphalian peace, was to bring relief to the ghetto and peace among the continuously squabbling Jewish parties.

In that period the chief rabbi and six esteemed citizens elaborated a new modus vivendi which was intended to secure internal peace in the ghetto by means of a new, juster order. It was not the fault of this order that this did not come about and that several decades later the Jews again found themselves in a tragic position . . .

PRAGUE
HEBREW LITERATURE

Prague – "the mother city of Israel" – owed its generally recognized status in Ashkenazi Diaspora inter alia also to the high standard of Jewish culture, in the first place literature, which had developed in Prague from the very beginning of Jewish settlement and had been gradually enriched both by the variety of contents and genres and by the application of the languages spoken by the Jews of Prague.

The document proving that the Jewish population of Prague spoke Old Czech dates from the 13th century: it comprises several thousands of Old Czech glosses – explanations of Hebrew expressions – included into their interpretative religious works by the scholars **Abraham ben Azriel** and **Isaac ben Moses** called Or Zarua after his work. From the 16th century onwards written documents begin to contain the colloquial language "Juden-deutsch". From the break of the 18th and the 19th centuries German began to assert itself through the influence of Jewish Enlightenment and official Germanization and from the mid-19th century Czech appears as a result of the legal emancipation of the Jews. Outstanding from all language strata which have created the uniform Prague Jewish literature in the course of centuries, however, is the Hebrew literature, the most original writings, grown from the thousand years' old tradition which had originated before the origin of the Diaspora and was alive and creative on the soil of the Prague Jewish Town for almost another thousand years.

Its principal and biggest component consisted in religious works, either interpretative or legal in character. They originated in all Jewish communities of the Diaspora from their very beginning, from the erection of synagogues and the establishment of the office of rabbi as the spiritual head of the community. It originated from the living foundations of traditional Jewish education based on the continuous study of the two foremost authorities of Judaism – the Torah and the Talmud. The provisions of the Torah and the Talmud governed the life of Jewish communities both on the religious and the practical levels and whole generations of scholars studied, commented and elaborated them with regard to the problems brought about by every day life. The Prague school of tosafists (i. e. authors of supplements to the Talmud) from the 12th–13th centuries, which included also **Abraham ben Azriel** and **Isaac ben Moshe**, created this very type of Hebrew literature which has remained valid and most widespread for whole centuries.

The Prague Jewish community as the biggest privileged centre and subsequently the representative of Jews in Bohemia necessarily attracted recognized authorities from the ranks of scholars who were elected Rabbis and Presidents of the talmudist school. They did not solve only the religious and legal problems of their communities, but were addressed also by the rabbis from other towns, and often even from other countries. The collections of re-

The sign of a Prague Hebrew print (1603). – The sign of the Prague Hebrew printing shop of the Gersonides.

sponds – answers to enquiries, which reproduce concrete religio-legal problems and, after appropriate analyses, suggest adequate solutions, belong – similarly as sermons – to the literary works of these spiritual authorities and simultaneously to the sources which contribute to the picture of the history and the life of individual communities. The commentaries and interpretations of the Torah, the Talmud and the medieval codes, responds and sermons became, thanks to the general historical and political conditions of existence of Ashkenazi communities, the principal genres of their Hebrew literature, serious genres, which comprised also religio-philosophical and polemic writings and, from the 16th century, also mystical writings.

In this way a number of authors have been incorporated into the history of Prague Hebrew literature, who acted as rabbis and presidents of the the the famous yeshiva – talmudist school, such as:

Yom Tov Lipmannd Mülhausen (second half of the 14th – mid-15th centuries), the author of the apologetic writing Sefer nicahon (The Book of Victory);

Elisser ben Elija Ashkenazi (1512–1586), the commentator of the Pentateuch and the founder of the Prague Burial Society; in the 70s of the 16th century his successor in the office of rabbi, **Isaac ben Abraham Chayut,** the author of several classic interpretative works;

the most famous of all Prague Jewish scholars, **Jehuda Liwa ben Bezalel – Maharal** or **Rabbi Loew** (1512–1609), whose epitaph on the tombstone in the Old Jewish Cemetery includes, inter alia, also the titles of his nine greatest writings (Gur Arye – The Lion Cub, commentary to the Torah; Gevurot ha shem – The mighty Feats of God; Derech chayyim – The Way of Life; Tiferet Jisrael – The Glory of Israel; Netivot olam – The paths of the World; Beer ha-gola – The Well of Exile, etc.);

Mordecai ben Abraham Jafe (1530–1612), the successor of Rabbi Loew, whose commentaries, interpretations and ethic writings bear a collective title of Levushim (The Garments);

Solomon Ephraim Luntschitz (1550–1619), talmudist and preacher;

Yom Tov Lipmann Heller (1775–1654), one of the pupils of Rabbi Loew and the author of a six-volume commentary to the Talmud known as Tosafot Yom Tov (Yom Tov's Supplements), which is being studied and acknowledged by conservative rabbinic circles even at present, at the cost of other author's writings.

From the number of authors of the traditional religious branch of Jewish literature flourishing in Prague in the 17th century mention should be made of **Shimshon Bacharach** (1607–1670) who worked in Moravia, Bohemia and Germany and died as chief rabbi in Worms, further **Aharon Shimon Spira,** the member of an outstanding Prague family of scholars and rabbis from the 17th and the 18th centuries and, last but not least, **David Oppenheim** (1664–1736). Oppenheim – like Rabbi Loew a century before him – became the chief rabbi of Prague after several years' work in Moravia. He became famous chiefly for his activities as collector; he amassed a noteworthy collection of books written in Hebrew and in Juden-deutsch which numbered about one thousand manuscripts and six thousand prints, including also rare Prague editions. At present this collection forms part of the Bodleian Library in Oxford.

Another continuously recognized author of the traditional Jewish culture is Oppenheim's successor in office, the Chief Rabbi of Prague **Ezechiel Landau** (1713–1793) whose collection of responds, Noda bi-Yehuda (Known in Judea), is being consulted even at present in ritual problems. The history of Jewish culture comprises also the Landau's polemic with the famous **Jonathan Eybenschütz** (1690–1764) who worked as preacher and president of the yeshiva in Prague and had to face there an accusation for leaning to the Sabbathian sect. Ezechiel Landau, the representative of the conservative direction of traditional rabbinic studies, had a number of successors from the number of scholars who were his contemporaries or the members of further generations. Their number included e. g. the president of the Prague yeshiva, **Meir Fischls Bumsl-Bunzlau** (d. 1769), **Zerah Eidlitz** (1725–1786), **Bezalel Ranschburg** (d. 1820), rabbi **Eleazar Fleckeles** (1754–1828) and **Simon Lichtenstadt-Lasch** (1796–1868). In opposition to this conservative line of Jewish culture stood the arising science of Judaism (Wissenschaft von Judentum),

*Mordecai Jafe: "The Robe from the City of
Susa", Prague 1609, the Gersonide printing
shop. The title page of a Prague Hebrew print
(1603).*

לבוש ד האורה

ביאור על רש״י שעל התורה · חבר איש
נורא . כ׳ חיבוה ואור תורה · ראס
ויספרת : הכינת · אם חקיר · הנתון
הנעלה · מהד״ר מרדכי יפה · י״ם ואהל
בקק פוזנא · סמפוהלר׳ :

נדפס פה קק פראג
הטירא

תחת ממשלת ארוממ סקיסר רהולפוס
יר״ה

בבית הנגלה כמר חיים בר יעקב
הכהן

Famous Rabbis of Prague: David Abraham Oppenheim (1664–1736)   *Jonathan Eybenschütz (1690–1764).*

which methodologically drew on the ideas of Jewish Enlightenment – the haskala – and linked up with the general development of humanities of the 19th century. The leading representative of the Judaic science in Prague was the chief rabbi **Shelomo Juda Rapoport** (1790–1867), a scholar who considered Hebrew literature an important source of the study of Jewish history and culture. Apart from his own vast work he left also extensive correspondence which he led with his colleagues – members of the school of Judaic science from all over Europe. Their number included also **Zacharias Frankl** (1801–1875), who had been born in Prague, the founder and editor of the periodical of the school, Monatsschrift für die Geschichte und Wissenschaft des Judentums (Monthly Journal for the History and Science of Judaism); further the preacher in the Old Shul, **Saul Isaac Kaempf** (1813–1892), the author of the works on the wealth of Jewish culture in medieval Spain; and in the 20th century the chief rabbi and director of the Talmud-Torah school in Prague, **Heinrich Brody** (1862–1942), one of the greatest connoisseurs of classical Hebrew literature and particularly poetry. Those last named published their principal works in German – the language known to the widest circles of those interested in Jewish history and culture.

Apart from the prevailing genres of traditional rabbinic studies, however, the Hebrew literature of Jewish Prague created also the works forming part of artistic genres, both prose and poetry. Unfortunately not many of them have been preserved and their creation itself had remained, until the period of Enlightenment and emancipation, under the influence of the conservative intellectual trend of Judaism.

Until the Renaissance the artistic prose in our territory was represented merely by fragments of annalist and travel records. Only from the end of the 16th century chronicles and minor works of historical prose began appearing, interspersed with autobiographies and memoirs; also scientific works, primarily from the field of natural science, appeared the literary standard of which ranks them on the boundary between artistic and scientific prose.

The first work of this type which has been fulfilling the role of entertaining and instructive reading in the Ashkenazi area, is the travel book by **Petachia of Regensburg.** His author had close relations to Bohemia and Prague, because his brother, the tosafist **Isaac ha-Lavan** (White) lived in Prague, and it cannot be excluded that Petachia himself had worked in Prague for some time. He undertook his journey probably in 1175–1185, some ten years after another famous Jewish traveller, the Spanish Jew **Benjamin of Tudela.** As it is testified to by the introduction to is itinerary "he departed from Prague, which is in Bohemia, travelled to Poland, from Poland to Kiev which is in Russia, and from Russia he walked six days to the river Dniepr . . ." Then he continued his journey via Crimea, Turkmenia and Armenia to Arab countries and to Persia, finally to head from Halab and Damascus for Galilee and Jerusalem, which was the chief goal of his journey. Although only a fragment of Petachia's itinerary has been preserved, it is obvious that it acquainted its readers with the places through which its author had travelled, their population, outstanding Jewish scholars who had lived there, memorial places and legends pertaining to them. **Petachia from Regensburg,** naturally, was not the only Jew from Prague who has left us his testimony of his pilgrimage to Palestine, the country to which thousands of pilgrims headed in the course of centuries. However, until the 18th century the Jewish itineraries did not emancipate themselves from the framework of the narrative in which reality had been mixed with legends. This is testified to also by the small work by **Gershon ben Eliezer Jidls** from Prague called Gelilot Erec Jisrael (The Territory of the Land of Israel), written in the first quarter of the 17th century; this itinerary, written in the colloquial Juden-deutsch, not in Hebrew, represents a sort of guidebook "for all those who travel to the land of Israel".

Indubitably the most widely read Hebrew writing of secular content penned by a Prague Jewish author is the chronicle Zemach David (the Wand of David) by **David Gans** (1541–1613). The personality of this Renaissance scholar itself deserves attention. David Gans, who had been born in the city of Lippstadt in Westphalia, received the traditional talmudist education from famous teachers in Bonn and Frankfurt, from where he went to the yeshiva of Cracow, headed by the famous halachist, Moses Isserles. Under

*David Gans, "Nehmad we-naim", manuscript
pages.*

his influence Gans began to study more profoundly the sciences to which he
had been attracted earlier: philosophy, mathematics, astronomy, geography
and history. When he came to Prague in 1564, he found successively two
teachers who stimulated further his yearning to know the world, its form and
its history – Sinai ben Bezalel and his brother, Jehuda ben Bezalel – Rabbi
Loew. In the sixties Gans left for Nordheim in Saxony for a short time to
study mathematics and geometry. However, he soon returned to Prague and
did not leave it until his death on Agust 22, 1613.

156

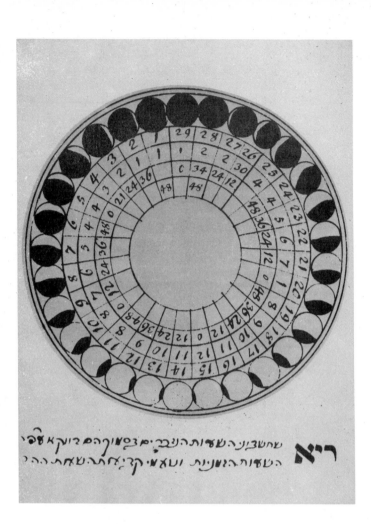

The relative peace and tolerance enjoyed by the Prague Jewish community at the end of the 16th and the beginning of the 17th centuries permitted also free relations of its outstanding members with the Christians. Also David Gans made use of this situation and established contacts with the astronomer Tycho Brahe, his assistant Johann Müller and with Johannes Kepler. In his book Nehmad we-naim (The Pleasant and the Dear) Gans mentions in several places his talks and correspondence with these outstanding representatives of Renaissance science. He also writes that he participated personally

David Gans: "Zemach David", Prague 1592, the Gersonide printing shop.

 את צמח דוד עברד מהדיה תצמח

ספר
צמח דוד

ראה זה דבר חדש שכבר לא הוה לעולמים · קצור מופלג בדורות
הקדמונים · אדם נח אברהם ושאר אנשי תמימים · וכל אלם תנאים
אמוראים המחוכמים · רבנן סבוראי גאונים ורבנים הדסים ז"ל · עד
שנותינו ה' אלפים שנ"ב ליצירת עולמים · גם בחלק השני ודברים
גדולים רשומים · והגעשים בזמני מלכי בכל פרס יון ואדום · פעשי
גדולים מכל אקסרים שמלכו לעולמים · מיולים הקסר הראשון
שמלך על רומי · עד זמן אדונינו הקסר רודולפוס ה"ה איש חטים ·
מאורעת מדינת צרפת ספרד ואיטליאה העצומי אשכנז פולין פיהם
ושאר עמים · מסכוכים מלחמות ושפיכת דמים · דברים
חדשים נוראים חעמים · אשר קראום ביבשה ויםם
דברים אשר לא נמצאו בדברי הימים · כי רלא
שערום גם אין אחר מן החכמים ·
בם יתענגנו נפשות
עוים ·

חבר לותו איש מסכיל חכם חרפיס וכנון דעת כגדיר דוד נאבוזון
וקהל ממו ב'מראל צמח דוד · לסינת טעמלי הנזכרי נהקרב ·

נדפס פה ק'פראג הבירה

תחת ממשלה יורינו הקיסר רודילפוס ירה על בני המשומתפים
בריטו הי"ק כמר עלמה כהן וכן מחיו ויק וחכים הבחו'כאל משה כהן
וה'תה התהלתי ביום ד' ברה סיון שוב לפק

three times in the observations in Tycho Brahe's observatory in Benátky nad Jizerou and that he translated for this outstanding astronomer the so-called Alphonsine tables from Hebrew into German. His Nehmad we-naim represents a unique work by an Ashkenazi author summing all existing knowledge of Jewish and non-Jewish scholars on geometry and astronomy; in the atmosphere of conservative Central European Judaism, however, it had remained neglected and even had to wait for its first printed edition to the middle of the 18th century. An entirely different acceptance, however, even from Gans' contemporaries, was accorded to his extensive historiographic work, the chronicle Zemach David.

158

This work consists of two parts. In the first part the author recorded briefly the history of the Jews from the biblical creation of the world to 1592, when the book was printed; the last paragraph is devoted to the mayor of the Prague Jewish Town, Mordecai Maisel, who had just completed the construction of his synagogue. The second, more extensive part, called "The Days of the World" contains a detailed annalist description of the history of the world. This division of the book into two separate parts was intentional, as the author writes in the preface to the first part: "To separate the sacred (i. e. the history of the Jews) from the ordinary (i. e. from the general course of history) I have devoted to the former a special part, so that the matters of the living God will not be mixed with the transient matters of dry grass." His prefaces in general contain Gans' ideas of history, its study and the role of historiographic literature as well as its effect on the reader. Gans explains in detail the reasons which led him to writing this work, enumerates sources – Jewish and non-Jewish – from which he drew his facts, and finally analyses the use of historiographic books and their reading for their readers and of the acquired knowledge of history. Particularly the preface to the second part, the world chronicle, is a real summary of the Renaissance view of a Jewish scholar on the humanities.

The fact that David Gans had written the first real historical work in the Central European Diaspora, brought him high regard of the scholars of the enlightened Judaic science. The lasting success of his chronicle with its readers, which was manifested by its ever new editions, regularly supplemented with the events of further centuries, however, is based on the variety of contents and the easily comprehensible manner of presentation which was accessible to all strata of readers. The book does not consist merely in the simple communication of historical facts and events. Zemach David is a real literary work, the first great literary work of secular content which belongs to Prague Jewish literature.

Other popular Hebrew writings of historical character, much smaller than Gans' Zemach David and propagated mainly by copying, originated in the first half of the 17th century. The first of them, the autobiography of **Yom Tov Lipmann Heller,** Megillat eva (The Scroll of Adversity), was written in 1628 and tells about the danger which threatened the author after he had been accused of attacks against Catholic faith and imprisoned by Viennese authorities. Although Heller proved his innocence and was acquitted (inter alia also on the intervention of Jacob Bassevi, the Court Jew, who paid for him the required fine of 10,000 thalers), he had to leave Prague after thirty years of work. The autobiography Megillat eva has been favourite reading for centuries and its copies both in Hebrew and in "Juden-deutsch" have been preserved to our day. It has undeniable literary qualities and the brilliance of its style confirms both the professional standard of Heller – the preacher and his universal talent which he applied also in the field of poetry.

On the other hand, the small chronicle or rather diary, describing the events during the siege of Prague by the Swedes in 1648, belongs to the production of semi-popular urban chronicles. It is called Milhama be-shalom (War in Peace) and it was written by a Prague Jew, the secretary of the chief rabbi of Prague, **Aharon Simon Spira**, viz. **Jehuda Leb ben Joshua Porit-Porges**. The Milhama be-shalom covers the events from the capture of Prague Castle and the Lesser Town of Prague by the Swedes on July 26, 1648, to the conclusion of the Peace of Westphalia and on to the festivities in July, 1650. Apart from the course of the siege of Prague the author recorded also the course of events in Bohemian countryside, often based on the reports of eye witnesses. When depicting the events in Prague itself Jehuda Leb afforded considerable attention to Swedish attacks – the struggle for the stone (Charles) Bridge, where he describes a mobile barricade erected by the Swedes, the excavation of trenches and placing of mines, and particularly the "general attack" of October 25th and 26th, immediately before the declaration of peace. On the part of the defence particularly interesting is his description of the defence of the bridge, the participation of the companies of the nobility, burghers, students and ecclesiastics and, naturally, the reports on the participation of the Jews in the defence of the town. These last mentioned parts of the diary represent a valuable source to the history of the Prague Jewish Town at the end of the Thirty Years' War. Once again they mention the important task of Prague Jews, viz. to organize fire service, which persevered also at the time of peace; according to the data in Milhama be-shalom the Jews intervened e. g. also during the fire which broke up after the explosion of the arsenal in Prague Castle at the beginning of 1649.

In respect of its factual and literary aspects the Milhama be-shalom is equivalent with other preserved documents of the period of chronicle, diary and memoir character, which originated in the urban and rural intellectual strata in the 17th century. At the same time it manifests a direct and intentional links with the Renaissance Hebrew chronicles represented in our territory by the work of **David Gans**. The form of the chronicles, which originated in Prague in the 18th century and depict the events of 1741-1754, i. e. the expulsion of the Jews from Prague and the war suffering at the beginning of the reign of Maria Theresa, is similar. These anonymous monuments of Hebrew historical prose, however, have been preserved in manuscripts only.

As it follows, artistic prose in Jewish Prague was limited chiefly to historical narrative, whether of general character or concerning the lives of individual persons. Another type of prose concerned with individual details includes a further popular form of Hebrew prose, the so-called family megillats. They are minor writings in Hebrew and in "Juden-deutsch" which usually have the form of a scroll (megillat) in imitation of the liturgical scroll of the Book of Esther. They contained narratives of real, deathly dangerous events or situations from which the hero had escaped successfully, and were read during annual family holidays commemorating these escapes. The number of preserved family megillats dating from the 17th-19th centuries testifies to the fact that this custom was considerably widespread in Bohemia and Moravia. In the end also Heller's Megillat eva is such a family scroll the narrative of

160

which is set into the wider framework of the Thirty Years' War; the same type of biographic literature was imitated also by **Moses Meir Perels,** the author of the genealogy of the family of Rabbi Loew. **Moses Meir Perels** (d. 1739) belonged to the Jewish intellectuals of Prague; he was the secretary of Prague Jewish community and a member of the presidium of the Burial Society for over twenty years. On his mother's side he was a descendant of Rabbi Loew and at the beginning of the biography which he himself called Megillat juhasin Maharal mi-Prag (The Scroll of the Generations of the Maharal of Prague) he paid homage to Loew's wife, Perl. It is the story how the young bride Perl supported her impoverished parents by the sale of bread; for one loaf she received a web of cloth instead of money from an unknown cavalryman. When she unwrapped it she found a great many ducats. Her father regained his former wealth and she could marry Jehuda ben Bezalel, her bridegroom. This story, recorded by Moshe Perels for the first time, has become an integral part of the legends on Rabbi Loew.

The youngest prosaic Hebrew works which originated in Prague belong to the period of Enlightenment and of the struggle for Jewish emancipation. Their number includes, for instance, a history textbook written and published for the pupils of the chief Jewish school of Prague by their teacher and ardent adherent of Enlightenment, **Peter Beer** (1758–1838) under the title of Toledot Yisrael (The History of Israel). Approximately at the same time **Juda Jeiteles** (1773–1838), the member of an oustanding Prague family of natural historians issued the biography of his father, the physician Jona Jeiteles, called Bne be-neurin (The Youth). Another member of this family, **Moses Wolf Jeiteles,** wrote the history of the Prague Burial Society called Zikkaron le-yom aharon (The Memory of the Last Day). This group of enlightened Hebrew literature includes also a part of the work of **Marcus Fischer** (1783–1852), the text-office secretary, writer and poet, who enriched the history of Jewish literature with a very successful fake. His Ramschak Chronicle, written in "Juden-deutsch", had been considered for long an original medieval source of the history of the Jews in Bohemia, similarly as the "Old Czech" manuscripts of Dvůr Králové and Zelená Hora, which originated in the same period and in the same patriotic spirit as the Ramschak, had been held for genuine for a long time.

To complete this survey of the Hebrew prose written in Prague mention must be made of scientific literature, which concentrated on natural sciences and originated within a relatively short period between the end of the 16th and the end of the 17th centuries. After the astronomico-geographic work of David Gans, Nehmad we-naim, the most important work in this field of studies is the book by **Joseph Solomon del Medigo** (1591–1655), a polyhistor from Crete, who was concerned with mathematics, physics, astronomy and medicine as well as philosophy. He was the pupil of Galileo Galilei and in Prague, where he spent the last years of his life, he supplemented his vast knowledge with further information. Although his writings were issued in other countries, he left part of his scientific bequest in the Jewish Town of

Joseph Salomo del Medigo
aus Creta
Im Alter von 37 Jahren 1628

Prague in the knowledge of his pupils. One of them, **Jissachar Beer Teller** (d.
1687), published a medical book, called Beer mayim hayyim (The Well of
the Water of Life) written in "Juden-deutsch" as a handbook giving the necessary knowledge of practical medicine; it has been preserved in a single
copy. The predecessor of Beer Teller, **Rivka,** the daughter of the physician
Meir Tiktiner (d. 1605) had even less luck: her practical handbook for housewives with the title of Meneket Rivka (Rebecca's Nurse), written in "Juden-deutsch", is known only from references in literature of a later date.
    In contrast to scientific studies practiced in the Jewish Town of Prague are
the works, representing a juxtaposed pole of thinking, which originated from
the then culminating mystic studies. In Prague they were represented primarily by the members of the Horowitz family – pupil of Rabbi **Loew Sabbatai
Sheftl ben Akiba** (1565 – prob. 1620), the author of the writing Shefa Tal
(The Torrent of Dew), and **Jeshaia ben Abraham Horowitz** (1555–1625), called
SHELO (after an abbreviation of the title of his cabalist compendium Shne
luhot ha-berit (Two Treaty Tablets). In the course of the 17th century and
chiefly in the 18th century, however, the centre of cabalist studies was trans-

ferred to Moravia, where it was enhanced inter alia by strong contacts with hassidic circles of Poland and Latvia.

In the poetry of the Ashkenazi region the religious poetry prevailed, particularly the genre of liturgical elegies (selihot) with historical subjects. This highly popular type of poetic compositions was created by the Ashkenazi Hebrew poetry from the eleventh century as a response to the tragic events taking place in the individual communities. In the majority of cases, therefore, the elegies were connected with concrete places and concrete times to such an extent that they were not included into the generally accepted collections of prayers, but came to form part of liturgical collections in certain regions only and only for the day which, with regard to the character of the recalled event, was promoted to local holiday or semi-holiday.

For the poetry in the territory of Bohemia and Moravia the documents testifying only to two composers of these historical poems exist – the rabbis of Prague, **Avigdor Kara** (d. 1439) and **Abraham ben Avigdor Kara** (d. 1542). In their poetic work which has been preserved to the present it is the well known E t k o l h a - t e l a a (All that Misfortune) by Avigdor Kara, composed in the memory of the "bloody Easter" in Prague in 1389 that represents a genuine historical elegy. Similarly the only preserved composition of Abraham Kara, A n a E l o h e A b r a h a m (Oh, Thou God of Abraham) was inspired by the uncertain situation at the time of the eviction of the Jews from Prague in 1541.

The historical poetical works which originated in the 17th century concern the raid of the Passauers in 1611 and the uprising of the Bohemian Estates and the siege of Prague by the Swedes in 1648. Another elegy tells about the great, so-called French fire of the Jewish ghetto in 1689. The presidium of the Prague Jewish community decided to commemorate all these events by annual memorial services. For the semi-holiday 2 Adar (on which the Passauer raid fell in 1611, i. e. February 15th) the then chief rabbi of Prague, **Solomon Ephraim Luntschitz,** composed three poems; for the 14 Heshuan (10th November in 1620, when, after the Battle of the White Mountain the victorious Imperial army occupied Prague) two elegies were composed by **Jom Tov Lipmann Heller,** who was equally talented a poet as talmudist and preacher. The elegies inspired by. the Swedish siege of Prague at the very end of the Thirty Years' War were the work of the then Prague chief rabbi, **Aharon Simon Spira;** according to the testimony of Spira's secretary, **Jehuda Leb ben Joshua,** they were printed during the very siege.

Poetic compositions concerning two big fires of Prague ghetto in 1689 and 1754 have been preserved in two versions, in Hebrew and in "Judendeutsch". While the Hebrew elegies are anonymous liturgical texts intended for the annual service and commemoration of both devastating events, the colloquial language versions are of reporting character approaching the semi-popular character of Bohemian and German broadside ballads. We also know their authors: S r e f a l i d (The Song of the Fire) of 1689 was composed by **Jehiel Michael ben Zalman Shamash;** the other song of the same title of 1754 **Abraham Moses ben David Laz.**

The Songs on the Fires composed in "Juden-deutsch" are merely two examples from the rich production of folk and semi-folk literature in this language which originated in Prague in the 17th and the 18th centuries and a part of which is represented in the Oppenheim's colection of Prague prints. There are also further songs on calamities which befell the town (e. g. plagues), moralist songs and ballads as well as narratives analogous with the Czech and German books of popular reading (on Magelona, on Styrian Knight and Danish Princess, on Melusina). Remarkable is the small composition called Shen Maase (Beautiful Story) on the arrival of Jews to Prague, written by two Jewish women – **Bela Horowitz,** wife of Josef Hazan, and **Rachel Raudnitz,** wife of Leb Poritz. The semi-popular literature in "Juden-deutsch" did not miss even the Prague yeshiva; in 1720 the David Oppenheim's students performed a Purim play with biblical motifs, Akta Esther mit Ahashverosh.

The Hebrew literature of all genres which developed in Prague in the course of the millenial history of Jewish community belongs to the foundations on which the thinking and contents of the subsequent German and Czech branches of Jewish literature built and from which they drew their inspiration. To these foundations also the last Prague poet writing inter alia in Hebrew returned, viz. **Jiří Langer** (1894–1943) known chiefly for his book of Hassid legends, The Nine Gates. He returned to the bequest of philosophers and mystics, story tellers and poets, first by his translation of classic Hebrew poetry, which he published closely before the outbreak of the Second World War under the title of "The Songs of the Condemned", and thenby his own Hebrew collections of poetry, Piyutim we-shire (Songs and Poems on Friendship) and Meat zori (A Drop of Balsam).

The preservation of the treasures of Hebrew literature of all times is due indubitably to Prague letterpress, famous even beyond the boundaries of Bohemia for its high quality. The Prague Hebrew printing shops have a rich history. As early as at the beginning of the 16th century a four member consortium of printers and publishers originated in Prague, from the works of which also the oldest preserved Hebrew Prague print originated – the collection of liturgical songs dated 1514. One of the members of this consortium was **Gershon Kohen,** the subsequent founder of the most important Prague printing shop, the privileged Gersonide printing shop. This shop, protected by the privilege issued to "Herman the Impressor" in 1527, existed until the end of the 18th century, from 1784 in combination with the second oldest Prague Hebrew printing shop of the **Bak family,** Both shops – the **Gersonide and the Bakian** – similarly as the printing shop of **Abraham Heida-Lemberger** and others which originated in Prague to exist perhaps only a few years, had provable contacts with Christian printing shops. From them they obtained e. g. block engravings and, on the other hand, produced matrices of Hebrew type for their needs. Already the attractive woodcuts in the oldest preserved print of benedictions of 1514 recall the engravings illustrating Czech books from the break of the 15th and the 16th centuries. Prague Hebrew prints, particu-

The Haggadah of Prague (1526).

The coat-of-arms of Prague from the Pentateuch (1530).

The Pentateuch of Prague (1530).

וְאֶת מַס • וַיִּתְּנוּ עָלֵינוּ עֲבוֹדָה קָשָׁה כְּמָה
שֶׁנֶּאֱמַר וַיַּעֲבִדוּ מִצְרַיִם אֶת בְּנֵי יִשְׂרָאֵל בְּפָרֶךְ :

וַנִּצְעַק אֶל יְיָ אֱלֹהֵי אֲבוֹתֵינוּ וַיִּשְׁמַע יְיָ אֶת קוֹלֵנוּ
וַיַּרְא אֶת עָנְיֵנוּ וְאֶת עֲמָלֵנוּ וְאֶת לַחֲצֵנוּ :

*Illustrations from the Haggadah
shel Pesach, Prague, 1777.*

בְּעֵבֶר הַנָּהָר יָשְׁבוּ אֲבוֹתֵיכֶם מֵעוֹלָם תֶּרַח אֲבִי
אַבְרָהָם וַאֲבִי נָחוֹר וַיַּעַבְדוּ אֱלֹהִים אֲחֵרִים :

וָאֶקַּח אֶת אֲבִיכֶם אֶת אַבְרָהָם מֵעֵבֶר הַנָּהָר
וָאוֹלֵךְ אוֹתוֹ בְּכָל אֶרֶץ כְּנַעַן וָאַרְבֶּה אֶת

שִׁיר כִּי אֵין מַחְסוֹר לִירֵאָיו כְּפִירִים רָשׁוּ וְרָעֵבוּ וְדֹרְשֵׁי יְיָ לֹא
טוֹב כִּי לְעוֹלָם חַסְדּוֹ : בָּרוּךְ אַתָּה יְיָ אֱלֹהֵינוּ מֶלֶךְ הָעוֹלָם

וֶוען אין גֶבֶענְשְׁט הוֹט אִחְבֶט אַן דִים טִיר מוֹיל

שְׁפֹךְ חֲמָתְךָ עַל הַגּוֹיִם אֲ
וְעַל מַמְלָכוֹת אֲשֶׁר בְּ
כִּי אָכַל אֶת יַעֲקֹב וְאֶת

דִיין גוֹיִם לֶארִין לוֹ
דֶן דִים דִיךְ נִיט קֶענִין
דִים דִיין נֶ״אין נִיט אָן
יַעֲקֹב בֶּר דֶּארְבֶּן מוֹל

larly the Gersonide prints from the 16th and the 17th centuries, belong to the foremost works of European Renaissance bookprint and the preserved copies are gems of world collections. One of the most famous Gersonide prints are the editions of the Pentateuch of 1518 and 1530, the Pesach Haggadah of 1526, a collection of penitent prayers – selihot – of 1529 and others. Apart from liturgical and general religious literature, however, the Gersonides and the Baks contributed to the propagation of Jewish culture in Prague and in the Central European Diaspora also by the publication of a great number of the works of older and contemporary scholars and rabbinic authorities. It is from the Gersonide printing shop, for instance, that the majority of the first editions of the works of Rabbi Loew came, similarly as the repeated editions of the works of his successors, **Mordecai Jaffe, Solomon Ephraim Luntschitz, Yom Tov Lipmann Heller,** and others. The Gersonides issued also the famous chronicle of **David Gans,** Zemach David (1592) and the first printed edition of the itinerary of **Petachia of Regensburg** (1595), similarly as the occasional historical elegies penned by **Luntschitz, Heller** and **Aharon Simson Spira.** And the Gersonide and Bak printing shops poured forth also the small prints of songs and entertaining stories in "Juden-deutsch".

In the course of the 17th and the 18th centuries, after the sufferings and heavy financial consequences of the Thirty Years' War and the years which followed it, the Prague Hebrew prints were losing some of its beauty, but continued to fulfil their educational, popularizing and entertaining purposes. From the mid-18th century their artistic aspect approached ever more the decorations of the Czech or German books of popular reading, broadsheets and calendars. Even in Hebrew prints simple, sometimes pathetically primitive folk woodcuts began to prevail, such as in the editions of the Pesach Haggadah and of holiday prayers issued by the Gersonide-Katz printing shop in 1754 and 1763.

The number of printers and publishers of Hebrew books in Prague is closed by **Moses Israel Landau** (1788–1852), the grandson of the great Prague scholar and chief rabbi, **Ezekiel Landau,** and one of the foremost representatives of Prague Jewish Enlightenment. In the middle of the 19th century his printing shop was not only a shop, but also an institution, propagating by the published books the ideas of Enlightenment and emancipation to all Jewish communities in Bohemia, Moravia and abroad. It was the Landau's publishing house that issued the commented translation of the Pentateuch by **Moses Mendelssohn,** the complete edition of the Old Testament and the Talmud as well as the works of enlightened writers such as **Peter Beer,** the members of the **Jeiteles** family, the chief rabbi of Prague, **S. J. Rapoport** and the works of the publisher himself. After the death of **M. I. Landau** the tradition of the Prague Jewish bookprinting was continued until the thirties of the 20th century by the publishing houses of **Pascheles** and **Brandeis.** However, the books which issued from them to disperse all over Bohemia corresponded already with the spirit of new times – the postemancipation and assimilation endeavours which characterized the then Jewish Town of Prague.

The Jews in Prague
German Literature

The phenomenon of "Prague German Literature" or, to be more accurate "Prague literature written in German", has been attracting attention of literary scientists as well as the reading public for a number of decades. This literature represents the by far most important complex of literary works in German language ever written outside the compact German language territory. Out of the half-million of people, which was the population of Prague at the break of the 19th and the 20th century, only a little over thirty thousands spoke German as their mother tongue. In the course of the short period of only a few decades, however, this community yielded a considerable number of outstanding writers. These authors, who wrote in German, were mostly Jews, the Jewry representing an important element in the cultural life of Prague. This fact was accentuated as early as 1917 by one of the Prague German writers, **Paul Leppin** (1878–1944) when he wrote: "We Germans ... in Prague ... have good, fine art, excellent press, theatre which is revitalized by new ideas, literature the quantity and quality of which represent almost a record. It must be admitted that the majority of these things, more than ninety per cent, must be credited to Jews ... What appears original and typically Prague-like are the works of Jewish specificity, adapted to the requirements of a Slavic city ... Without Jews the spiritual life in German Prague would exist probably only as a miserable trickle."

The development of this Jewish German literature in Prague, which was amply supported by the Prague German theatre and Prague German journalism, was concurrent with the development of Jewish emancipation and assimilation; its problems were connected also with the problems of Zionism.

In the first period which culminated in the revolutionary year 1848, the German Jews in Bohemia and Moravia enthused about political, national and religious liberty, being imbued with the ideas of emancipation brought about by the Enlightenment. Their participation in journalism and columnistics was marked from the forties of the 19th century. This literature achieved another culmination at the turn of the 19th and the 20th centuries with the development of neo-romanticism, a literary movement the melancholic, elegiac, mysterious, demoniac and fantastic elements of which were particularly stimulated by the atmosphere of Prague. Absolute peak of its development was attained by this German-written Prague literature in the first half of the 20th century, when some of its authors came to occupy the front ranks of world literature.

Prague was a place where the elements of three cultures were meeting, mutually intermingled and clashed for centuries. "German, Czech and Jewish factors affected simultaneously the creative spirit ... and the thrice cultivated soil yielded blossoms of such uniqueness that could not have grown anywhere else", **Oskar Wiener** (1873–1944), a Prague German Jewish poet maintained as early as 1919 in the preface to the anthology "Deutsche Dichter aus Prag". And another German writing author from Prague, **Johannes Urzidil** (1896-1970) spoke about four springs from which the Prague writers of German language drank: apart from the German, Czech and Jewish spirits he adds "the Austrian spirit in which they were all born and educated". Also other authors, such as the German traveller **Alfons Paquet** (1881-1944), saw in Prague the point of intersection of Western and Eastern cultures: "Should the world not have been created so historically and should it have been possible to divide it into beautiful, pure areas, Prague would have been for long a natural capital of that central Europe which spreads between Minsk and Brussels."

This merging and intermingling of cultures was not without problems. The cultures fertilized one another, but created also a specific mutual tension. The ideas about the specific character of their coexistence resulted in the formulation of the so-called triple ghetto theory. Its suggestions can be found already in the study by **Josef Körner** (1888-1950), a Prague German literary historian, which was published in 1917, and in the review of Max Brod's (1884-1968) novel, "Tycho Brahe's Weg zu Gott", penned by the Czech literary critic, F. X. Šalda (1867-1937). Later on **Pavel (**also** Paul) Eisner** (1889-1958), translator and literary historian of Jewish descent, who mastered Czech equally well as German, formulated this theory in more accurate terms and applied it to the situation of **Franz Kafka** (1883-1924) and generalized it for the whole Prague literature written in German. He maintained that the Prague German literature originated in the last decades of the Austro-Hungarian monarchy in an unnatural insular environment, surrounded by a sound Czech national community and that its creators lived on the Prague German island as in a triple ghetto: social, racial and national, i.e. bourgeois, German-Jewish and German ghetto. There were no German folk strata in Prague – Prague Germans were bourgeois, merchants, clerks, industrialist, intellectuals. Apart from that the Prague German colony consisted of Jewish and non-Jewish bourgeois, so that even within it there was a certain invisible wall. And finally the triple ghetto was completed by the isolation of the Germans from their Czech surroundings. This theory is supported also by some statements of Prague German writers themselves. For instance, the afore mentioned **Oskar Wiener** pointed to the tragic fate of Prague German poets who had remained always only the sons of a society which had to rely on itself and had been separated strictly from its Slavic environs. And another Prague German-Jewish writer, **Willy Haas** (1891-1973) saw Prague at the beginning of the 20th century as a whole divided among three worlds: the world of aristocracy, mostly of foreign (Spanish, Italian, French, Scotch, Irish) origin, living in Baroque palaces in the Lesser Town, which had been endowed with property and high offices of State by the Hapsburghs after the Thirty Years'War and which spoke the so-called k.u.k (Imperial and Royal) aristocratic German, i.e. a mixture of the German of Alpine countries with French and Czech expressions; the world of the so-called "German" Prague, on the other bank of the river Vltava around the Municipal Park (subsequently Vrchlický's Park near the Wenceslas Square) and the Příkopy (Graben) Street, whose tone was determined by rich Jewish families, settled in Prague perhaps from the 11th century and having traditions of their own, their rabbis, scholars and alchemists.; and finally the world of the Czech Prague with ancient traditions, to which the future belonged. "These three worlds live next to one another, strictly mutually closed, house by house, but separated by ages old abysses."

These "three worlds" of **Willy Haas,** however, do not coincide accurately with Eisner's theory of **three ghettos,** because they neglect the difference between the bourgeois stratum of Jewish and non-Jewish origin. And it is these very proportions of the population within the German speaking enclave that are significant for the Prague German literature. The influx of Jewish population to the capital from the countryside, which began in the 19th and continued in the 20th centuries, significantly influenced the composition of German Prague. While in 1880 some 20% of all Jews from Bohemia and Moravia lived in Prague, in 1900 it was almost 30 % and in 1930 over 45%, i. e. almost one half. Parallelly with this growth of Jewish population the decrease of the overall number of German population continued, so that about 1900 the whole two thirds of the German speaking population of Prague were Jews. The feeling of language and cultural appurtenance as well as personal friendships between German Jewish and non-Jewish authors decidedly prevailed over the feeling of racial difference. This is testified to not only by numerous examples of their cooperation and personal contacts, but also by the fact that numerous non-Jewish Prague writers writing in German, drew the subjects of their works also from Jewish environment and were often erroneously considered Jews, such as **Gustav Meyrink** (1868–1932) or **Paul Leppin.** That was also the reason why antisemitism, which had been spreading in Germany and Austria from the end of the seventies of the 19th century, could not acquire decisive influence within the Prague German enclave. On the other hand, this enclave was confronted directly with the mostly undifferentiated anti-German and anti-Jewish moods of its Czech surroundings and perhaps this circumstance, too, welded it together rather than divided it.

The boundary between the Czech speaking and German speaking population of Prague, the Czech and the German cultures, was not as unsurmountable as the triple ghetto theory would seem to indicate. Prague German literature had also an important historical function – the function of cultural mediator between the Czechs and the Germans, and it acquitted itself of it with honour, as it is testified to by the translating work of **Otto Pick** (1887–1940), **Rudolf Fuchs** (1890–1942), **Franz Werfel** (1890–1945), **Camill Hoffmann** (1879–1944), **F. C. Weiskopf** (1900–1955), **Louis Fürnberg** (1909–1954), **Paul Eisner** and others. The purposive cooperation of the writers writing in German with Czech cultural workers culminated in the thirties, at the time when the Czechoslovak Republic was threatened by fascism. However, in the preceding decades the relatively rich and finely differentiated cultural atmosphere of Czech Prague did not remain without influence on the Prague German writers, either. The specific Prague atmosphere of cultural interpenetration affected the writers particularly in that respect that the orientation of the writers who lacked the background of German folk life in Prague became more cosmopolitan and European. After all, they were not enthusiastic themselves over the idea of a strictly closed cultural ghetto in the majority of cases. By way of example let us quote at least **Max Brod** (1884–1968): "I refuse that theory absolutely. Perhaps it fits the much too sceptic Prague of German Jews, but certainly not the much freer, hopeful and, although not exactly naive, yet somewhat childlike mood of the Prague circle."

✳ ✳ ✳

Prague German literature did not appear out of the blue. It could link up with rich tradition reaching back to the Middle Ages, when outstanding German minnesängers decorated the royal court of the Přemyslids. Particularly the Napoleonic wars brought to Bohemia a number of important German romantic poets who enlivened the Prague literary scene. Czech mythology, Czech history and particularly Prague itself have become favoured subjects of German literature ever since.

The partitipation of writers of Jewish descent in literature written in German in the first decades of the 19th century was relatively small. In the majority of cases they only studied in Prague, and having completed their studies they left for Vienna or elsewhere, such as **Justus Frey,** actually Andreas Ludwig Jeitteles (1799–1878), **Moritz Gottlieb Saphir,** actually Moses Saphir (1795–1858), **Ludwig Frankl** (1810–1894) or **Ignaz Kuranda** (1811–1884).

The full drive of the Jews and their penetration into Prague German literature began in 1848. Emperor Joseph II (1741–1790), influenced by the ideas of Enlightenment, abolished the laws restricting the freedom of movement of the Jews and permitting only the eldest son of the family to marry, and ordered the Jews of his empire to attend German schools "for better education and for better use of the Jews for the State", as the decree of May 13, 1781 had it. These humanizing measures enabled the influx of the families of Jewish merchants from the province to major cities and to Prague, where they succeeded relatively quickly to attain a relatively high standard of living and culture. Good German education, consequently, was nothing exceptional for Jewish boys. **Alfred Klaar** (1848–1927) subsequently characterized this situation as follows: "... From the Josephian time, but particularly in the first half of the 19th century, the closeness and restricted character of the Prague Jewish Town gave rise to a strong spiritual stream ... For centuries, in suppression and closeness, not only the forces of the reason had been sharpened there, but also the living metaphysical needs and movements were maintained. In pious circles ... a pronouncedly theosophic direction prevailed, in enlightened circles great yearning for liberation. Nowhere else, perhaps ... the cult of German classics was cherished more sincerely than in a great number of Jewish families in Prague ..."

Alfred Meissner (1822–1888). *Moritz Hartmann (1827–1872).*

The first generation of German writing authors in which these facts manifested themselves positively was grouped around the periodical "Ost und West" issued in Prague between 1837 and 1848 by **Rudolf Glaser** (1801–1868) and around the annuals "Libussa", published in 1842–1860 by **Paul Aloys Klar** (1801–1860), the founder of the well known institute for the blind. The annual was participated in by several outstanding authors of Jewish descent. Best known among them is **Moritz Hartmann** (1821–1872), the son of a wealthy family from Dušníky near Příbram, who studied medicine and philosophy in Prague from 1837. Here he made acquaintance of **Alfred Meissner** (1822–1888), **Isidor Heller** (1816–1879) and other literary men and published his first poems in Glaser's "Ost und West". However, it was only later, when he had been living in Germany, that he was captivated by the picture of Bohemia as it was painted by the famous French authoress, George Sand (1804–1878) in her novel "Consuelo" (1842–1843) with the subject taken from the Hussite movement. Influenced by this reading, Hartmann published in Leipzig in 1845 a collection of poems, "Kelch und Schwert" in which he, as a poet from the land of the Hussites, bemoans the loss of Bohemian freedom after the Battle of the White Mountain and opposes the Hapsburg rule. The collection was very successful, having captivated the Czechs and the Germans in Bohemia alike. However, its anti-monarchist tone aroused the displeasure of the authorities. In 1847, after his return to Prague,

Hartmann was arrested, but his trial was interrupted by the revolutionary events in 1848. Hartmann took an active part in politics and in 1848 he participated inter alia in the Slavonic Congress on the Žofín Island, which requested equality for Slavonic nations. The town of Litoměřice elected him its deputy for the Frankfurt Parliament, where he took a left-wing attitude, near the German nationalism. His subsequent poems and stories, however, did not increase his fame; from among them only his novel "Der Krieg um den Wald" took place on Bohemian soil; it deals with the scenes from the farmers' revolt in the 18th century.

Hartmann's brother-in-law, **Siegfried Kapper** (1821–1879) was born in Smíchov, then not yet a quarter of Prague, in No. 13, Nádražní Street. After studies of medicine he worked as medical practitioner in various places, from 1866 in Prague. He joined the young radical Czech and German writers and conceived the idea of a joint emancipation struggle of the Czechs and the Jews. He tried to acquaint the Germans with the wealth of Czech and Yugoslav poetry and made it the target of his work. His first collection of poems, "Slavische Melodien" (1844) contains echoes of Slavonic poetry, the second collection, written in Czech, "České listy" (Bohemian Letters) (1846) accentuates the Czech patriotism of the Jews. However, his endeavour remained without response on the major part of Czech cultural public, although his friends included also some Czech poets, such as Karel Sabina (1813–1877) and Václav Bolemír Nebeský (1818–1882). Kapper was also the author of the first German translation of the most famous Czech romantic Byronic poem, "Máj" (May) by Karel Hynek Mácha (1810–1836). Kapper's work includes also the subjects concerned with the Prague ghetto, particularly in the collection "Prager Ghettosagen" (1896).

Prague ghetto, as a literary subject, however, was discovered by other authors. Among the Prague German writing poets this subject was treated for the first time by **Salomon Kohn** (1825–1904). His romantically tuned novel from the Prague ghetto at the time of the Winter King, Frederic of Palatinate (1596–1632), "Gabriel" (1875) was very successful; it was translated into several languages and was published again even after half-a-century. Of greater literary value, however, are Kohn's short stories from the ghetto.

The first conscious programmatist in the German written literature in Bohemia, however, was **Leopold Kompert** (1822–1886). In his works with educational tendencies he endeavours to liberate the Jews from the restrictions of the ghetto, presenting a programme of Jewish assimilation and Czecho-German-Jewish symbiosis.

He was born in the ghetto of an East Bohemian town of Mnichovo Hradiště, in No. 58, as the son of a wool merchant and the grandson of the local rabbi who exercized great influence on the boy's development. His impressions from the childhood, lived in an intact Jewish community, subsequently became an inexhaustible source of his literary work. It was only when he was ten years old that he encountered the world outside the ghetto, when he began attending the German Piarist grammar school in Mladá Boleslav in 1833, where he was the school fellow of Moritz Hartmann. When his parents could

Title page of Leopold Kompert's book of stories "Aus dem Ghetto", Leipzig, 1848.

Aus dem Ghetto.

Geschichten

von

Leopold Kompert.

Leipzig,
Verlag von Fr. Wm Grunow.
1848.

no longer afford his studies, he left for Prague in 1836 and subsequently moved to Vienna, to Bratislava and to Hungary, where he worked as preceptor. The time and place distance enabled him to mould in a literary form his ancient experience of the life in the ghetto. That is probably also the reason why Kompert's works are characterized by idealization, a reconcilement of discrepancies and mild, kindhearted humour.

He published his first printed work in Bratislava, in the periodical "Pressburger Zeitung"; at the instigation of the founder of the Viennese periodical, "Sonntagsblätter" who afforded publication possibilities to his countrymen of Jewish origin, he wrote a collection of sketches and short stories from Jewish environment, "Aus dem Ghetto" (1848).

Kompert was a conscious Austrian patriot and in his whole life he did not cease to be grateful to Joseph II for having shown the Jews the way of how to emancipate themselves from the ghetto and integrate with society by means of education. He was proud of his mother tongue – German – and in national struggles he sided with the German Austrians. His work dates to the time in which general faith in progress prevailed and when a number of laws was issued which brought the Jews emancipation and to which Kompert sentitively reacted in his books. Kompert's whole life convincingly illustrates and documents his conviction that it is possible to be simultaneously a Jew, an Austrian and a German writer. He occupied important posts in the Viennese Schiller Foundation as well as in the Jewish community and his literary work earned him the degree of doctor honoris causa in Jena.

Kompert's endeavour was to show the Jews the way out of the ghetto to general knowledge and full civic responsibility. He was of the opinion that the Jews should turn primarily to the soil and handicrafts to eliminate all differences between them and other races and cherished a utopian hope that the day would come when the Christian and the Jewish religious systems would be modified and would merge, which would lead to the solution of all problems seemingly insoluble otherwise. That is the programme of Jewish assimilation which he formulates in his literary work. The Jews must consummate their liberation from the ghetto by leaving the traditional cult of nonmanual work and take up physical work – handicrafts and agriculture. He dealt with the subject of Jewish agrarian colonization in his novel "Am Pflug" (1855). It takes place between 1849, when the forcefully imposed constitution, preserving the principle of civic equality, enabled the Jews to own farms and land, and 1853, when this possibility was restricted again.

The second Kompert's novel, "Zwischen Ruinen" (1875) is concerned with the problem of the mixed marriage of a Jewish factory owner and a Christian girl from a weaver's family. In 1867 the Jews in the Hapsburg empire were finally fully emancipated by a law and a fully equivalent civil marriage without any legal obstacles was introduced shortly afterwards. Until then a mixed marriage was possible only if the Jewish partner had been christened beforehand. In Kompert's novel both partners in civil marriage have retained their faiths. Kompert thus demonstrated his belief in the possibility of good coexistence between the Christian world and the Jewry.

German patriotism, concealed in Kompert's works by the conciliatory programme of coexistence of the Czechs, Germans and Jews, acquired sharper, more aggressive features in the work of the most important Bohemia-born author of the second half of the 19th century, **Fritz Mauthner** (1849–1923). He was born in Hořice near Hradec Králové, where his father owned one of the local weaving mills. In 1855 the family moved to Prague, where Fritz attended first the Piarist grammar school in Panská Street until the autumn of 1861, and then the German grammar school in the Lesser Town. After his final examination in 1869 he became the student of law at the University of Prague. Apart from law he attended also lectures on political economy, philosophy, journalism and Oriental studies. Without completing his studies with a degree he left Prague in 1876 and settled in Berlin, where he worked as journalist. He gained literary fame, which eluded him after the publication of a volume of sonnets "Die grosse Revolution" (1872) and after the performance of the drama "Anna" in the German Land Theatre (the present Tyl Theatre) in Prague on May 23, 1874, by parodic studies published in a Berlin newpaper and issued in 1878 in book form under the title of "Nach berühmten Mustern". The young writer, who wished to be recognized also as the author of serious novels, joined the naturalist movement and after the model of the French novelist Emile Zola (1840–1902) he intended to write a cycle of novels which would depict the life of the whole epoch. He wrote the first novel of the Berlin naturalism, "Der neue Ahasver" (1882), aimed against the wave of antisemitism then arisen in Berlin. The central character of the novel is an erudite Jewish doctor of Prague and the action takes us not only to Berlin, but also to the ghetto of Prague, with its dirty narrow streets, dark corners and crooked houses, subsequently made famous by the novel "Der Golem" by **Gustav Meyrink** (1868–1932).

Although Mauthner situated his most extensive socio-critical works in Berlin or in classical times, the impressions of his youth spent in Bohemia had remained alive all his life and had left traces also in his prosaic works. In his novels "Die letzte Deutsche von Blatna" (1887), whose locale recalls his native Hořice, and "Die böhmische Handschrift" (1897) based on the well-known faked historical manuscripts, he depicted national quarrels in Bohemia, granting his sympathy explicitly to the Germans.

From 1909 Mauthner lived in Meersburg on the Lake Constance, devoted his time exclusively to philosophical problems and wrote his greatest works, "Beiträge zu einer Kritik der Sprache" (1901–1902), "Wörterbuch der Philosophie" (1910–1924) and "Der Atheismus und seine Geschichte im Abendland" (1920–1923). His experience from Bohemia, however, inspired also his philosophical work and Mauthner even began writing his autobiography of which he completed only the first volume: "Erinnerungen. Prager Jugendjahre" (1918).

Fritz Mauthner's personality and his student years in Prague inspired the literary work of his cousin **Augusta Hauschner** (1850–1924). She was born in Prague, in the Old Town, No. 924 Dušní Street, in an esteemed and wealthy Jewish family as the daughter of a factory owner, Salomon Sobotka. In 1871 she was married and moved to Berlin, where she stayed also after her husband's death. However, she never severed her relations with Prague, where she went often visiting her relatives and read from her works in literary soirées.

She began writing only after her husband's death. Her social novel "Zwischen den Zeiten" (1906) takes place in a small town in the highlands between Bohemia and Moravia the whole population of which works in the local textile factory. Under an obvious influence of Emile Zola Hauschner tried to depict the factory as a monster dominating its environs, full of misery, vice, callousness and animality, and devouring all people from its wide surroundings. It is interesting that all characters, with the exception of the heroine who wants to bring light and culture to the workers and their families, but fails, are Czechs.

One of the most interesting and most characteristic pictures of Jewish Prague is painted in another of her novels, "Die Familie Lowositz" (1908). Hauschner returned once again to Prague environment in a short historical novel "Der Tod des Löwen" (1916) depicting the last years of the life of Emperor Rudolph II (1552–1612). A very effective background consists of Prague Castle, the aristocratic palaces in the Lesser Town, the churches, the Old Town and the Jewish ghetto, where the sickly dreamer Rudolph II seeks the key to the secrets of the world and man from the cabalist scholar, Rabbi Loew. The emperor's sickness is the sickness of the time, and his death marks the end of the whole epoch.

The writer's close relation to Prague is documented also by her last, but obviously unfulfilled intention to write a novel of her native town, "Das goldene Prag".

✳ ✳ ✳

In the seventies of the 19th century, in which the action of Hauschner's novel "Die Familie Lowositz" takes place, the Austrian liberalism was on the summit of its power in Bohemia. After 1880 the majority of the lower middle class in the boundary regions of Bohemia began adopting German nationalism and antisemitism; at the same time the workers emancipated themselves from the leadership of the liberals. North Bohemia with Liberec (Reichenberg) at the head became the centre of the Austrian social democratic movement. Alienation set in between German Prague and German countryside in Bohemia and Moravia. Rural journalism ignored consistently the production of Prague literary circles. This development threatened the Jews. Therefore, at the end of 1885, at the instigation of the Prague lawyer, Dr. Friedrich Duschnes, and the former industrialist Siegmund Mautner, the Centralverein zur Pflege jüdischer Angelegenheiten (Central association for the care of Jewish affairs) was founded. Initially it was intended for the protection of civil rights of the Jews in Bohemia, but subsequently it developed far reaching humanitarian, social and cultural activities.

At the same time the discrepancies between the Germans and the Czechs were becoming more profound. In the second half of the 19th century the Czechs were enjoying great economic and cultural boom. From the nineties the Czech bourgeoisie fought not only to attain exclusive position in Bohemia and Moravia, but also to change the balance of power in the Hapsburg monarchy. These Czecho-German clashes were of key significance for the Austrian monarchy. From the beginning of the eighties the language disputes represented an adequate pretext for nationalist agitation. These disputes culminated in the so-called Badeni riots in 1897. The Government of K. Badeni (1846–1909) issued a language edict in April, 1897, permitting the use of Czech in lower official instances of civil and judicial administration in the territory of Bohemia and Moravia even in the so-called internal intercourse, i.e. actions without the participation of the parties. Although this edict solved the language problem very inconsistently, the Czech politicians presented it as the basic step to the elimination of national oppression. For German nationalists it became the signal for anti-Czech demonstrations which grew into pogroms of Czech minorities in the boundary regions. Similar upsurge of nationalist moods took place also in the Bohemian camp. When the Badeni's edict was abolished at the beginning of 1898, Czech nationalists instigated anti-German and anti-Jewish demonstrations during which windows were broken, shops ransacked and houses set on fire in Prague. The experience of those days and months had left indelible traces in the memory and subsequently in the books of a number of German authors, beginning with German nationalists, such as the Jihlava-born **Karl Hans Strobl** (1877–1946) or the North-Bohemian writer **Julius Kraus** (1870–1917), who studied in Prague at the time, and ending with Prague humanist authors of Jewish descent, such as **Max Brod** (1884–1968), **Egon Erwin Kisch** (1885–1948) or **Willy Haas** (1891–1973). Less than two years afterwards a vulgar antisemitic campaign took place, aroused by the allegedly ritual murder of a Czech girl by the Jew Leopold Hilsner in Polná. Professor T. G. Masaryk (1850–1937), subsequently the President of the Czechoslovak Republic, intervened then very sharply against the antisemitic witch-hunters.

Disputes, clashes and changes in the balance of political powers and the antisemitic moods could not remain without influence on the life of the Prague German enclave. As early as 1871 the artistic association Concordia was founded under the auspices of the central association, Deutsches Casino (at present the Slavonic House, No. 859, Na Příkopě Street). Its foundation took place in the inn U Celestýnů, No. 709 in Dlouhá Street, on the occasion of the celebration of the 80th anniversary of the Austrian dramatist Franz Grillparzer(1791–1927) on the instigation of **Alfred Klaar** (1848–1927), writer and editor of the Prague newspaper Bohemia, and **David Kuh** (1819–1878), publisher of the newspaper Tagesbote aus Böhmen.

Alfred Klaar, with his proper name Alfred Karpeles (1848–1927), was born in Prague, in the Old Town, in No. 229, Huss Street. After studies of law he worked as journalist and from 1885 he was professor of German literature at the Prague German Realschule. He was interested chiefly in the problems of Austrian and German theatre and wrote also his own dramatic works of low significance. As a universally erudite and sharp critic he became – according to the characteristic by Paul Leppin - a "local hero" in Prague, who took up a dominant position in the world of art and in Prague society and was considered the only authoritative representative of Prague German literary endeavours for years.

Even after Klaar had left for Berlin in 1899, the Concordia, under the patronage of **Friedrich Adler** (1857–1938) and **Hugo Salus** (1866–1929), was recognized as an authority which took up a German nationality-conscious attitude; however, its artistic credo was epigonist and did not afford any possibilities for artistic experiments and self-assertion of the younger generation. Therefore, younger artists founded circles of their own, such as the Verein deutscher bildender Künstler in Böhmen (Association of German Creative Artists in Bohemia) in 1895, which originated "in an intentional contrast to the monopoly of the Concordia on the formulation of literary taste", or later on the association Jung-Prag (The Young Prague).

The splitting of German associations took place as early as the break of the eighties and the nineties. In 1892 the nationalist Germania separated from the liberal Lese- und Redehalle der deutschen Studenten in Prag (Reading and Speaking Hall of German Students in Prague). The growth of antisemitism resulted in the foundation of literary, German national and finally Zionist Jewish organizations. The activities of the Centralverein zur Pflege jüdischer Angelegenheiten was continued by the activities of an association with analogous aims, the Centralverein deutscher Staatsbürger jüdischen Glaubens (Central Association of German Citizens of Jewish Faith), whose members included also the fathers of Max Brod, Franz Werfel, Franz Kafka and Willy Haas. The foundation of the antisemitic association Germania was countered by Jewish students by the foundation of the Verein jüdischer Hochschüler Bar-Kochba in Prag (Association of Jewish Students Bar-Kochba in Prague) in 1893 which soon joined the Zionist movement and in 1913 issued an important collection "Vom Judentum". In the same year as the association Bar Kochba also the first lodge of the Jewish order B'nai B'rith was founded. The German artistic life in Prague could develop since that time only under the pressure of various interests. Great role was played by the frictions of various parties and groups as well as private sympathies and antipathies. Willy Haas recalls this atmosphere: "The whole town was somehow disenchanted, it seemed to have inexplicably disintegrated into different fragments ... Circles around every individual were so close, the boundaries intraversable ...".

❋ ❋ ❋

The recognized literary taste was governed for many years by the ideas of **Friedrich Adler** and **Hugo Salus**.

Friedrich Adler (1857–1938) had ambitions to become the successor of Goethe and was also respected as such. He was born at Kosová Hora near Sedlčany and experienced a sad childhood and youth. As an orphan, entirely dependent on the assistance of relatives, he came to Prague in 1867 and lived there all his life. He attended first the grammar school in the New Town, from the seventh form in the Lesser Town. He was highly talented for languages, in the sixth form he was said to know six languages. In spite of that he had to try three times before he passed his final examination. The years of his studies of law were more cheerful. He established inspiring contacts in the Lese- und Redehalle der deutschen Studenten the president of which he became. In 1883 he graduated, in 1890 he passed a barrister's examination and in 1891 he opened his own office which, however, he gave up in 1896, when he became the secretary of the Prague Chamber of Commerce. Later on, after the origin of the Czechoslovak Republic, he became interpreter of the House of Deputies of the Czechoslovak Parliament and consultant of the Ministry of Schools and National Education.

He soon began writing poetry, but did not publish. He was introduced to literature by the well known Austrian journalist and publicist, Karl Emil Franzos (1848–1904). The experience of sad youth lent Adler's poems a social

Friedrich Adler (1857–1938).

tone which became fashionable in the eighties and contributed to Adler's relations to the Berlin naturalists. Nevertheless he published his first collection
of poems, "Gedichte" as late as 1893. His poetry is contemplative, not
very original, but characterized by extraordinary formal dexterity which Adler had acquired also thanks to his rich translating experience with Italian,
Spanish, French, English as well as Czech and modern Greek. His collection
of satiric verses "Vom goldenen Kragen" (1907) became – primarily
thanks to the illustrations by Karl Teschner (1879–1948), painter from Karlovy Vary (Karlsbad) – a charming typical Jugendstil booklet.

More important than his own poetry are Adler's translations. German national conviction did not prevent his friendship with the outstanding Czech
poet Jaroslav Vrchlický (1853–1912) whose poems he published in German
translation in 1895. It was in Adler's translation that the Nobel Prize winner,
the writer **Bertha von Suttner** (1843–1914) quoted the verses of Jaroslav
Vrchlický and Svatopluk Čech (1846–1908) in her lecture on pacifism for the
Concordia in 1895, held in the Deutsches Haus, No. 859, Na Příkopě Street.

Greater success than his lyrical poetry was reaped by Adler's dramatic
works. He took over the subjects from Calderón (1600–1681), Tirso de Moli-
na (1584–1648) and other classics. Apart from the comedy "Zwei Eisen in
Feuer" (1900) which was staged for the first time on March 24, 1900 in the
New German Theatre (at present Smetana Theatre) in Prague, he wrote the
comedy "Don Gil" (1902) which had a great success not only in Prague,
but also in Munich, Berlin, Karlsruhe and elsewhere. Both plays were translated i. a. into Czech and performed on Czech stages, viz. in the Švanda Theatre in Prague-Smíchov and in the Vinohrady Theatre. The most independent

181

Portrait of Hugo Salus (1866–1929), physician,
poet and dramatist, by Max Švabinský, 1900.

of Adler's works is the cycle of one-act plays "Freiheit" which was performed for the first time on December 7,1904, in the New German Theatre in Prague. The same theatre put on also his play "Der gläserne Magister" (1909) on January 5, 1910, the dramatization of a story by Miguel Cervantes de Saavedra (1547–1616).

Friedrich Adler was spared the horrors of Hitler's regime. He died in February, 1938, aged 81 years, and was buried in the Jewish cemetery Na Malvazinkách in Prague. His wife and his two daughters were deported to Terezín (Theresienstadt).

Hugo Salus (1866–1929) was Adler's literary rival. He came from a family which rose from the Jewish poor. He was born in Česká Lípa in North Bohemia, attended grammar school first in Česká Lípa and subsequently in the towns where his father, a veterinary surgeon, had been posted – in České Budějovice and Litoměřice. On his father's wish he studied medicine at the University in Prague, where he graduated in 1891 as doctor of medicine. After compulsory practice in the hygienic institute and the maternity clinic he settled in Prague in 1895 as a medical practitioner in gynecology. By the publication of his works in the well-known satirical Munich periodical "Der Simplizissimus" and in "Die Jugend" (after which the German variant of the Art Nouveau, der Jugendstil, was christened) Salus became known to a relatively wide circle of readers. He adopted impressionism and the sentimental and idyllic neo-romanticism in the Biedermeier mood and his predilection for Czech music, particularly that by Bedřich Smetana (1824–1884) and Antonín Dvořák (1841–1904), as well as his sense of plastic arts influenced his poetry.

His melodious, dreamy, tender, moody, lyrical poems combine the melancholy inherited from the Jewish ghetto with the melancholy of Slavonic Prague. His lyrical register, however, is limited and does not show any creative development. Salus sought his themes in nature as well as in Jewish, Christian and primarily classical legends and myths. However, more than the classical poetry he loved its imitation in the gallant and pastoral rococo poetry of French provenance. He excels in fine miniatures and genre pictures. His verses are reflexive, frivolous and mildly satirical, formally perfect, but lacking the force of direct experience. His tendency to idyllic mood and expression of yearning for simple homely happiness won him popularity among the wide strata of his bourgeois readers. His numerous lyrical poems on Prague and the epic rendering of Prague legends reflect the city with the Vltava embankment and the silhouette of Prague Castle, the Lesser Town with its quiet streets, Baroque palaces and garden terraces as well as the Jewish cemetery and the Old-New Synagogue.

Salus tried also to win success in the dramatic field. His most successful play, ''Römische Komödie'', was performed in the author's presence in the New German Theatre in Prague on March 18, 1910.

In his national ideas Salus underwent a certain development. He was a German-conscious Jew and initially did not agree with Zionism.

Like Friedrich Adler also Hugo Salus was a friend of the foremost Czech poet of the time, Jaroslav Vrchlický, whose alleged Jewish origin – the allegation being obviously due to the Jewish motifs and subjects of his works – was fictitious. The number of Salus' acquaintances included also the dramatist and director of the dramatic department of National Theatre, Jaroslav Kvapil (1868–1950), Czech authors F. S. Procházka (1861–1939), Antonín Macek (1872–1923), Jaroslav Hilbert (1871–1936), František Herites (1871–1936), the sculptor J. V. Myslbek (1948–1922) and the painter Max Švabinský (1873–1962) who drew also Salus' portrait.

Salus' poetic glory, however, waned relatively quickly. To the new generation his verses seemed already obsolete; on the other hand, their melodiousness was appreciated by the composer Arnold Schönberg (1874–1951) and Max Brod who set some of his poems to music. Max Brod also devoted to Hugo Salus a passage in his autobiography "Streitbares Leben", and Franz Werfel included him as a literary character in his last work "Stern der Ungeborenen". Rainer Maria Rilke (1875–1926) worshipped Salus in his youth as a master of lyricism. Hugo Salus has remained alive as a legendary cultured poet with an intellectual mien and a typical black wide-brimmed hat. He was buried in Prague, in the Olšany cemetery, Department X, Field 1, No.155.

✳ ✳ ✳

At the break of the century Hugo Salus and Friedrich Adler represented Prague German literature, generally recognized by the contemporary Prague German society, and through the Concordia association determined its fashionable literary taste. Younger artists, who did not want to adjust to this conventional taste, began founding circles and groups of their own which, however, were of short duration and soon disintegrated again. Their number included chiefly such groups as the Freie deutsche Künstlervereinigung, headed by **Leo Heller** (1876–1941), the Jung-Prag, the generation grouped around the lyrical broadsheets "Frühling" and the periodical "Wir", whose uniting spirit was **Paul Leppin** (1878–1945).

Young people associated in the group of Jung-Prag were not from students' circles; therefore, they were not taken seriously either by the Prague German society or by the press. They wrote poetry, provoked the bourgeois by their eccentric behaviour and did not conceal their good relations to young Czech writers for which they were criticized by German press. Their number included the poets **Oskar Wiener** (1873–1944), **Ottokar Winicky** (1872–1943), the journalist **Walter Schulhof** (1878–1902), the graphic artist **Hugo Steiner** (1880–1945), the sculptor **Karl Wilfert jr.** and others. They convened in the café Renaissance and discussed art. They decided to implement the idea of R. M. Rilke and invite to Prague the German impressionist lyrical poet **Detlev von Liliencron** (1844–1909), who was received with enthusiasm both by the "official" writers, Friedrich Adler and Hugo Salus who tried to acquaint him with Jewish Prague, and by the Jung-Prag group with Oskar Wiener at the head who accompanied him through the romantic streets of the city and subsequently devoted to Liliencron's visit an essay "Mit Detlev von Liliencron durch Prag" (1918).

The young generation gathered around Paul Leppin, the publisher of the lyrical broadsheets "Frühling" (1900) and the periodical "Wir – Deutsche Blätter der Künste" (1906) which were considered to represent the generation. The number of their contributors included, apart from Leppin, **Camill Hoffmann** (1879–1944), Ottokar Winicky, Oskar Wiener, **Victor Hadwiger** (1878–1911), R. M. Rilke, Max Brod and the Viennese lyrical poet **Paul Wertheimer** (1878–1937), the writer **Stefan Zweig** (1881–1942), the painter and puppet theatre player **Richard Teschner** (1879-1949) and others. This review did not survive its third issue, but brought its co-authors and Prague literary life new stimuli. The number of Paul Leppin's friends included also the subsequent Berlin director **Franz Zavřel** (1879-1918), the well-known actor **Alexander Moissi** (1880-1935) and the Prague banker Gustav Meyer, subsequently the writer **Gustav Meyrink** (1868-1932).

Paul Leppin (1878-1945), the "uncrowned King of Prague bohème", as he was called, was not of Jewish descent. He lived in Prague his whole life and in his lyrical poems and numerous prosaic works he painted a picture of Prague as a romantic, demoniac and mysterious city.

At the beginning of the twentieth century Prague became one of the favourite subjects of German literature with fantastic features. It was at that time that the myth of Prague as a beautiful, mysterious, fatal city originated, and Prague German poets participated decisively in its creation. Pavel Eisner tried to characterize their specific relation to Prague as follows: "National metropolis has a specific position in German literature written in Bohemia. Being the heart of a foreign nation, it is the seat and the heart of all that is foreign; it is a place inhabited by strange phantoms of the past, the place of liquidation and loss, uncertain ground swaying underfoot, the romping ground of shadows of day and night. The view of Prague in German literature is pronouncedly phantasmagoric; it is a city breeding intangible secrets and tormenting riddles. A vampire city attracting the German soul by its gorgonic horror, like Carthage used to attract Roman mercenaries . . . a complex feeling called Hassliebe in German (love-hate) and which is a typical erotic feeling. Prague itself is a lovingly hated and hatingly loved female creature." This picture of Prague as a beautiful, simultaneously loved and hated woman to whose charm the poet succumbs, can be found also in the preface to Wiener's anthology "Deutsche Dichter aus Prag". For Wiener, Prague is "a city of eccentrics and visionaries, the unquiet heart of Central Europe" which everyone who gets acquainted with it, must love cravingly. "However, this devotion is a painful attachment. It is like a passion felt for an intoxicatingly beautiful, but whimsical woman . . . Many gathered their strength and tore themselves away from this dark Salome . . . But even those who were not destroyed by their passion are sick with an undying yearning for Prague.".

Even Karl Hans Strobl, who lived in Prague only during his study years, conceded: "I have not spoken yet with any man who had been in Prague, to whom that city has not become an affair. Not an affair with a sweet girl which is exhausted in one night and terminates with a hangover the morning after, but a passionate erotic relation to a mysterious woman which cannot be exhausted . . . to whom we must cling with our thoughts and our senses, even though fate has separated us from her already."

The literary interest in the mysterious Prague was connected also with the interest in the mysterious person of Golem. The Jewish legend of artificial man made of clay and enlivened by the magic force of a word, connected with the personality of the Rabbi of Prague, Jehuda Loew ben Bezalel, (approx. 1512–1609) buried in the Old Jewish Cemetery in Prague, appeared in written form only in 1837 and propagated after the publication of a collection of Jewish tales and legends "Sippurim" (issued by Wolf Pascheles in Prague in 1853). According to the tale told by L. Weisel, printed in this collection, Golem was a clay figure made in 1580 in Prague by Rabbi Loew "according to today no longer existing instructions of the cabala" and enlivened it by the magic force of the so-called shem, i.e. a strip of paper inserted into his mouth.

Both of these themes – fantastic Prague and the Golem – found their way even into cinema. In 1913 the film "Der Student von Prag" was shown for the first time, a fantastic story with the romantic subject of a double. The scenario was written by the German writer Hans Heinz Ewers (1871–1943), the film was directed by the Danish director Stellan Rye and the title role was played by the famous actor Paul Wegener (1874–1948). In 1914 Paul Wegener made his first Golem film jointly with Hendrik Galeen, which was followed by two others.

In 1914 also **Paul Leppin** published his novel "Severins Gang in die Finsternis", subtitled "Ein Prager Gespensterroman". In this novel Prague appears for the first time in the fantastic light as a mysterious, fatal city exerting a sinister influence on the hero. Prague quarters and streets – Vinohrady, Nusle, the Old Town, Ferdinand (at present Národní) Street, the Botanic Garden, the Pilsner beer restaurant in Štěpánská Street opposite St. Stephen's church, the Old Town Square, etc. are more than scenery and locale of the story depicting the wandering of Severin, a petty clerk and decadent dreamer yearning for a romantic erotic adventure. The Czech literary critic F. V. Krejčí (1867–1941) said in his review: "Prague is here something more important than the young Severin, because it is Prague that creates that environment, that atmosphere filled with the poison of melancholy and destructive eroticism, poisoning Severin as a merely passive victim. Prague as a demon, as a seductress, damping his will by the sepulchral stench of its historicity and the melancholy sensuous moods – it is Prague that determines "Severin's journey into darkness"."

Paul Leppin not only accentuated the fantastic features of Prague, but afforded a new, original content to the personage of Golem in his drama "Der Enkel des Golem" which had its first performance in the New German Theatre on December 8,1934. According to contemporary critics this play, which was never issued in book form, was particularly effective in the presentation of the atmosphere of ancient Prague in which myth merged with reality. "Sometimes the whole Prague appears as a reflection of the mysterious Golem; then again Golem appears as a diminutive symbol of the haunting picture of the city . . ." Max Brod wrote in a contemporary review.

The combination of the picture of fantastic Prague with the myth of Golem crystallized into a world success in the well known novel by Gustav Meyrink, "Der Golem" which presented Prague, and primarily its Old Town and its Jewish alleys, as a city of twilight, flickering shadows, mysterious apparitions, ghosts and visions.

186

Gustav Meyrink (1868–1932).

Gustav Meyrink, actually Gustav Meyer (1868–1932), came to Prague with his mother, actress Marie Mayer, engaged in the Prague New German Theatre in the 1884–1885 season. However, when a new director came to the theatre in 1885, she left for Petersburg, leaving her 17-year-old son in Prague. After his studies at the grammar schools and medium-grade commercial school Gustav Meyer, as soon as he came of age, founded a banking and exchange establishment "Meyer and Morgenstern" in the centre of Prague, No. 2 Ovocná Street (subsequently 28th October Street) in 1889. The firm was erased from the Company Register in 1894, when Meyer became independent and opened "The First Christian Exchange Office" in No. 33, Wenceslas Square. Meyer – Meyrink was not a Jew. The exchange office obviously moved subsequently to the Black Rose passage in the street Na Příkopech and later on to No. 14, Jungmann Street. The elegant banker, who became co-founder of the Prague theosophic lodge "The Blue Star" in 1891, roused both sympathy and antipathy of Prague society by his eccentric behaviour. Max Brod and Paul Leppin made his acquaintance in the café Continental, No. 1047 in the street Na příkopě. The tension between Meyrink and Prague society culminated in his dispute with the members of Prague officers' corps, which was heard by the District Court in the Ovocný trh Street in December, 1901, and January, 1902. This case was almost parallel with another affair: on January 18, 1902, Meyrink was arrested and accused of financial fraud which he had allegedly commited as banker. On April 2, 1902. he was released and the prosecution stopped. However, his enterprise was ruined and Meyrink was discredited.

187

He lived in Prague almost twenty years and lived on a number of addresses, inter alia also in the centre of Prague, in No. 10, Ferdinand (at present Národní) Street, in No. 14, Ferdinand (at present Janáček) Embankment in Smíchov, in No. 15, Jungmann Street near the Wenceslas Square, in No. 62, Havlíček (at present Bělehradská) Street in Vinohrady, in No. 15, Přemyslovská Street on the boundary of Vinohrady and Žižkov, and finally in the tower near the Nusle Stairs above the Botič. In May 1904 he left Prague for good and later on he wrote: "If anybody asks me: 'Would you like to live in Prague again?' I reply: 'Yes, but in memory only; in reality not a single hour.' In the night I often dream about Prague and its demoniac charm. When I wake up, I feel as if I got rid of a nightmare. Since I have left Prague I have been living – not counting two years in Vienna – in Germany and I have seen many German cities – even such as have beautiful medieval buildings like Prague and which have a similarly bloody past. None of them, however, has that incomprehensibly remarkable atmosphere. They are as if disinfected and you walk in them as if you were walking through tedious museums."

Prague not only left an indelible mark on Meyrink's life, but determined also his work. It appears in it in the shape which the writer loved so dearly: mysterious medieval Prague, full of monuments recalling long-gone-by times and ancient legends, the city of Golem, to which Emperor Rudolph II called alchemists and mysterious scholars. That is the picture of Prague Meyrink presented most impressively in his most successful novel "Der Golem" (1915). In it he modifies originally the Jewish tale of Golem, linking it with a contemporary story from the break of the century. In Meyrink's novel Golem revives every 33 years and appears in Prague ghetto as a spook rousing fear and panic among its population and becoming the personification and symbol of the soul of the crowd. At the same time he appears as a double of the hero and narrator of the story, Athanasius Pernath, and his spiritual leader on his way to self-knowledge. The background of this Pernath's way, which is the central theme of the novel, consists in the exotically moulded and anthropomorphized Jewish Town of Prague at the time before and during its clearance which took place in 1893–1917 as well as other parts of Prague. Prague is described in concrete terms, with topographic details. It is clearly stated that the locale of the story is the ghetto of Prague, the text of the novel mentions a number of authentic Prague buildings and localities, such as the Old-New Synagogue, the Týn Court, the Castle, the Golden Lane, the Stag Moat, the Daliborka tower, the Fürstenberg Garden in the Lesser Town, the stone Charles Bridge, etc. At the same time these concrete topographic details have a symbolic meaning and can be interpreted as the phases of the spiritual development of the hero of the novel.

In his novel Meyrink utilized the fact that he knew from experience the ghetto of Prague before its clearance, as well as his personal acquaintance of some personalities of Prague whom he expressly mentions in the novel. Their number includes also the poet **Oskar Wiener,** initially Wien (1873–1944). He was born in Prague, in No. 248, Liliová Street, in the Old Town, in the family of the merchant, Ignatz Wien, who was the founder of the first Prague felt hat factory. He should have become a merchant, too. However, after a short career of clerk he devoted his life to literature. He lived his whole life in Prague, first in the "Wien" villa in Bubeneč, later on in No. 75, Královská (at present Sokolovská) Street in Karlín. As a Jew he was deported to the ghetto of Terezín in July, 1942, where he died in April, 1944.

Similarly as Leppin and Meyrink, also Wiener loved old, romantic Prague. The new, modern, busy city which originated after the clearance of the ghetto was alien to him. He drew the themes and melody of his poems from the darkened Prague alleys and nooks, from the bizarre contrast of the Old Town and the modern city and from the cultures of the two contending nations as well as from Jewish traditions and legends. His collections of poems were characterized by a medley of moods, in which melancholy was combined with the lightness of a broadside ballad. Melody, rhythm and a folk tone of Wiener's verses inspired some composers, the most important among whom was Max Reger (1873–1916).

Apart from Liliencron Wiener considered the German lyrical poet Richard Dehmel (1863–1920) his poetic teacher, and it was at the latter's instigation that he began composing songs and verses for children. Wiener's collections of children's verse, the most successful among which was the book "Der lustige Kindergarten" (1907) ranked among the best books for children of the time.

Wiener was endowed with rich fantasy. In the style of Prague Neo-Romanticism he wrote the sketches and prosaic stories collected in "Verstiegene Novellen" (1907) and "So endete das schöne Fest" (1910). Of extraordinary charm for the lovers of old Prague are particularly Wiener's stories taking place in the environment of the Stromovka park and of the gardens around the Baroque castle of Troja.

The atmosphere of Prague combined with an erotic theme appears also in a not too successful novel "Im Prager Dunstkreis" (1919). Particularly good is the characterization of the environment of the individual Prague living quarters and localities, in the first place, once again, the Stromovka park with its mansion, as well as of the Lesser Town with the restaurant "The Golden Well", the Old Town, the Agnes' Convent, the neighbourhood of the Olšany Cemetery, etc.

Wiener was interested also in literary history, a fact testified to by his studies and editorial work. Specific relation to Prague has the book "Alt-Prager Guckkasten. Wanderungen durch das Romantische Prag" (1922). In poetical almanacs "Der Heimat zum Gruss" (1914) and "Deutsche Dichter aus Prag" (1919) he collected the contributions of a number of German poets living in Bohemia and Moravia at the time when many of them had already left Prague and Bohemia to seek their luck in nearer or farther foreign countries.

The number of poets of Jewish descent in Wiener's anthologies included the authors of older and younger generations. The journalist and dramatic critic **Josef Adolf Bondy** (1876–1946), born in No. 91 in Prague-Josefov (the house was torn down obviously during the ghetto clearance) lived mainly in Berlin. The journalist, dramatic author and critic **Heinrich Teweles** (1856–1927) lived in Prague. Similar intensive interest in journalism characterized also **Emil Faktor** (1876–1942). He was born in Prague in No. 1150, Biskupský Dvůr, in the proximity of the present-day White Swan department store. After his studies of law he worked as editor and dramatic critic in Prague periodicals "Bohemia" and "Montagsblatt aus Böhmen". His collections of lyrical poetry "Was ich suche" (1899) and "Jahresringe" (1908) contain emotional as well as reflective, dreamy as well as melancholic verses characterized by cultured form. On March 23, 1914, his play "Die Temperierten", with the subject of marital infidelity was performed for the first time in Prague. The autor lived for twenty-five years in Berlin.

After the Nazis had seized power in Germany Emil Faktor sought refuge in his old country. In 1933 he asked for Czechoslovak citizenship which he was granted on December 7,1935. On his return to Prague he changed several addresses. He lived in No. 423, Skořepka, in the Old Town, in No. 1322, Zderaz, near the Charles Square in the New Town, in No. 1853, Jinonická Street on the opposite river bank, then in No. 226, Palacký (at present Křižík) Street in Karlín and in Žižka (at present Perner) Street, in No. 150, Pštross Street near the Charles Square in the New Town and finally in Lhotka (at present part of Prague), in No. 90/77, Na Borovém Street. However, the flight to Prague and the Czechoslovak citizenship did not save his life. In October, 1941, he was deported from the so-called Protectorate Bohemia and Moravia to the concentration camp in Lodz, where he died in 1942.

Prague Neo-Romanticism left indelible traces also in the work of the lyrical poet and prosaist **Leo Heller** (1876–1941). The author, who lived chiefly in Berlin, cooperated with numerous periodicals of the most varied orientation. He considered himself principally city lyricist and wrote chiefly cabaret poetry. He wrote some sincere verses also about Prague where he moved at the close of his life.

One of the foremost representatives of Prague Neo-Romantic lyrical poetry was **Camill Hoffmann** (1878–1944). He was born in No. 78 in Kolín-Zálabí, in the family of Jewish merchant and innkeeper, frequented the German grammar school in the Old Town Square in Prague, Kinský Palace, and then the medium-grade commercial school. He too left Prague in 1902 for Vienna. From 1911 he worked as journalist in Dresden. He published his first poems in Paul Leppin's lyrical broadsheets "Der Frühling". Hoffmann's impressionist lyrical poems, characterized by dreamy, volatile sentiments, melody and formal maturity, revive Bohemian landscape.

In 1918 Hoffmann returned to Prague and as an experienced journalist he was entrusted by T. G. Masaryk, the President of the new Czechoslovak Republic, with the preparations for the new government daily, "Prager Presse" which began to appear in 1921. At that time Hoffmann was already in Berlin, where he worked at the Czechoslovak legation as a Counsellor and press attaché. He was particularly active as a mediator of Czech culture to the German public, having translated into German Masaryk's "Weltrevolution" (1925) and Čapek's "Gespräche mit Masaryk" (1935). He continued writing poetry, but stopped publishing it after the beginning of his diplomatic career. After the Munich accord in the autumn of 1938 Hoffmann was recalled from Berlin and pensioned off. He returned to Prague, where he lived as a Ministerial Counsellor, rtd. in the Lesser Town, No. 492/1, Durdík Street, and in Žižkov, in No. 315, Na Balkáně Street. On April 20, 1942, he was arrested in the street, and together with his wife deported to the ghetto of Terezín. The poems he wrote there are mostly irretrievably lost. On October 28, 1944, he was deported from Terezín by the last transport to the extermination camp in Oswieczim (Auschwitz), where he died.

The atmosphere of the Prague Neo-Romanticism yielded also the author of fantastic novels, one of the most widely read German writers between 1918 and 1933, **Leo** (actually Leopold) **Perutz** (1882–1957). He was born in Prague, and although he had lived in Vienna most of his life, the old, mystery-laden Prague left indelible traces in his work. His father, Benedikt Perutz, came from an old and revered family of Rakovník; in his youth he came to Prague, where he worked his way up to the position of a well-to-do owner of a textile factory. Leo Perutz attended the Piarist school, where he became schoolfellow and friend of the subsequent journalist and novelist **Arnold Höllriegel**, with proper name **Richard A. Bermann** (1883–1939). In 1899 the factory of Benedict Perutz in Prague was destroyed by fire and the family, including the then seventeen-year-old boy, moved to Vienna.

Leo Perutz attempted to write from the very time of his grammar school studies. He published his minor works in "Teplitzer Zeitung" and lent his unpublished works to his friends **Arnold Höllriegel** and **Ernst Weiss,** (1882–1940) a writer from Brno, to read. His first novel, "Die dritte Kugel", (dealing with the events of the life of the Spanish conqueror of the Aztec empire, Fernando Cortéz (1485–1547), was published in 1915, in the middle of the First World War. It was begun while he was still living in Prague.

The period of 1918–1933 was the most productive era of Perutz' life. He wrote a number of historical as well as contemporary stories, novelettes and plays. His works are characterized by a unique combination of history and fiction, realistic events and fantastic elements, because the irrational, according to Perutz' opinion, is a factor which must be taken into account in human life and history.

The antifascist exile meant for him a painful gap in his work. The 54 years old author chose Palestine as his new home. He was not a Zionist, and once he wrote with irony and egocentric self-irony: "Zionism fulfilled its historical mission by bringing me to Palestine; now it has no other tasks." The establishment of the state of Israel and the military clashes with the Arab minority and the neighbour states moved Perutz to consider another emigration in

1948. "I have always been in favour of a binational state here, and now I belong among the defeated," he wrote then in one of his letters. He did not leave Israel, but travelled all his life between Tel Aviv and Austria, where he died of a coronary thrombosis.

The last book published in his lifetime was the novel "Nachts unter der steinernen Brücke" (1953) on which he had worked for almost thirty years. The work consists of integral episodes depicting the stories, tales and legends from Prague of Rudolph II. Apart from historical personalities there is also a number of marginal and historically undocumented figures. In accordance with Perutz' concept of historical novel, the reader learns about great historical events from the very viewpoint of these figures from the periphery of history. The refined composition of the novel consists in the symbolism of numbers (for instance the number of seven – the subject of the first, seventh and fourteenth chapters are Rabbi Loew and the cabala) and in the asymmetric structure: the story of the novel is not told chronologically, but only in the course of reading the reader discovers the framework and realizes that the stories are told by the preceptor Jacob Maisl, a descendant of the famous Maisl family, to his unruly pupil Leo Perutz at the time of the clearance of Prague ghetto at the beginning of our century. In this novel Leo Perutz erected a monument to his native city. He said himself: "In my whole life I have not lost the Prague of my childhood. I have always followed the phantom of Prague ghetto and have sought it everywhere."

✳ ✳ ✳

Of central importance for Prague German literature of the period preceding the First World War is the personality of **Max Brod.** It was his role to fill the gap between the older generation, represented by F. Adler, H. Salus, P. Leppin and O. Wiener, and the emerging youngest generation which was only preparing to enter literature at that time. R. M. Rilke, G. Meyrink, E. Faktor, L. Heller and C. Hoffmann had left Prague already and thus Max Brod represented the "intergeneration" missing link. The feelings of the young, then beginning writers, were aptly characterized by Brod's friend, Oskar Baum (1883–1941): "The grandfathers, who came from small towns, were educated in the traditional piety of the ghetto, the fathers were cosmopolitan in accordance with the political fashion, with the reservation that their education and their world outlook were formed by the school and by the press incited by state nationalism. They had no time to be concerened with themselves; breathlessly, in sober and active devotion to work, they endeavoured to achieve the maximum social assertion and material security. And the sons ... full of intellectual superiority over everything, including the past, felt like the final product."

The negative attitude of the sons to their fathers' world was characteristic of expressionism, a literary and artistic movement, the emergence of which in Germany generally coincided with the time of arrival of the new generation of young Prague writers. However, the attitude of the young and their creative work had specific Prague features of its own. Of particular significance for their development and refinement was **Karl Kraus** (1874–1936), native of Jičín, writer and journalist of Vienna, an analyst and critic of bourgeois liberal forms of thinking and living. On December 12, 1910, the first out of the 57 Kraus' lectures took place in the Lese- und Redehalle der deutschen Studenten. Kraus influenced not only the development of the opposition attitude of the young Prague writers, but also their sympathies and antipathies. At the same time, however, the Prague authors, in whose number the Jews prevailed, dissociated themselves decisively from the Pangerman Zionism; but for all their sympathies for Czech literature the national aspirations of the Czechs remained alien to them similarly as Zionism for some time. Characteristic in this respect is the reminiscence of **Hans Kohn,** printed in the Prague Jewish periodical "Selbstwehr" in 1926: "Twenty or fifteen years ago we were a small circle, rooted in Prague, which we loved passionately . . . Judaism was alien to us, a distant legend. We did not know any Jews who would not be from Bohemia or, in the best case, from Vienna. We were fully assimilated in German culture of those days or to that part of it which was compatible with our Jewish temperament . . . Assimilation was for us, similarly as for all others, a reality, and Zionism only a gesture, or a programme, Judaism a traditional or accepted fact and by far not a problem."

The way to Zionism was shown to a number of young intellectuals by the "Drei Reden über das Judentum", presented in 1909 in the Prague students' association Bar Kochba by the philosopher **Martin Buber** (1878–1965). They started an extensive discussion collected in the volume "Vom Judentum" issued by the Bar Kochba association in 1913.

In 1907 the editor Franz Steiner founded in Prague a Jewish periodical "Selbstwehr". Later on, in 1918, **Felix Weltsch** (1884–1964), fellow student and friend of Franz Kafka, became the editor, and together with Hans Lichtwitz, who became the Israeli diplomat Uri Naor later, made of it a periodical of high standard and the most widely read Jewish weekly in the territory of Czechoslovakia. The editors of the Selbstwehr published also the collection "Das Jüdische Prag" in 1917.

The endeavours of the young writers' generation were represented best by the association Johann Gottfried Herder-Vereinigung, which originated in 1910 in the framework of the Prague lodge of the B'nai-B'rith. This association developed wide cultural activities and organized, inter alia, also literary evenings in which the young authors read from their works. The association had contacts with the circle of Berlin writers around **Kurt Hiller** (1885–1972) and **Ernst Blass** (1890–1939) and with the group of Viennese authors gathered around **Hugo von Hoffmannsthal** (1874–1929). Externally the association was represented by the periodical "Herder-Blätter", published in Prague by Willy Haas, Norbert Eisler and Otto Pick, which presented to the public the Prague German literary avant-guarde, subsequently called by some literary critics "Prager Schule". The first number of the periodical appeared in April, 1911.

Max Brod (1884–1968).

Until October, 1912, when the magazine stopped appearing, five numbers were issued. They contained the contributions by then more or less unknown Prague writers who rallied round **Max Brod**: **Oskar Baum, Franz Kafka, Franz Werfel, Willy Haas, Rudolf Fuchs, Otto Pick, Franz Janowitz** (1892–1917), **Hans Janowitz** (1890–1954) and others. One of the most productive contributors was Max Brod, who pioneered and mediated the works of Franz Werfel, Franz Kafka, Oskar Baum and other Prague authors.

* * *

Max Brod (1884–1968) was a universal personality. He studied law, was a philosopher, critic, poet, prosaic and dramatic writer, composer and active musician (he composed songs, and accompanied on the piano e.g. the Czech composer Josef Suk (1874–1935).

He was born in No. 1031, Haštalská Street in the Old Town of Prague in an old Jewish family whose family tree extended as far as the famous Rabbi Loew. Max' father, initially an ordinary bank clerk, rose to the position of vice-director of the Böhmische Unionsbank in Prague. From the age of four Max' childhood was overshadowed by a backbone ailment the consequences of which were minimized thanks to the untiring care and enormous energy of his mother. Together with his friend and subsequent philosopher and publicist, Felix Weltsch, Brod attended the elementary school of the Piarists in the New Town of Prague, in No. 1, Panská Street, where the Prague middle-class German Jews sent their children. His namesake, the publicist Leo Brod, (b.

194

1905) characterized it subsequently as follows: "The Piarists ... were a spiritual order which bound its members to teaching children free of charge ... They were active particularly in Austria and Poland. Their conduct and costume were similar as those of the Jesuits, and when the Jesuits were removed from schools by Emperor Joseph II, the Piarists took their place. Particularly in Bohemia and Moravia they took over the elementary and medium grade schools and in Prague a German elementary school in Panská Street existed even at the time when all medium-grade schools had become state schools and operated until 1918. The number of its pupils included Mauthner, Brod, Kisch, Werfel and others."

Having completed the Piarist school, Max Broad studied at the German grammar school in Štěpánská Street, where the number of his younger fellow students included also Franz Werfel and Willy Haas. Together with his friend Weltsch they enrolled for the study of law in 1902 at the Prague university, where he graduated in 1907. During these student's years Brod met also Franz Kafka, one year his senior. They met for the first time in 1902 in the Lese- and Redehalle der deutschen Studenten in Prag, but became close friend of Franz Werfel, too, whom he aided effectively in his literary beginnings. The friends often undertook walking tours in the woods in the environment of Prague, attended lectures in the Bar Kochba association as well as the cabaret Montmartre in the Old Town which performed from 1911 in the Řetězová Street in the house "At Three Wild Men" (at present No. 7). They associated in the Johann Gottfried Herder-Vereinigung and met in the café Arco at the corner of the Hybernská and the Dlážděná Streets. They discussed literature and art and Werfel read his first poems. The cohesion and cooperation of this young Prague poetic generation found its expression also in the annual "Arkadia" published in 1913 by Max Brod.

A great experience for Max Brod and many of his friends of the same generation were the lectures of the guest of the Bar Kochba association, Martin Buber, about Judaism. Apart from Buber the development of Max Brod to Zionism was influenced also by the meeting with the East Jewish dramatic group which had its guest performances in Prague in 1911 and was the first Max Brod's encounter with the East European Judaism. However, according to his own confession, the decisive impulse came from the response aroused by his novel "Ein tschechisches Dienstmädchen" (1909). This story of the love of a young German official of Vienna and a Czech girl, taking place in Prague, was criticized in the Czech, German and Jewish press. He was impressed particularly by the review by Leo Herrmann (1881–1951) published in the "Jüdische Volkstimme", a Zionist daily, issued in Brno from 1901. The reviewer stated with contempt that the young author obviously believed that the problems of nationality could be solved in bed. Leo Herrmann was one of the leading personalities of the Bar Kochba association and the contributors of the "Selbstwehr" weekly, and it was he who had initiated Martin Buber's invitation to Prague.

Brod's Judaism was also the impulse to a parliamentary interpelation of the deputies of Henlein's party, who protested against awarding the Czecho-slovak State Prize intended for German artists to Max Brod in 1930, basing their objections on Brod's declaration that he was of Jewish and not of German nationality.

The rich experience of a Jewish life is reflected in the whole of Brod's literary work – his heroes – like the Jews – are persecuted, degraded, tortured. Their temporary defeats, however, are not total defeats; in one way or other they attain their goals. This corresponds with Brod's conviction that the salvation both for the suffering Jewish people and for the whole mankind will come from Judaism.

Brod's literary work is extraordinarily extensive. Apart from religio-philosophical works, critical essays and numerous translations it contains also dramas, poems and, last but not least, novels and stories. Brod is an arresting narrator of originally tinted erotic stories. However, the focal point of his work is in his historical novels, the most important of which is the trilogy "Ein Kampf um die Wahrheit", comprising "Tycho Brahes Weg zu Gott" (1915), "Rëubeni, Fürst der Juden" (1925) and "Galilei in Gefangenschaft" (1948). The story of many of his works takes place at least partly in Prague.

Brod was the first to recognize Kafka's literary talent and did not comply with his wish that his literary estate should be destroyed after his death. On the contrary, by the posthumous publication of his works he founded his literary fame. He presented to the public also Franz Werfel, Friedrich Torberg (1908–1979), Robert Walser (1878–1956) and others. He devoted consistent attention also to Czech culture and his participation in its publicity in other countries is indubitable – let us mention at least his translations of librettoes and lyrics to the songs of Leoš Janáček (1854–1926), Bohuslav Foerster (1859–1951), Vítězslav Novák (1870–1949) and others. He opened the way to the world also for Jaroslav Hašek's (1883–1923) famous novel "The Good Soldier Schweik" whose success he aided also by his dramatization in which, directed by Erwin Piscator, the title role was played with enormous success by the well known actor Max Pallenberg (1877–1934). Brod's interest in the composer Bedřich Smetana (1824–1884) and in the atmosphere in which he worked is testified to by the biographic novel with picturesque cultural and historical background "Die Verkaufte Braut" (1962) concerned with the librettist of the opera, Karel Sabina (1813–1877).

Brod lived in Prague until the beginning of 1939 and but for the Nazi occupation he would have never left it. He was convinced that it was the very triad of the German, Czech and Jewish elements in the environment of Prague that was so stimulating for creative writing.

Having graduated in 1907, Brod worked first as a probational clerk at the Land Court in Ovocný Trh Street, No. 587, later on as a clerk in an insurance company and at the Directorate of Posts. Similarly as Kafka he felt his work as a burden. Therefore be welcomed the end of this drudgery when in 1924 he was offered the post of dramatic and music critic of the newspaper "Prager

Max Brod's memorial tablet in the Jewish Cemetery in Prague – Strašnice.

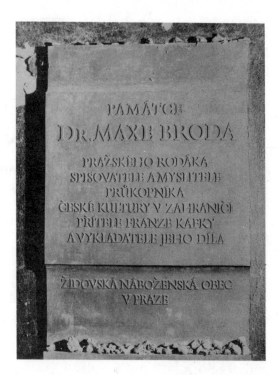

PAMÁTCE
DR. MAXE BRODA
PRAŽSKÉHO RODÁKA
SPISOVATELE A MYSLITELE
PRŮKOPNÍKA
ČESKÉ KULTURY V ZAHRANIČÍ
PŘÍTELE FRANZE KAFKY
A VYKLADATELE JEHO DÍLA

ŽIDOVSKÁ NÁBOŽENSKÁ OBEC
V PRAZE

Tagblatt". Simultaneously he worked as a press officer of the Czechoslovak Government and after the origin of the Czechoslovak Republic he founded the National Jewish Council with offices in No. 22, Celetná Street, in the Old Town of Prague and discussed the rights of the Jewish community in Czechoslovakia with the President, T. G. Masaryk.

In March, 1939, Brod emigrated to Palestine, where he settled in Tel Aviv. In the last decades of his life he published a number of books, often of reflective and reminiscent character, depicting the atmosphere of his native Prague and affording valuable material for the study of the whole literary and cultural epoch. Well known are Brod's autobiographic and memoir volumes "Streitbares Leben" (1960) and "Der Prager Kreis" (1966) in which he recalled, apart from a number of well known names also some which had fallen into oblivion since. His novel "Rebellische Herzen" (1957) is a roman-à-clef dealing with the dynamic life in the editorial office of "Prager Tagblatt" and in which a significant role is played by such authentic Prague localities as the promenade on the Příkopy, where the father of R. M. Rilke used to walk with his friends, the night club Femina (in the Black Rose passage), the Štěrba's café and others.

197

Memorial tablet on Franz Kafka's native house, No. 5, U radnice Street, Old Town of Prague.

The signboard of the shop of Franz Kafka's father.

In 1954 Brod visited Germany, where his brother, the writer **Otto Brod** (1884–1944) died as one of the victims of Nazism and to whose memory he dedicated the autobiographic novel ''Der Sommer den man zurückwünscht'' (1952). Four years before his death, in 1964, he visited Prague to open by a Czech address the exhibition on the life and work of Franz Kafka on June 23, 1964. During his visit he lived in the Palace Hotel in Panská Street. He died in 1968 and was buried in the old cemetery in Tel Aviv. On behalf of Czech public the Czech publicist Luděk Pachman took farewell of him.

✳ ✳ ✳

The writer who attained the greatest universal fame from the number of Prague authors of Jewish origin was **Franz Kafka** (1883–1924). He was born on July 3, 1883, in the Old Town of Prague, in the house "At the Tower" (at that time No. 4/24, Jáchymova Street). This corner house next to the St. Nicholas' church was destroyed by a fire in 1897 and was rebuilt in 1902, only the portal having been preserved from the old house. On July 3, 1966, a memorial relief by academic sculptor K. Hladík was unveiled on the house stand-

Franz Kafka's parents, Hermann and Julia Kafka.

Franz Kafka in his childhood.

ing at the crossing of the Kaprova, Maiselova and U radnice Streets (No. 5/24).

Franz Kafka's father, Hermann Kafka, came from the Bohemian village of Osek near Písek in South Bohemia, where he lived until 1881, when he moved to Prague. He grew in a Czecho-Jewish environment, he spoke better Czech than German, and in the first years of his stay in Prague he felt like a Czech and was considered as such. At that time he was a member of the council of the synagogue in Jindřišská Street, the first Prague synagogue with Czech religious service. However, the social rise of Prague Jews was conditioned by their relation to German society and German culture, and so Hermann Kafka gradually abandoned Czech language, joined German society and the religious community of the Cikán Synagogue and subsequently the community of the Pinkas Synagogue, and sent his children only to German schools. In 1882 Hermann Kafka opened a haberdashery shop, at first in No. 12, Celetná Street, which he expanded into a wholesale trade store later on, thus ensuring the status of a wealthy citizen. Later on he moved the shop to No. 3, Celetná Street, and finally to the Old Town Square, to the part of the Kinský Palace adjoining the Týn Church. His property and social rise was influenced indubitably also by his marriage to Julia Löwy, a daughter of a wealthy and cultured German-Jewish family from Poděbrady.

On September 20, 1893, Franz Kafka began attending the German state

The Golz-Kinsky Palace in the Old Town Square on the ground floor of which Hermann Kafka had his shop. The German grammar school, attended by Franz Kafka, was in the same building.

grammar school in the Baroque Kinský Palace in the Old Town Square, in the same building in which his father's shop was situated. In July, 1901, he passed his final examination and in the autumn he enrolled at the Prague German University to study law. However, he frequented also lectures in Germanistics and art history. In 1902 he toyed with the idea of continuing his studies in Munich; he even left for Munich for a few days, but returned to Prague soon to complete his legal studies.

. Kafka did not enjoy the study of law; he was attracted to art and literature. His first literary attempts dated from the time of his studies; none of them however, has been preserved. He often went to both the Czech and the German theatre, participated in lectures and literary evenings in the Lese- und

Franz Kafka in the Old Town Square (1920–1921 ?)

Portrait of Franz Kafka.

Redehalle der deutschen Studenten, where he made acquaintance, in the winter of 1901–1902, of Max Brod, subsequently his closest friend.

On June 18, 1906, Franz Kafka graduated and became Doctor of Law. The required year of judicial practice was spent at the criminal and civil court in Prague, No. 587, Ovocný Trh Street, behind the rear facade of the then German Land Theatre. Immediately afterwards, in October 1907, he applied for employment with the insurance company Assicurazioni Generali, whose offices were in No. 832, at the corner of the Jindřišská Street and the Wenceslas Square. In less than one year, however, he left his employment and joined the Workers' Accident Insurance Company for the Kingdom of Bohemia in No. 7, Na poříčí Street, where the job afforded him more time for his writing. In this insurance company Kafka was employed until his premature retirement due to ill health in July, 1922.

After hours Kafka rested, went for walks and after a late supper he began to write and continued often till late at night. Max Brod, with whom he contracted a close friendship in 1908, introduced him to Prague literary and night life, in which Brod always participated more intensively than Kafka. He acquainted him with his friends, Felix Weltsch and Oskar Baum, and together they went for walks in the nearest environs of Prague. During the holidays they travelled together abroad. In 1908 and 1909 the Munich review "Hyperion" printed some excerpts from Kafka's longer prosaic work, "Beschreibung eines Kampfes" and several shorter sketches. At the same time Kafka published his first sketches in the Prague "Bohemia". It was at that time, too, that he began to keep his diaries systematically.

When the association of the Prague Jewish youth, Johann Gottfried Herder-Vereinigung, originated in 1910 and the young writers began issuing the "Herder-Blätter" in 1911, they invited also Kafka to contribute. Kafka was also one of the first writers invited to read publically his works in literary evenings organized by the association. It took place on December 4, 1912, in the Jugendstil Palace Hotel in No. 897, Panská Street; Kafka read "Das Urteil" which was printed in Brod's annual "Arkadia" son afterwards.

The period of Kafka's relations with the Herder-Vereinigung coincides partly with the period in which Kafka became interested for the first time in the specificity of Judaism. In 1911 he came into the first contact with the religion of East European Jews, viz. through the vagrant East European Jewish dramatic company from Lwow (Lemberg), presenting its guest performances in the café Savoy in the Old Town of Prague in yiddish. Kafka became interested in Jewish history, in hassidic legends and began to learn Hebrew. The number of his teachers included also **Jiří Mordecai Langer** (1894–1943), brother of the Czech dramatic author František Langer (1888–1965), and **Friedrich Thieberger** (1888–1958), son of the Rabbi of Prague and brother of the poetess Grete Thieberger, married to the writer Johannes Urzidil. While – according to his diaries – the hassidic stories were dear to Kafka's soul and attracted him permanently, his relation to Zionism was uncertain, although he always sympathized with its social attempt at building agricultural communities.

The year 1912 ranks among the most productive years of Kafka's life. On August 13, 1912, he made acquaintance, in Max Brod's company, of Felicia Bauer, a clerk from Berlin, with whom he fell in love and whom he both did and did not want to marry. This clash of wishes, the weighing of all pros and contras, split Kafka's life and culminated – as Kafka himself was convinced – in the outbreak of tuberculosis in August, 1917. In the Autumn, 1912, however, it had a very productive influence, resulting in the origin of the first of Kafka's great works: the story "Das Urteil", the first chapter of the novel "Der Verschollene", published posthumously by Max Brod in fragmentary form under the title of "Amerika" and Kafka's longest story, "Die Verwandlung". On the break of 1912 and 1913 also Kafka's first book appeared, "Betrachtung", comprising eighteen shorter prose works. The same publisher published subsequently further Kafka's books, among which the fragment of a novel "Der Verchollene", published under the title "Der Heizer" (1913) brought Kafka the Kleist Prize for 1915 and became Kafka's first work translated into a foreign language. It was translated into Czech with the author's permission by Milena Jesenská and printed by the Czech anarchist poet S. K. Neumann in April, 1920, in his literary review "Kmen".

When the First World War broke out, Kafka had to vacate his flat in his

*Franz Kafka with
his fiancée,
Felicia Bauer.*

parents' house in No. 36, Mikulášská Street, for his sister Elli with her two
children. Kafka rented a room first in No. 10, Bílek Street (at present near the
Intercontinental Hotel), later on – in March 1915 – in No. 18, Dlouhá třída
street (at present No. 16), in the house "At the Golden Pike". In August,
1914, he began writing his most famous novel, ''Der Prozess''. However,
he was not content with his rooms – he was ultrasensitive to noise and the

talks and noises from adjoining flats disturbed him in his literary work. Therefore, in 1916 he stayed and worked for some time in a small house in the Golden Lane in Prague Castle, which was rented from its owner, Mrs Michlová, by Kafka's youngest sister, Ottla. It was there that Kafka wrote in the winter of 1916–1917 in the evenings and at nights a number of shorter prose works and stories, which he published in 1919 in the collection "Ein Landarzt".

In March, 1917, he rented a two room flat in the Schönborn Palace in the Lesser Town, at the foot of the Petřín Hill, in No. 365, Na Tržišti Street (at present the embassy of the USA). There he continued to write further stories, among which the story "Beim Bau der chinesischen Mauer" was obviously inspired by the well-known Prague feature, the Hungry Wall in the Petřín Hill, i.e. in the immediate vicinity of Kafka's flat. In this flat one August night in 1917 Kafka's fatal illness – tuberculosis of the lungs – was heralded by hemoptysis.

While previously Kafka left Prague only sporadically and for short periods, the years of his illness were marked with vain trips for health to the countryside, to hospitals and sanatories – to Siřem to his sisters Ottla, to Želízy near Mělník, where he met the Czech Jewish girl Julie Vohryzková, to the Italian Merano, from where he wrote his first letter to the Czech girl, Milena Jesenská, etc.

During his stay in Müritz at the Baltic Sea coast in July, 1923, Kafka made acquaintance of Dora Dymant, a girl of about twenty from an East Galizian Jewish family, with whom he even lived together in Berlin at the end of September, 1923. At the beginning of March, 1924, however, his state deteriorated so much that he had to be brought to Prague on March 17, 1924. It was his last stay in Prague. On April 10, he was taken to the pulmonary sanatorium Wiener Wald, from there to the University Clinic of Professor Hajek in Vienna and finally, at the end of April, to the sanatorium of Dr. Hoffmann in Kierling, not far from Vienna, where he died on June 3, 1924, nursed to the last moment by Dora Dymant. On June 11, 1924, he was buried in the Jevish cementery in Prague–Strašnice. His parents were buried in the same grave subsequently. On June 19, 1924 a commemorative ceremony took place in the Kleine Bühne in the Senovážné Square in Prague, organized by the then dramaturgist of Prague German municipal theatre, Hans Demetz, with the speeches of Max Brod and Johannes Urzidil.

Numerous Kafka's works have not been preserved. A part of the manuscripts were burned in the author's presence and at his request by Dora Dymant, another part was confiscated by the Gestapo during the search of Dora's flat in Berlin. Thus also an irreplaceable part of Kafka's manuscripts fell victim to the Nazis.

* * *

Kafka's friend **Oskar Baum** (1883–1941) was born in Plzeň, in No.

Franz Kafka with his sister Ottla in Siřem near Žatec.

Oskar Baum (1883–1941).

132/133, in the old town, as the sixth child of a well-to-do draper, Jakob Baum. In Plzeň he also began attending the grammar school. His studies, however, were terminated prematurely; in 1894, during one of the boys' scuffles with nationalist undertones a piece of broken glasses deprived the weak-sighted boy of eyesight completely: Baum was sent to the Viennese institute for the blind, Hohe Warte, where he lived for eight years. After successful piano and organ examinations he left the institute in December, 1902, and went to live in Prague, where he worked at first as organist in the synagogue in the Jerusalem Street and then earned living as a piano teacher. Baum's literary interests had deep roots. His first attempts reached back into his childhood. His first published book was a collection of three stories "Uferdasein" (1908) issued with a preface by Max Brod. Stefan Zweig called it "the most captivating German document of the life without light". Similarly as Baum's next novel, "Das Leben im Dunkeln" (1909), depicting inter alia also the educational system in the Viennese institute for the blind, it was deeply lived and felt picture of the life of the blind, an accurate description of their feelings and observations and enabled the reader an insight into their psychology. The autobigraphic book "Ein Versuch zu leben" (1926) was translated into Czech in the same year and welcomed also by Czech liter-

*Café Arco in Hybernská Street in which not
only political and social, but primarily literary
plans were hatched.*

ary criticism. At that time Baum was a recognized writer of some renown in
Czechoslovakia and worked as music critic in the "Prager Presse" from 1922.
The social novel "Die Schrift, die nicht log" (1931) was awarded the
State Prize of the Czechoslovak Republic intended for German artists in
1932.

Although Baum did not become a Zionist, his relations to the Jewish problem underwent a certain development, a fact testified to by his novels standing at the beginning and at the end of his literary career – "Die böse Un-
schuld" (1913), a genre picture of the life of Jewish families in a small
Czech town, expressing the conviction that all problems can be solved only
by reason, and "Das Volk des harten Schlafs" (1937), attempting, at
the time of the beginning persecution of the Jews by the Nazis, to rouse the
Jewish nation to a militant attitude by showing it a positive historical example.

In 1938 Baum, like all Jewish journalists, lost his job in the "Prager Presse". He was spared of the deportation to Terezín only thanks to his death after an operation on March 1, 1941, in the Prague hospital in No. 521, Kateřinská Street. He was buried on March 4, 1941, in the Jewish cemetery in Prague-Strašnice.

The circle of Max Brod's Prague friends was increased after Kafka's death by **Ludwig Winder** (1889–1946), writer and journalist. His first prose work, a novel from journalist environment, "Die rasende Rotationsmaschine" was published in the spring of 1917. It was also the first Winder's book which aroused some response of literary critics and interest of the reading public. However, it was only the novel "Die jüdische Orgel" (1922), taking place in Jewish environment of a small town and presenting the problem of guilt and penitence in a story of a son of a fanatically religious father, that represented the literary breakthrough of the 33-year-old author. In 1924 he also made his first appearance on the stage as the author of the play "Dr. Guillotin" which was performed in numerous theatres, also in Prague. The novel "Die nachgeholten Freuden" (1927) was the first work written in German attempting to present an epic picture of the post-war reality in Czechoslovakia. The novel "Steffi oder Familie Dörre überwindet die Krise" (1934) published in Czech translation by the Czech writer Helena Malířová (1877–1940) even earlier than the German original in the Kittl's publishing house in Moravská Ostrava (1935) was awarded the State Prize for 1934. Winder's last novel written in Prague, "Der Thronfolger", concerned with Ferdinand d'Este, was banned in Germany and in Austria. It was published in the Humanitas publishing house in **Zürich** in 1938 and in Czech translation by F. Borový's publishing house in Prague in the same year. In his English exile Winder wrote three novels, of which only the novel "Die Pflicht", concerned with the problems of the resistance movement in the Protectorate Bohemia and Moravia and the psychological ways leading to it, found a publisher and was issued with the English title of "One Man's Answer" (1944).

Some of Brod's friends left Prague not under the pressure of Nazi occupation, but far earlier. Among them was also one of the best known German Prague poets, **Franz Werfel** (1890–1945). He was born in Prague, in No. 11, Jezdecká Street (at present Havlíček Street), opposite today's Masaryk railway station, as the first child of a very wealthy Jewish family. The house recalls the fact by a commemorative tablet mounted in September, 1990.

From the autumn, 1900, he attended the German grammar school Na Příkopě, next to the Piarist school, where, too, the majority of pupils were Jews. His marks were not too good and in 1904, having repeated third form, he went to the grammar school in Štěpánská Street, where the number of his fellow students included Willy Haas and Paul Kornfeld. Apart from then the circle of his friends included also the subsequent actor Ernst Deutsch and the subsequent poet Franz Janowitz. The friends read their literary attempts in their circle. Through Willy Haas Werfel made acquaintance of Max Brod

Franz Werfel (1890–1945).

Memorial tablet of Franz Werfel on the house in Havlíček Street.

who presented Werfel's poems in a literary evening in Berlin for the first time to the public in the winter of 1911.

When Werfel passed his final examination in 1909, he went, according to his father's wish, to practice with a shipping firm in Hamburg. However, he did not enjoy the work, worked carelessly and at the end of May, 1911, he returned to Prague. In the autumn he started his one-year voluntary military service in the barracks in the Hradčany. From the spring, 1911, to the autumn, 1912, Werfel spent his last year in Prague and thanks to his first collection "Der Weltfreund" (1911) he became immediately a well-known poet.

In October 1912 he left for Leipzig, where he published further books of poetry "Wir sind" (1913) and "Einander" (1915). His lyrical poems and particularly his dramatic works, in the first place his "magic" trilogy "Spiegelmensch" (1920) made him one of the foremost representatives of the German expressionism.

He was also the first German-writing author to be awarded the Czechoslovak State Prize in February, 1928. At that time he returned more than once in his work to the subjects drawn from the experience of his Prague youth or from Bohemian history. Already the story with a characteristically expressionist title "Nicht der Mörder, der Ermordete ist schuldig" (1919) took place partly in Prague, particularly on the Štvanice island. The experiences of his grammar-school years were transposed into reminiscences in the story "Der Abituriententag" (1928). Also the novel "Barbara oder die Frömmigkeit" (1931) has strong autobiographic elements. Also the lo-

209

Paul Kornfeld (1889–1942), drawing by D. A.   *Willy Haas (1891–1973).*
Delaville.

cale of some episodes of the novel "Der veruntreute Himmel" (1939) is
the environment of Prague.

Similarly as other authors of Jewish origin also Werfel looked with growing fears at the advancing racialism in Germany. In 1938 he emigrated to
France, from where he succeeded in escaping under dramatic circumstances
before the German invasion to the USA, where he settled in California. From
the magnificent success of the novel about the miracle of Lourdes, "Das Li-
ed von Bernadette" (1941) he was generally considered a Catholic and
exposed to attacks on the part of his Jewish fellow-citizens. Unfortunately, he
did not manage to write the planned big Jewish novel with the working title
"Der Zurückgebliebene" or to return to Europe, as he wished. He died of
a repeated coronary thrombosis on August 26, 1945.

Apart from Franz Werfel the German expressionism was influenced also
by another Prague Jewish writer, **Paul Kornfeld** (1889–1942), who won
a front-rank position among the expressionist dramatic writers with his dramas "Die Verführung" (1917) and "Himmel und Hölle" (1919). His
novel "Blanche oder Das Atelier im Garten" was published in 1957,
fifteen years after its author's death in the concentration camp in Lodz in January, 1942. His name, together with the names of all other victims of the holocaust, is engraved on the wall of the Pinkas synagogue in Prague.

✳ ✳ ✳

Similarly as Werfel and Kornfeld also the third fellow student from the Piarist school and grammar school in the Štěpánská Street, **Willy Haas** (1891–1973) left Prague. After the First World War he worked in Berlin and Leipzig, returning to Prague only after the Nazis had seized power in 1933. He lived there until the occupation of Czechoslovakia in 1939, when he emigrated to India. After 1945 he did not come back to Czechoslovakia, returning there only in his memories, in the first place in his book of memoirs "Die literarische Welt" (1958), painting a picture of German literary life before the First World War.

The circle of Haas' friends and collaborators included also **Otto Pick** (1887–1940) with whom Haas published in Prague in 1933–1934 the periodical "Die Welt im Wort". It was to be a continuation of Haas' periodical "Die literarische Welt" the publication of which in Germany was brought to an end by the Nazi régime. Similarly as Haas also Pick came from a German Jewish family, studied in Prague and worked chiefly as dramatic critic in German press. In 1921–1938 he was a columnist of the newspaper "Prager Presse". While Pick's poetic and prosaic works, mainly stories, have been forgotten, he is often appreciated as one of the foremost translators of Czech literature (O. Březina, F. Šrámek, brothers Čapek, J. S. Machar, V. Dyk and others) into German. Representative are also his anthologies: "Tschechische Erzähler" (1920) and "Deutsche Dichter aus der Tschechoslowakei" (1922).

* * *

One of the German Jewish authors who have merged most closely with the Czech atmosphere of Prague, is the reporter and journalist **Egon Erwin Kisch** (1885–1948). He was born as a son of a textile shopkeeper in the house "At Two Golden Bears" in the Old Town of Prague, in No. 475, the corner house of the Kožná and Sirková (at present Melantrichova) Streets. He was a perceptive visitor and an untiring dancer in Prague public houses, beginning with the luxury brothel "U Goldschmiedů" over the cabaret Montmartre to the lowest dives of Prague riff-raff. The collections of his short stories, sketches and reportages "Aus Prager Gassen und Nächten" (1912) and "Prager Kinder" (1913) are witty probes into the life of Prague underworld.

From the strata of the lumpenproletariat Kisch drew also the subject of his only novel "Der Mädchenhirt" (1914) depicting the life of a pimp and taking place in the Prague island of Kampa. The starting point of the story is based on an actual event – the explosion of the boiler of the steamer Franz Joseph I on the Vltava on May 19, 1898. Kisch always knew how to use topical sensations in his literary work. This is testified to also by the reportage on the espionage affair of Colonel Alfred Redl, chief of the espionage department of the Austrian general staff, who committed suicide in the rear wing of the Liechtenstein Palace, No. 13, the Lesser Town Square, on May 19, 1898. From the autumn, 1921, Kisch lived in Berlin, where he was arrested after

the Reichstag fire on February 28, 1933, imprisoned in Spandau and in March, 1933, on the basis of the intervention of Czechoslovak authorities, released as Czechoslovak citizen and "evicted from the Prussian State territory" to Czechoslovakia. He presented his experience with Nazi prison to the public in the form of reportages "Aus den Kasematten von Spandau", published in Prague in the "Arbeiter-Illustrierte-Zeitung" and subsequently in book form. In Prague Kisch joined the antifascist movement and to demonstrate his solidarity with German emigrants he moved to France in the summer of 1933. When he became a real exile after the Nazi occupation of Czechoslovakia, he left for the USA at the end of 1939 and then settled in Mexico.

In March, 1946, he returned to Prague, where he lived in a villa in Střešovice, No. 133 in the street U laboratoře. However, his health was ruined and he died in 1948. After his cremation his ashes were laid to rest in the urn grove of the Prague crematorium in Strašnice.

Kisch' collections of criminalist and memoir reportages and sketches "Prager Pitaval" (1931) and "Marktplatz der Sensation" (1932) have remained very popular among his readers until the present day.

The unity of the Jewish, German and Czech elements was personified in **Rudolf Fuchs** (1890–1942) who endeavoured to mediate the contacts between the Czech and the German cultures by his translations. He devoted much of his time to the translation of Bezruč "Silesian Songs" a selection of which he published with a preface by Franz Werfel in 1917, in the middle of the First World War. In 1937 he published their complete translation together with his essay "Petr Bezruč, Dichter wider Willen". The anthology "Erntekranz aus hundert Jahren tschechischer Dichtung" (1926) contains his translation of the works by Czech poets. For his endeavour to achieve rapprochement between the Czech and the German nations Fuchs was awarded the Czechoslovak Herder Prize in 1937.

Fuchs died in English exile in a traffic accident; his remains were brought to his country and laid to rest in the Jewish cemetery Na Malvazinkách on October 12, 1956.

✱ ✱ ✱

Also **Louis Fürnberg** (1909–1957) did much to mediate between the Czech and the German cultures. He was born in Jihlava and spent his childhood in No. 130 in Rybáře, at present a part of Karlovy Vary, where his father had a factory. In 1927 he began studying a commercial school in Prague. However, he soon left school and worked as a communist journalist. In 1932–1936 he led an agitation and propaganda theatrical group "Echo von Links". When the Nazis occupied Czechoslovakia on March 15, 1939, he was detained, when trying to escape across the Polish border. Nevertheless, in August 1939 he succeeded in emigrating to Palestine via Italy and Yugoslavia. The number of his best known prosaic works includes the "Mozart-Novelle" (1947) related to the first performance of Don Giovanni in Prague in the autumn of 1787.

On his return to Prague in 1946 Fürnberg worked as correspondent of foreign communist press and cooperated with the foreign broadcast department of Prague radio. After the February communist coup d'etat in 1948 he worked at the Ministry of Information and later on at the Czechoslovak Embassy in Berlin. In 1954 he moved to the German Democratic Republic.

Of similar political conviction was also another Prague writer of Jewish descent, **Franz Carl Weiskopf** (1900–1955). In 1937 he published a book of his translations of Czech and Slovak poetry "Das Herz – ein Schild" in the left-wing emigrant publishing house Malik in Prague. In 1937 he was awarded the Czechoslovak Herder Prize.

Also the novels he had written in Prague in the thirties and the forties were oriented on the struggle with fascism. They were "Die Versuchung" (1937) and "Himmelsfahrtskommando" (1944) which takes place in Prague. In 1939 he emigrated to Paris and later on to New York. In his unfinished trilogy "Kinder ihrer Zeit", the most successful of which was the first part, published first in English and after the war also in German as "Abschied von Frieden" (1950), he depicts Prague of the time closely preceding the outbreak of the First World War with much local and period colour. However, he was not interested in the problems of Jewish specificity.

Franz Carl Weiskopf (1900–1955).

Substantially more intensive relation to Judaism was manifested by Jewish authors from Moravia who lived only a part of their lives in Prague – Hermann Ungar and Ernst Weiss.

Hermann Ungar (1893–1929) came to Prague in 1913 to study law at the German University. After graduation in 1918 and a short stay in Cheb (Eger) Ungar worked as a bank clerk in Prague and from 1922 at the Czechoslovak Embassy in Berlin. He visited Prague, the native town of his wife (who was born in Smíchov), only sporadically. In 1923, when he was spending several days in Prague, his second book was published in Berlin, the Prague novel "Die Verstümmelten" giving a suggestive picture of a big city, unconcerned with the fate of the individual, and developing the subject of man's alienation from himself and from the ambient world, so characteristic of Ungar's work.

Ungar's friend **Ernst Weiss** (1882–1940) was a son of a Jewish textile merchant. In 1902 he came to Prague, where he spent one year studying medicine, but continued his studies in Vienna and returned to Prague only intermittently in 1906. He spent a longer period in Prague only after the termination of the First World War. At that time he lived in Prague for two years, working as a surgeon in the General Hospital. He was intensively influenced by the magnetism of Prague, but only for a short time, because in 1921 he left for Berlin. However, his visits to Prague, where his mother lived, were frequent.

From his work it is particularly the novel "Franziska" published in 1916 under its original title "Der Kampf" that is linked with Prague. Another link with Prague is represented by a whole field of Weiss' work, viz. his dramatic attempts. Two of his plays were performed first in Prague: "Tanja", a drama from the Russian revolution, was first performed on October 11, 1919, at the Chamber Theatre of the German Land Theatre in Prague, and the drama "Leonore" was first performed on June 30, 1923, at the German Minor Theatre.

The number of authors who had left Prague after a short stay to live in Germany includes also **Hans Natonek** (1892–1963). He was born in Prague in a relatively well-to-do family. His father was one of the directors of the Triester Lloyd insurance company. Jewish origin did not play any substantial role in the family; the father was a free-thinker and the son belonged to Catholic Jews who were assimilated and integrated into German culture. In 1917 Natonek moved to Leipzig, where he worked as journalist and writer. The strongest relation to Prague is manifested in his novel "Kinder einer Stadt" (1932), the story of four Prague journalists, whose style of living and values collapsed with the collapse of the Austro-Hungarian Empire in 1918 and who are trying to build a new existence on the ruins of this collapsed world. Each of them seeks support in another political or intellectual movement. In spite of that they remain bound together by their Prague origin, being the children of one city.

When the Nazis seized power Natonek, who obtained German citizenship in 1927, was deprived of it again. He also could not publish. Nevertheless, he hesitated to leave Germany, and it was not until May, 1935, that he crossed the boundary in secret and without documents to return to his native Prague. There, having obtained the right of domicile and the Czechoslovak citizenship in 1936, he contributed to a number of German as well as Czech newspapers and periodicals. He also wrote a novel with autobiographic features "Die Strasse des Verrats" (published posthumously in 1981). The immediate threat to Czechoslovakia made Natonek flee again, this time to Paris, from where he emigrated later to the USA.

✳ ✳ ✳

While Max Brod and Willy Haas were the personalities around whom Prague German writers grouped particularly before, but also after the First World War, it was **Hermann Grab** (1903–1949) who, according to Max Brod's assumptions voiced in his book "Der Prager Kreis", should have become such a personality for the youngest generation of Prague German writing poets.

Grab's first short story "Die Kinderfrau" was published in the Prague daily "Prager Tagblatt" in 1934. One year later he published his first book, the novel "Der Stadtpark" (1935). The fate of Hermann Grab, who lived first in Paris (from 1939) and later on in the USA, where he had felt always a foreigner, linked with Europe and Prague, and where he died in 1948 in

New York, as well as the fates of a number of his heroes, are typical in many respects of the fate of one whole stratum of Prague population – the German Jewish patriciate; the fall of the Austro-Hungarian Monarchy tore the firm ground from under its feet and the Nazi occupation of Czechoslovakia meant its definite end.

* * *

The Prague German literature was brought to an end by the destruction of Czechoslovakia by the Munich accord in 1938 and the subsequent annexation of the so-called Protectorate Bohemia and Moravia by the German Reich in March, 1939. Prague German writers, most of them of Jewish descent, fled to exile to the most varied countries all over the world: Palestine (Max Brod, Leo Perutz, Louis Fürnberg), Britain (Ludwig Winder, Otto Pick, Rudolf Fuchs), the USA – often after the previous stay in West European countries (Franz Werfel, F. C. Weiskopf, Hans Natonek, Hermann Grab), Mexico (E. E. Kisch). In France which was a transient station for many, Ernst Weiss found a voluntary death. Many of those who had survived the hardships and sufferings of emigration, did not have enough strength left to return to Europe. And those who did not want or did not manage to leave Prague before the Nazis came perished mostly in the concentration and extermination camps (Oskar Wiener, Emil Faktor, Camill Hoffmann, Paul Kornfeld, Georg Mannheimer).

After the war Prague, swayed by anti-German and anti-Jewish ressentiments, could no longer become a centre of German culture. The last and lonely German poet of Jewish origin, who lived there until 1973, was **Oskar Kosta** (actually Oskar Kohn, 1888–1973). However, an obituary for Prague German literature was written as early as 1945 by Pavel Eisner: "... The Second World War almost liquidated the Jews in our country; and those who were left will no longer be German Jews propagating German culture. Exeunt omnes ... The blood, often so alien to the Czech nation in its cultural and pseudo-cultural manifestations, was purged in the red twilight before its doom to the highest ethos; and the last of their race were hallowed by the peace with those to whom their fathers, blinded by the false sun from elsewhere, could not find way."

GOLEM OR MYTHS AND LEGENDS
OF THE PRAGUE GHETTO

Who would not know the legend about Golem, the artificial man created by miraculous rabbi Loew of Prague?

It is a legend which reflects Man's titanic endeavours to wrench the secret of birth from nature and to create artificially a creature endowed with the semblance of life.

The first mention of Golem, endowed with life by rabbi Loew, appeared long – as many as one hundred years – after the death of his alleged creator. It is, however, an ancient legend which crops up in different variants and forms in many oriental nations. Golems appeared in different places and in different periods in the past. They had different forms, but the same idea: the transformation of dead into living matter and then into an element serving Man.

Let us now acquaint ourselves with one of the many existing forms of the Golem legend – the one which exists in Prague.

According to this tradition Golem came into being on the twentieth day of the month of Adar, i.e. in March of the year 5340 on the Jewish calendar, which corresponds to the year 1580 of our epoch. (The word Golem has its base in Old Hebrew and various meanings are attributed to it. As a rule, however, it was used to mark things or substances without form, creatures without a soul and intelligence.)

Golem was created by rabbi Loew either on the soil of the Old-New Synagogue, or, according to another version, somewhere on the edge of Prague in an undefined brick-field. The rabbi was assisted in creating Golem by his son-in-law and one of his favourite pupils, perhaps by the name of Sosson. From clay the three of them kneaded a human figure of 150 centimetres in height. The birth ritual proper began four hours after midnight and when the clay mass had gained the form of a human figure those present began to leave one by one. This departure meant the beginning of the ritual proper, the coming to life of the mass, the ritual which culminated with the placing of a secret formula under Golem's tongue. Each of the three persons present represented a different element: the rabbi's son-in-law fire, his pupil Sosson water and rabbi Loew himself air. When the first of the rabbi's assistants walked seven times round the clay mass in anticlockwise direction the mass became so heated that it radiated heat like glowing red-hot iron. When the second assistant walked round Golem in the same manner steam forced its way out of the trunk of the figure, the body became moist, nails grew on the fingers and the skin acquired a polish. Rabbi Loew then placed a secret formula of life in the figure, whereupon Golem came to life. (In other versions of the legend no mention is made of a secret formula. Here the quotation by all those present of verses from the seventh chapter of the second book of Genesis served as the life-giving formula.) Golem was then arrayed in garments and given the

*Rabbi Loew and Golem, a drawing by Mikoláš
Aleš, 1899.*

name of Josele, whereupon he left with his creator for the Jewish Town, where he lived and served in rabbi Loew's family. He was good-hearted and a little clumsy, but he willingly did everything that was asked of him. He could do many things, but there was one thing he could not do – speak. He also worked as a servant in the synagogue (shames) with the exception of the Sabbath, when his creator removed the secret formula and thus made him immobile again. Josele lived a quiet life and the only change in its regular rhythm was the alternation of ordinary days and Saturdays, the alternation of life and death.

What was Golem's end?

One Saturday, when the consecration of the Sabbath was approaching, the grand rabbi finished the solemn song, but forgot to remove Golem's secret formula. In an attack of rage and madness Golem began to use his enormous supernatural strength to destroy everything that got in his way. Rabbi Loew arrived from the synagogue just in time to remove the secret formula and thus take away life from him. The soulless mass collapsed on the floor and disintegrated. Golem's remains were allegedly taken to the Old-New Synagogue and it is said that at that time rabbi Loew prohibited access to the loft of the synagogue. This prohibition was ignored by the well-known Prague Jewish writer Egon Erwin Kisch when he decided to set foot on the loft of the synagogue and seek the remains of Golem there. In his reportage "Po stopách Golemových" (In Golem's Footsteps) he describes how, after overcoming great difficulties, he gained permission from the caretaker of the synagogue to climb on to its roof. He writes:

"The foundations of the synagogue are so deep below street level that one is relatively low even here above and through a dormer window in the roof we can see directly in front of us the clock on the small tower of the Jewish Town Hall, whose hands run in the opposite direction. Light comes through several dormer windows here. A bat is hanging upside down on one of the beams. For whole centuries there has been gravel between the deep, convex crests of the vault above the supporting wall. If the clay creature of the great rabbi Loew is buried there it is buried there until judgement day. If it were exhumed, the house of God would collapse."

So much for Kisch's rational reportage. The writer did not find Golem in the loft of the synagogue, but he readily came forward with another version of where it might be possible to discover him.

According to a manuscript which E. E. Kisch found in the Hungarian-Galician village Vola Michova Golem's remains were removed soon after their depositing by the same servant whom rabbi Loew had allowed to assist during the bringing-to-life ritual. The servant removed Golem's remains to the house of his relation Asher Balbier in Cikánská Street in the ghetto where, along with Asher he tried – similarly as rabbi Loew had done – to bring him to life. Their attempt was fruitless. The only thing they are alleged to have achieved was that Golem had his revenge in the form of the death also of Asher's children during the plague which broke out in Prague. The coffins of these children were taken away from Prague along with the last remains of the clay from which Golem had been created. These were buried in March 1592.

This is one of the many versions of the Prague history of Golem.

We do not know exactly when the first legend about Golem was recorded. It was initially handed down by word of mouth and even in those early days it was mostly situated in the environment of the Prague ghetto. The legend may have been imported into Prague and revived as late as in the romantic period. The Prague ghetto was one of the biggest in Europe and in spite of it – or just because of it – it was the constant target of Christian religious fanatics. If to this we add the "alchemistic" atmosphere of the court of Rudolph II and his fondness for mysterious sciences, it can easily be imagined that the ghetto was a suitable background and setting for tales of the nature of the one about an artificial man.

The legend about Golem was recorded and published in print in 1909 in Hebrew in a collection called NIFLAOT-MAHARAL, i.e. the miracles of rabbi Loew. Before that, in 1847, the volume called SIPPURIM had been published for the first time in German in Prague. This title indicates a collection of Jewish popular legends, tales, myths, stories and chronicles. On the basis of previous legends Chaim Bloch compiled a book entitled "Der Prager Golem" which was first published in magazine samples and later in book form in Berlin in 1920. A special effect of the book lay in the atmosphere of fear and uncertainty which reigned in the closely packed little streets of Prague's ghetto for whole centuries. Due to this special Prague atmosphere of the tale it was presumed that the first records of the legend were written directly by the renowned rabbi's son-in-law several years after his death. This was only a guess, however.

Another German-writing writer, Gustav Meyrink, who published a fantastic novel about Golem in 1915, also took the Prague ghetto's legend about Golem as his base. This novel soon gained world fame and the figure of Golem, which had so far lived only in the Prague tradition, became the subject of specialized studies. It was also treated in other works of a belles-lettres nature and it can be presumed that it indirectly marked also the work of Franz Kafka. It even marked the approaching persecution of the Jews during the Second World War.

And so it is not surprising that the Prague Golem was a prefiguration of cybernetics, an artificial human being, i.e. a robot, of the kind seen by the Czech writer Karel Čapek in his book RUR and realized by Norbert Wiener, the founder of cybernetics.

Numerous writers and film producers have devoted their attention to the figure of Golem. In 1914 the Golem theme was also treated by the dramatist Paul Wegener, who also portrayed the figure of Golem in a film. The Golem theme was used in a film for the second time in 1920. Before the Second World War the French director Julian Duvivier gave origin to a French Golem and in Czechoslovakia Golem appeared in Martin Frič's well-known film

Pekařův císař a císařův pekař (The Baker's Emperor and the Emperor's Baker). (The most recent literary treatments of the Golem legend include a work by Nobel Prize winner Elli Weisel.)

$$* \quad * \quad *$$

Mention has already been made of the collection of Jewish legends published for the first time in the German language by the Prague Jewish publisher Wolf Pascheles in 1847 under the title SIPPURIM, "Eine Sammlung jüdischer Volkssagen, Erzählungen, Mythen, Chroniken, Denkwürdigkeiten und Biographien berühmter Juden aller Jahrhunderte, insbesondere des Mittelalters." (A Collection of Jewish Popular Legends, Tales, Myths, Chronicles, Memorables and Biographies of Illustrious Jews of All Centuries, especially the Middle Ages.)

This collection, which contains Jewish legends from the whole world, includes numerous legends and myths of Jewish Prague, legends of Prague's ghetto. These were recorded by the Jewish writers Georg Leopold Weisel, Salamon Kohn, Michael Klapp and others. It is quite understandable that this theme soon found its way also into Czech books. A cycle of legends of the Prague ghetto can be found in the work of Josef Svátek (1835–1897), Alois Jirásek (1851–1930), Adolf Wenig and others. In Egon Erwin Kisch's reportages tales with a Jewish theme also have a historical core.

The greatest number of legends is devoted to rabbi Loew, Mordecai Maisel and, in the first place, Golem. Legends about the Old-New Synagogue, the Old Jewish Cemetery, the Pinkas and the Maisel Synagogue also exist.

Legends About the Miraculous Rabbi Loew.

Many tales concern the relationship between the miraculour rabbi Loew and the Emperor Rudolph II.

... When the Emperor Rudolph II issued a mandate according to which all Jews were to be banished from Prague, the fellow-believers of the rabbi asked him to help them and himself. When he was refused an audience by the emperor he made his way to the Stone Bridge at the time when the emperor's coach was about to cross it. As the coach approached, rabbi Loew placed himself in its way. The assembled people started shouting and tried to drive the audacious rabbi away. They threw stones and mud at him, but instead of these fresh flowers fell on him. At this moment the emperor's coach drove up and the horses themselves came to a halt and stood as though carved out of stone. On observing all this the emperor motioned to the rabbi, who then approached the coach and handed the petition to the sovereign. The unfavourable order concerning the Jews was afterwards revoked.

... On one occasion Rudolph II invited rabbi Loew to visit him at the Castle in order that, through his magic art, he might evoke and humanize the great figures of Jewish primal fathers, the prophets Abraham, Isaac and Ja-

The Old Jewish Cemetery.

cob and his sons. Rabbi Loew promised to meet this request on condition that no one laughed when the figures of the patriarchs appeared.

The figures of the venerable prophets gradually appeared before all those present, including the emperor. Everyone gazed in wonderment at the dignified forefathers of the Jewish nation until Jacob's son Naphtali appeared among them. Contrary to the others, he was small, red-haired and freckled. The king could not refrain from laughing when he set eyes on him. At that moment, however, the ceiling of the room began to drop lower and lower. Not one of those present was capable of moving and everyone sat as though frozen. At the request of the emperor rabbi Loew stopped the ceiling from dropping further through the strength of his will. However, it never returned to its original height. The lowered ceiling still exists in one of the interiors...

... Once Rudolph II visited the rabbi in his in the ghetto. Although the rabbi's house looked old and unattractive, inside one room was more beautiful than another. The banquet which followed in no way lagged behind a royal feast. In order to commemorate the emperor's visit to his house, rabbi Loew had the imperial lion carved next to his own emblem, a cluster of grapes.

... At the time of rabbi Loew a destructive plague broke out in Prague's ghetto which killed only Jewish children. Neither pleas nor prayers saved the situation. When the rabbi fell asleep at night the prophet Elijah appeared to him and, in his dream, accompanied him to the Old Cemetery, where he saw children rise from the dead and run about the cemetery. The following day rabbi Loew ordered his novice to visit the cemetery during the night, tear the shroud off the first child that crossed his path and bring him to his house. The novice accordingly went to the cemetery and on the stroke of midnight he tore the shirt off a white apparition and rapidly took it to the rabbi, who told him to return to the cemetery and wait and see what happened. On the stroke of one hour after midnight the children returned to their little graves except the one lacking a shroud. It could not return to the depths of the earth without it and so it made its way to the rabbi's house with the plea that the novice return its shroud to it. The novice did so, but only on condition that it told him why so many children died. And so it came to light that the cause lay in two sinful mothers who had murdered their new-born babies. The child also betrayed the names of the wicked mothers and then returned to the cemetery to rest in eternal peace. The next day the rabbi convened the council of elders, who placed both mothers and their husbands, who were acquainted with everything, at the mercy of secular justice. The women were sentenced to death and the men to imprisonment. From then on children stopped dying.

How Mordechai Maisel Gained His Wealth

Once when walking through a forest a rabbi by the name of Jitzak came upon a group of sprites with a heap of gold and silver coins. When he asked who the money was for he received a somewhat uncertain reply. After exchanging his three gold coins for three ducats from the treasure he made his way home. There he wrapped a ducat in a piece of cloth and threw it out of the window. Then he waited to see who would pick it up. Towards evening a poorly dressed boy appeared. He picked up the rag with the coin and took it home. The same thing happened the following two days. The rabbi then had it announced that he had lost three gold coins and that he would reward the honest finder who returned them. The poor boy called at the rabbi's house and told him that he had found three gold coins, but that he was returning only two, because he had given the third to his mother, who had a shop with old iron, for purchases. He said he would return the third when his mother had made some money. In reply to the rabbi's question as to why he had picked up the rags with the coins the boy said that in a dream he was told to go to the rabbi's house in the evening and pick up what he found on the ground in front of it. The rabbi was now convinced that the poor boy by the name of Mordecai was the one for whom the treasure from the forest was intended. And so he decided to take the poor boy into his family. Mordecai did not agree with this, because he had a blind father at home whom he had to lead to the synagogue three times a day. It was finally agreed that Mordecai should live in the rabbi's house, but would go to the synagogue with his father during the day. After the elapse of many years Mordecai gained the hand of the rabbi's daughter in marriage. He became independent, established his own iron shop and did well. Moreover, he had a noble heart. He never forgot his humble origin and always helped the poor.

One day Maisel received from a peasant an old, heavy chest, perhaps full of stones, as a guarantee instead of money. The honest Maisel wanted to open the chest and return its contents to the peasant. However, he was unable to open the chest and so it was agreed that the peasant should return to Prague after the harvest and that by then the chest would be opened. If there was something valuable in it, Maisel would return it honestly to the peasant, or purchase the contents.

After the peasant had left, Maisel succeeded in opening the chest, which proved to be full to the top with gold and silver coins. As the peasant had left, Maisel decided to close the chest again and wait until the peasant reappeared after the harvest. A year passed, but the peasant did not appear and so rabbi Jitzak told his son-in-law about the heap of gold and silver he had seen in the forest. He convinced his son-in-law that the treasure inside the chest belonged to him.

Maisel's new wealth did not make him proud. He gave a part of the money he had acquired to the rabbi for the building of a new synagogue, which was named after him and is still known as the Maisel Synagogue.

The Old-New Synagogue

A legend tells us that the Old-New Synagogue was built by angels when the Jews had to migrate from the region after the fall of Jerusalem. The Jews arrived in Prague seventy-two years before the Czechs. They settled on the bank of the River Vltava and wanted to have their own stone synagogue, but because they did not know how to work heavy stones a host of angels appeared on the building site who said that God had ordered them to build the Jews a house of prayer. The synagogue was built without human labour and human activity. For the building of the synagogue the angels also used stones from the temple in Jerusalem on condition that they would be returned to Jerusalem after Solomon's temple had been rebuilt there.

Another version of the legend about the Old-New Synagogue has it that it was brought here directly from Jerusalem by angels. Once again a condition was laid down – this time that the Jews were not to change or repair anything on this synagogue, which, after the one in Jerusalem, was one of the oldest in the world. If in the course of the passing centuries something had to be repaired or built-on to the synagogue, the builder was always punished by misfortune or even death. For this reason the synagogue remained unchanged for long centuries.

The legend that the synagogue was built by angels is supported by another version which tells of the great fire which affected the whole ghetto in 1558. It spread with unprecedented force and at a high speed until it reached the

The Old-New Synagogue.

Old-New Synagogue. When it seemed that nothing could save the building God heard the pleas of the believers and sent down two white doves which sat on the crest of the roof and waved their wings until they turned back the flames and thus saved the synagogue. The doves were considered to be two of the angels who had originally built the synagogue. The real events formed the base of a legend which tells us why not even the appearance of the interior of the house of prayer was to be changed. This order was laid down in order to commemorate two big pogroms. In 1096, when the Crusaders passed through Prague, and in 1389, when the walls of the Old-New Synagogue were splashed with the blood of innocent victims. It was allegedly forbidden to whitewash the blood stains so that they might remain on the walls for all time.

The Pinkas Synagogue

An exceptionally poor and just Jew by the name of Pinkas, who earned a living by buying and selling old clothes, lived in Prague. His business failed to thrive and when his strength had almost run out a rich count afforded him assistance. However, Pinkas always thanked the Lord only for this help. This greatly annoyed the count and so one day he said: "My dear Pinkas, I have no money left, but you continuously thank the Lord for the help you receive, so turn to Him now, perhaps He will help you".

Pinkas returned home without any money and his wife and children had nothing to eat. When Pinkas was meditating on his fate in a small chamber, a dead monkey suddenly fell into it. In those days the families of wealthier citizens kept such monkeys. When Pinkas decided to burn the monkey in the stove, a gold ducat fell out of its mouth. A closer inspection showed that the body of the monkey was full of gold ducats. And so Pinkas's family was rid of all its worries and celebrated the sabbath as the wealthiest in the ghetto. In the middle of the celebrations Pinkas's former benefactor – the count – came to visit him. He was amazed when he saw the rich feast on the table and heard the story of the dead monkey. He told the surprised Jew that the monkey was his property and that it had escaped a few days previously. The honest Pinkas returned all the ducats to the count with the exception of those he had spent to celebrate the sabbath. The count refused to accept the ducats and explained how they had probably got into the monkey's stomach. He was testing the genuineness of the coins between his teeth and the monkey, who had been watching him, thought he was swallowing the money and, in an unguarded moment, imitated the count and swallowed some ducats.

From then on Pinkas did very well. He grew rich, but in spite of it he always remained a modest and God-fearing citizen. He was elected to the post of primate of the religious community and had new houses built for the poor in the street which later bore his name, similarly as the synagogue which he had built.

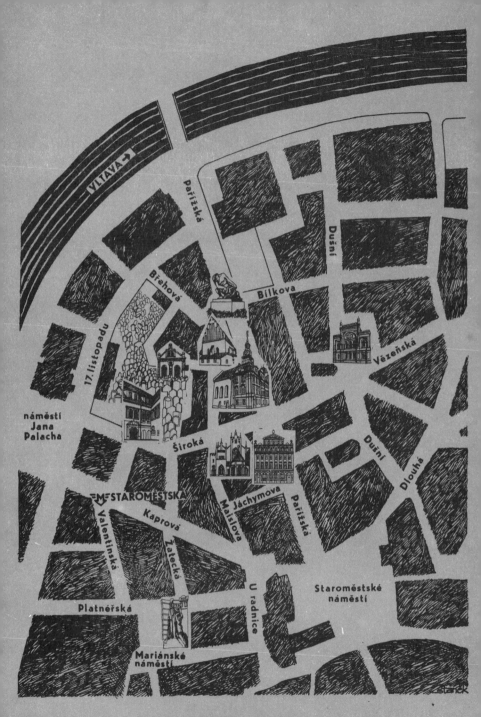

Plan of the Jewish Town of Prague (Dipl. ing. J. Staněk)

GUIDES
TO THE
MONUMENTS
OF THE JEWISH
TOWN
IN PRAGUE

THE JEWISH MUSEUM
IN PRAGUE

The Jewish Museum in Prague was founded in 1906 as the third of the big associated Jewish museums in Central Europe (Vienna 1895, Frankfurt 1897). The direct cause of its origin lay in the reconstruction of Prague's Jewish Town which began in 1895 after the slum clearance activity realized in the locality. The endeavour to found the museum culminated in May 1906 when the question of the salvation of monuments from the rich furnishings of the Hand and the Grand Court Synagogues, then intended for demolition, was negotiated.

The most important task was fulfilled during the institution of the musem society by Dr. Salomon Hugo Lieben (1881–1942), who had just completed his studies at Prague University and had already published his first work on the cultural history of Prague's Jews. Markus Brücker,

who secured most of the organizational tasks connected with the agenda of the museum, was his friend, Lieben's self-sacrificing assistant. Another fellow-worker of Dr. Lieben was Dr. Augustin Stein, a lawyer and town councillor. He was a well-known representative of the then contemporary Czech-Jewish movement and later also president of the Jewish religious community in Prague. The first president of the museum society was Dr. Adolf Hahn, a lawyer and a member of the presidium of the Grand Court Synagogue.

The statutes of the "Society for the Founding and Maintenance of the Jewish Museum in Prague" were approved by the provincial governor on 29 August, 1906 and published in print in Czech and German versions. The affairs of the society were handled by a twelve-member curatorium, which administered the society's property, drew up the annual budget, one of the tasks of the society, and submitted a report on their activity to the general assembly once a year. The financial means of the society were gained from membership fees, gifts and occasional gains from lecture and publishing activity. In 1906 the museum society had, apart from its founding, endowment and honorary members, 31 ordinary members, this number rising to 79 in 1907 and to 110 in 1908. In 1910 the number of ordinary members of the society was 254 and it can be presumed that this number grew also in

The Jewish Museum in Jáchymova Street is primarily a scientific centre. Collection of old Judaica.

the following years.

The programme of the museum formed an important part of the statutes. The society had to accumulate, preserve and exhibit articles of the synagogal and home cults, especially works of an artistic character, and archive materials, manuscripts and prints concerning Jewish history and literature and to secure pictures of Jewish monuments, personalities and articles. The three mentioned basic kinds of collections manifested well-balanced proportions even after thirty-five years of existence of the museum. Of the total number of 1,101 articles, the museum collection as a whole contained 453 cult arti-

cles, 339 archive materials, manuscripts and prints and 309 paintings, engravings and photographs, However, the most interesting part of the collecting programme of the museum is the territorial demarcation of its collecting regions into Prague, Bohemia and the historical countries of the Czech kingdom. This regional orientation was, in the framework of Jewish museum activity, specifically formulated in this way for the first time in general in the course of the origin of the Prague museum. S. H. Lieben himself saw the specific character and importance proper of the Jewish Museum in Prague in it, for it ensured that its collection was of a compact nature and historical significance.

As reconstruction work was being carried out in the centre of the Jewish Town at the time when the museum was founded, it had, for the time being, to be satisfied with the provisionary depositing of its collections in house No. 5 in Benediktská Street in a peripheral part of the Old Town. The installation of the collections in two rooms on the first floor of this house took place in 1907 to 1908 and in the middle of 1909 this, the first exposition of the museum was made accessible to the public.

The museum gained a new location for its exposition in rooms on the first floor of the new building of the Burial Society bearing No. 37 in Josefovská Street (now No. 7 Široká Street), completed by the architect B. Hypšmann in 1911 as one of the most modernly designed of the new buildings. Its position on a crossroad near the entrance to the centre of the Jewish Town was very convenient for the location of the exposition. Negotiations concerning the setting-up of the new interiors took place from the end of 1911, the date of the solemn opening of the new exposition of the museum being Sunday 28 April, 1912. Most of Prague's newspapers carried a report on the event. The hall of the museum was conceived as a small lapidarium. In a big interior an attempt was made to reconstruct the interior of a synagogue with monuments of synagogal art. Three smaller rooms formed what could be called the treasury of the museum because silver articles and manuscripts were installed in them. The new exposition, whose opening meant the successful culmination of all the activity of the museum society up to that time, was open free of charge to the public every Saturday and Sunday.

The early 20th century was marked by new and important activity on the part of the Jewish Museum. In 1923 the increased number of visitors necessitated lengthening of the visiting hours (from 9 to 18 hours every day except Saturday) and the introduction of an entrance fee of 2 crowns per person. The growth in the number of visitors to the museum is also witnessed by S. H. Lieben's guide to the exposition printed in Czech and German in 1924. Its constant endeavours to expand the exposition of the museum resulted in the society gaining the lease of the building of the no longer used hall of ceremonies of the Burial Society in Prague (building No. 243 in the street U starého hřbitova) for the purpose. This unsual building, erected in Neo-Romanesque style in the years 1906 to 1908 by the architect Gerstl, was suitable for the purposes of the museum due in particular to its situation near the entrance to the Old Jewish Cemetery, the most frequented monument of the former Jewish Town. The solemn opening of the new exposition in the hall of ceremonies took place on 9 May, 1926. The conception of the exposition was based on the previous successful installation in Josefovská Street. The Aron ha-Kodesh and the grille of the almemor from the Cikán Synagogue and monuments of synagogal art were installed in the main exhibition hall and a smaller room on the first floor. The lapidarium

The library of the Jewish Museum.

was installed on the ground-floor, while the neighbouring room contained the treasury of the museum.

The advantageous position of the new exposition was immediately reflected in a growth of the number of visitors to the museum. In 1928 it was visited by nearly 11,000 persons and in 1929 by at least 13,233 paying visitors. The gains from the entrance fees soon formed the most important item in the budget of the museum. At that time financial support was regularly afforded the museum by the Supreme Council of the Jewish Religious Communities in the Czechoslovak Republic, the Jewish Religious Community in Prague, the town council of Prague and other Jewish Religious Communities, lodges of the B'nai B'rith in Prague and other towns and numerous societies and private firms. In 1928 the number of members of the museum society reached 316 in spite of the considerably increased membership fees. In the twenties the Prague museum established cooperation with the Jewish museums in Vienna, Berlin, Wroclaw, Munich, Mainz and Kassel as well as with a number of other societies, institutions and specialized journals and also lent its collections for display at various exhibition events.

In the thirties the position of

Prague's Jewish Museum began slowly but continuously to worsen as a consequence of the economic crisis and specially of the changing political situation in neighbouring countries. The changed situation was reflected to the greatest extent in the restriction of tourism and the marked decrease in the number of visitors. Later a gradual decrease of subsidies and finally also of gains from membership fees came about.

After the conclusion of the Munich agreement in September 1938 and in the tense atmosphere of the Second Republic the Jewish Museum experienced another period of increased interest on the part of Jewish and non-Jewish visitors. After the occupation of the Czech Lands by the Nazi army on 15 March, 1939, however, its wider activity was actually made impossible and the number of visitors to its exposition dropped to the minimum. According to the statutes of the society the museum collections were to fall under the administration of the Jewish Religious Community if the society was dissolved and this undoubtedly happened in connection with the forced centralization of all the organs of the former Jewish autonomy in the years 1940 to 1941. The last entry in the museum's Visitors' Book is dated 24 November, 1941 and it is the last testimony to its activity. On the same day the first deportation transport left for the Terezín concentration camp.

The rapidly continuing deportation of Jewish citizens from the Protectorate of Bohemia and Moravia to concentration camps from the end of 1941 gave rise to the question of what to do with the property of abolished rural communities. Already in November 1941 the so-called "Treuhandstelle", an organization concerned with the liquidation of confiscated Jewish property, was formed in Prague. Representatives of the rural and monument department of the Jewish Religious Community in Prague now hastily sought a possibility of saving Jewish cultural monuments and therefore drafted, along with museum specialists invited for the purpose, a proposal concerning the setting up of a museum where historical and art monuments from the old Prague museum and cleared synagogues as well as from all the Jewish Religious Communities in Bohemia and Moravia and partly also articles from privately owned property would be concentrated. They regarded this solution as the last possibility of saving the whole cultural heritage of the one millennium of life of the Jews in the Czech Lands from forced removal and extinction. This had already happened in neighbouring countries which had fallen under the rule of the Nazis. At the same time they held the hope that after the war these monuments would be returned to their original owners and put to their original use again.

After lengthy negotiations concerning the proposals for the founding of a museum with the supreme Nazi organ for "the final solution of the Jewish problem" (Endlösung der Judenfrage) in the Protectorate (Zentralstelle für Jüdische Auswanderung) and after coming forward with numerous comments and suggestions the Nazis finally agreed to the founding of the Central Jewish Museum (Jüdisches Zentralmuseum) in Prague, led, of course, by entirely different motives than those of its creators. In the concentrating of Jewish cultural monuments the Nazis saw not only an easy way of becoming rich, but also a later possibility of misusing them for anti-Jewish propaganda, which was the main supporting element of Nazi ideology, or perhaps as a means of pressure in the course of negotiations with the allies.

Specialists who had been present at the origin of all three Jewish museums in pre-war Czechoslovakia participated in the projecting and activity of the museum; their number including in particular Dr. Josef Polák, former director of the museum in Košice in Slovakia and initiator of the founding of the Slovak Jewish Museum at Prešov, followed by Professor Dr. Alfred Engel, one of the creators of the Jewish Museum at Mikulov in Moravia and, until his death on 10 November, 1942, also Professor Dr. Salomon Hugo Lieben. This team was headed by the librarian of Prague's Jewish Religious Community, Professor Dr. Tobiáš Jakobovits. The Prague avant-garde architect František Zelenka helped to create the expositions and from the spring of 1943 the art historian Dr. Hana Volavková worked at the museum. The writer Dr. Jiří Weil and others also worked there. Apart from specialists, over forty persons were employed in the administrative department, the workshops and the storerooms in certain periods, but their number and composition constantly changed as a consequence of the unceasing deportation of Jews. In the course of two years the em-ployees of the museum created a work, remarkable for both its size and quality, which in normal conditions would have taken long decades to originate. And they did this in unimaginably difficult work and psychological conditions, under the constant threat of deportation or arrest and continual controls by the SS and in maximum work tension.

The Central Jewish Museum began to operate to the full extent on 3 August, 1942. In that period country communities were sent a detailed list of all types of articles along with instructions concerning their securing, recording and dispatch. All the museum documents bear witness to an endeavour to ensure the broadest and the most complete documentation of all monuments of Jewish culture. Later, in connection with the deportation transports, consignments of selected articles began to arrive in Prague in a continuously quicker sequence from all 153 pre-war Jewish communities in Bohemia and Moravia. Over 200,000 articles, books and archive materials, recorded on 101,090 catalogue cards, passed through the hands of the employees of the museum. Apart from this activity, which was extremely time-consuming, the workers of the museum were ordered to create clear, but closed expositions of selected articles in several cleared synagogues. These were intended solely for visitors from the ranks of the bosses and ideologists of the Nazi party.

Although the creators of the war expositions had to meet the requirements of the Nazis in fulfilling their task, they succeeded in creating a work whose modern conception

One of the expositions of the Jewish Museum – The Silver of Bohemian Synagogues.

won recognition also after the war. Started first of all was work on the installation of an exposition of Hebrew manuscripts and prints in the High Synagogue, prepared by Dr. T. Jakobovits. The interior of the Old-New Synagogue was supplemented with several items from its furnishings and Dr. J. Polák installed an exhibition depicting the development of this outstanding monument of medieval synagogal architecture in the vestibule and side aisles. The biggest exposition on the theme of Jewish holidays and rites was realized in 1943 under the supervision of Dr. Jakobovits, Dr. Polák, Dr. Volavková and architect Zelenka in the Klausen Synagogue. This exposition, intended to portray the historical development of the Jewish population in the Czech Lands throughout the millennium of its existence, was originally meant to be installed in the Pinkas Synagogue, but due to the essential increase of the number of architectural modifications of the building this idea was not realized. Instead the Zentralstelle expressed the requirement that a Museum of the Prague Ghetto be hastily installed in the building of the old museum. Intensive work on this project was carried out by Josef Polák and Hana Volavková in the first half of 1944. In the summer and autumn of 1944 most of the leading workers of the museum were deported and work within its walls was limited to completion of the expositions and the cataloguing of the collections. The final wave of deportation of employees of the museum in February 1945 wholly paralysed its further activity. After the war the Prague Jewish Museum renewed its activity already on 13 May, 1945 under the administration of the Council of the Jewish Religious Community in the Czechoslovak Republic. Dr. Hana Volavková, one of the few specialized workers of the war-time museum to survive deportation, was entrusted with the running of the museum. The first task of the post-war period was to secure all the monuments of the war-time museum as well as the numerous scattered war-time deposits of books and archive materials. Depositories of textile, silver and paintings were set up in the newly gained building in Josefovská Street, while the most important collections of books and archive materials were concentrated at the seat of the war-time museum in Jáchymova Street, where a reading-room with a study was established. Apart from the department of collections of synagogal art, the archives and the library, a department concerned with documentation of the war-time persecution of the Jews and a monument department were newly founded. Up to the end of 1949 loans of cult articles and prayer books were made to meet the needs of fifty-two renewed Jewish Religious Communities and articles from private property were restored to their rightful owners.

An important task in the first post-war year was also the reinstallation of the war-time expositions in the Klausen Synagogue and the Museum of the Prague Ghetto, which were solemnly opened in the precence of important representatives of public and cultural life and foreign guests (E. E. Kisch, M. Brod) already on 26 June, 1946. In the post-war years Hana Volavková organized short-term exhibitions of the wartime work of Otto Ungar (1946) and Karel Fleischmann (1947) as well as the exhibitions Old Prague in Paintings, Graphic Sheets and Models (1947) and From the Collection of Jewish Portraits (1948) in the exhibition hall on the groundfloor of the building in Josefovská Street. In the framework of the area of the Jewish Museum the museum also secured a tour of inspection of the Old Jewish Cemetery and the Old-New Synagogue, for whose maintenance it was also responsible. In the years 1946 to 1949 the expositions and exhibitions of the Jewish Museum were visited by approximately 200,000 persons.

In November 1949 the size of the museum collections, the need of securing their safety and specialized care and the conviction of the employees of the museum that its collections should be preserved as an indivisible whole forming a unique base for study of the history and culture of the Jewish population of Bohemia and Moravia led to the adoption by the Council of the Jewish Religious Community in the Czechoslovak Republic of a resolution according to which the museum was to be placed in the care of the state. In connection with the nationalization process restitution activity was completed and the Council of the Jewish Religious Community took over hitherto borrowed and newly classified cult articles and book funds as its own property. On the basis of a decree of the government of 4 April, 1950 the Jewish Museum was renamed the State Jewish Museum and

Dr. Hana Volavková was made its first director. The museum thus became a specialized institution on a national basis and a scientific institute with the task of systematically treating the history of Jews in Czechoslovakia throughout the whole millennium of their existence here.

Apart from the Klausen Synagogue and the Museum of the Prague Ghetto, the Council of the Jewish Religious Community also placed the High and the Pinkas Synagogues under the administration of the museum. Archeological research and reconstruction works were started in the Pinkas Synagogue already in August 1950 with the cooperation of the State Institute for the Care of Monuments. These were completed in 1954. On the basis of artistic designs created by the academic painters Jiří John and Václav Boštík the Monument to 77,297 Victims of the Nazi Racial Genocide of Jews in the Czech Lands was installed in the renewed interior of the Gothic synagogue for which a project of expositions depicting the development of Jewish communities in Bohemia and Moravia throughout their one millennium of history were prepared at the war-time museum. Dr. Volavková, who was present at the origin of the conception of this monument, wrote the following about it: "The alphabetically and topographically arranged names have lost the character of a document. Every family newly appears here as a whole and every solitary person has remained alone here. Degraded to numbers and transports during the war, they have found a new home and a human face. They are liberated by modest,

From the rich collections of the Jewish Museum: painted glass jug, Prague 1784.

piously written script, almost medievally by an anonymous art."

In the latter half on the fifties the Maisel and the Spanish Synagogue were placed under the administration of the museum. Until 1960 they were converted into depositories and expositions of synagogal textile and silver. The year 1958 also saw the adaptation of the synagogue in Michle, where over 2,000 Torah rolls were located. Of the short-term exhibitions held in this period let us mention, for example, the one documenting the Nazi racial persecution of Jews in the Small Fortress at Terezín during the occupation (1950), the exhibition of children's drawings from the Terezín concentration camp in the High Synagogue (1956) and in Paris (1957), repeated many times since then in various places at home and abroad, the Terezín Ghetto 1942–1945 exhibition of the war-time work of the painters Fritta, Karel Fleischmann, Leo Haas, František Nágl, Otta Ungar and Malvina Schalková in the Maisel Synagogue (1958) and the exhibition depicting the life and work of the Czecho-Jewish writer Vojtěch Rakous in the High Synagogue (1959). In the fifties and sixties the museum carried out very important acquisition activity in the sphere of further supplementation of the archives and collections of the war-time persecution department and in continuation of the all-round documentation of immovable monuments of rural Jewish communities. As regards the publishing activity of the museum, mention can be made of the new editions of the Guide to the Old Jewish Cemetery (1957, 1960) and to the exposition organized in the Klausen Synagogue

(1956), of the newly arranged catalogue of the exposition of the Museum of the Prague Ghetto (1957) and also of the two revised popular editions of the books Židovské město pražské (The Jewish Town of Prague) (1959) and Zmizelé pražské ghetto (The Vanished Prague Ghetto) (1961). Apart from the well-known bibliography of Jewish Prague (1952) and Otta Muneles's Starý židovský hřbitov (The Old Jewish Cemetery) (1955), a work by Hana Volavková entitled Pinkasova škola – památnik minulosti a našich dnů (The Pinkas School – A Monument of the Past and Our Days) (1954), acquainting readers with the results of the archaeological research and reconstruction of this building on a wider cultural and historical basis, was published in a separate edition of the State Jewish Museum called Židovské památky v Čechách a na Moravě (Jewish Monuments in Bohemia and Moravia). In 1959 Hana Volavková also prepared, along with the writer Jiří Weil, the first edition of the book called Dětské kresby na zastávce k smrti, Terezín 1942–1944 (Children's Drawings at the Halt to Death, Terezín 1942–1944), which since then has been published in unchanged form in numerous foreign-language editions.

The uniqueness of Prague Jewish Museum lies in the fact that since the time of its foundation it has been oriented exclusively regionally to the acquisition of monuments from Prague and the Czech Lands. A select collection of articles of all kinds which originated or were used throughout whole centuries in Czech or Moravian communities was also successfully accumulated at the pre-war museum. During the war this collection was enlarged many times through the collection of synagogal monuments from the 153 pre-war Jewish religious communities. Not only the most significant synagogal monuments of these communities, but also their archives, libraries and partly also documentation of immovable monuments were accumulated at the museum with the result that the historical picture of their life was transferred here practically in its whole entirety. Thanks to dedication inscriptions, their place and time of origin and the names of those who ordered them and in some cases also of their manufacturers can be determined. And thus these collections now not only form a rich base for the building-up of representative art-historical and ethnographical groups, but should also be treated above all as a document of the historical, demographic and economic development of the individual Jewish Religious Communities throughout the period of their existence. Just this character and the circumstances of the origin of the collections of Prague's Jewish Museum make them a real monument of all the victims of the holocaust and the destroyed Jewish Religious Communities in Bohemia and Moravia.

▶

From the collections of the Jewish Museum: an illustration from the manuscript of the Pesach Haggadah of 1728.

אֶחָד חָכָם · וְאֶחָד רָשָׁע · וְאֶחָד
תָּם · וְאֶחָד שֶׁאֵינוֹ יוֹדֵעַ לִשְׁאֹל
חָכָם מַה הוּא אוֹמֵר מָה הָעֵדֹת
וְהַחֻקִּים וְהַמִּשְׁפָּטִים אֲשֶׁר
צִוָּה יְיָ אֱלֹהֵינוּ אֶתְכֶם · וְאַף אַתָּה אֱמוֹר לוֹ

צוּרַת אַרְבָּעָה בָּנִים דִּבְּרָה תוֹרָה ::

From the collections of the Jewish Museum: an illustration from a liturgical manuscript (1728).

From the collections of the Jewish Museum: an illustration from a liturgical manuscript (1813).

THE SYNAGOGUES OF
THE JEWISH TOWN

The Old-New (Staronová) Synagogue, Červená Street

This synagogue is one of Prague's oldest Gothic monuments, the spiritual centre of the city's Jewish community, and it ranks among the oldest preserved synagogues in Europe. In spite of all slum clearance activities, the locality still has its medieval atmosphere. The synagogue stands on its original site, a few metres below the level of the other streets of the Old Town, in the street called Řeznická of the 17th century at the latest. The small square into which this street ran was called Dřevný plácek (Wood Place). In the 18th century the name Řeznický plácek (Butchers' Place) was given to the square. Butchers' shops once stood here, as the name of the square implied. These were painted red and this gave rise to the present name of former

Řeznická Street – Červená (Red) Street.

The origin of the synagogue, characterized also externally by a special, austere appearance, dates approximately in the years 1270 to 1280 and its construction was most likely connected with a privilege granted to Prague's Jewry by Přemysl Otakar II in 1254. This spa-

The obverse and reverse of a medal minted by the Jewish Religious Community in Prague to commemorate of the 700th anniversary of the foundation of the Old-New Synagogue (1290–1990).

244

tial layout has a long-standing tradition in the sphere of synagogal architecture. It was used already in the Romanesque period in the case of the building of the synagogue at Worms (late 12th century) and somewhat later also in the case of a similar house of prayer at Regensburg. Certain similar building elements make it impossible to exclude the fact that the Cistercian building workshop which participated in the construction of the South Bohemian monasteries at Zlatá Koruna and Vyšší Brod may have helped to build the synagogue. This is only a conjecture at present, evoked by a similarity manifested particularly in the leaf decoration of the capitals, consoles and tympana. It can perhaps also be presumed that the same royal stone mason workshop which at that time realized several buildings in the vicinity of St. Agnes's Convent "Na Františku" worked on the building.

A flight of steps leads to the vestibule, which is a low, longitudinal room adjoining the main double nave on the south. It is covered by a broken barrel vault, divided up by massive bands of vaults. In the 17th century two boxes were built-in here for the use of the tax collector. Entrance is gained to the main nave of the synagogue through a portal whose tympanum is covered with

*The Old-New Synagogue
– interior with the
historical banner.*

a relief of vine leaves and clusters of grapes growing on the spirally twisted branches of a tree. This form of decoration may perhaps symbolize the twelve tribes of Israel as the branches of one single vine bush.

The house of prayer proper is, surprisingly, relatively big and provides adequate space for the main component – the speaker's tribune (almemor). This rectangular interior is divided by two octagonal pillars into two naves. This type was usual in an interior of a semi-secular character, for example, in chapter halls, refectories, etc. of that period. It was therefore also suitable for a synagogue, which in the Middle Ages served not only for prayers and

teaching, but also for the handling of the legal matters of the community. The interior of a synagogue often had the character of a public place of assembly. It was frequently the office of the chief rabbi and sometimes also his school. A strongly profiled cornice runs round the walls of the Old-New Synagogue. Along with consoles and supports round the periphery of the interior massive pillars bear a five-part vault with ribs of a grooved profile. This vault was designed in such a way that the fifth rib was always inserted in the cross rib vault in the direction of the peripheral wall.

Standing in the centre of the house of prayer, surrounded by a Gothic grille of the 15th century, is the speaker's tribune (bimah, almemor) with a stand for the reading of the Torah. The rabbi also spoke from this place.

The high standard is an interesting monument. Its faded red cloth bears the following text: "Deputies of the Lord, the whole land is full of His glory. In 1357 the Emperor Charles IV granted the Jews of Prague the privilege of carrying a banner. This banner was repaired during the reign of the Emperor Ferdinand. Damaged in the course of long years, it has now been repaired in honour of our lord the Emperor Charles VI. Praise be to His Majesty on the occasion of the birth of his son, the Archduke Leopold. May His glory be raised to happiness. In the year of Tikon may His Empire be very strong. Year 1716".

This is the historical banner of Prague's Jewish community. It was one of the privileges of the Jewish Town and, as the inscription on it tells us, the Jews received it from Charles IV. The banner bears the star of David and pictured in its centre is a pointed Jewish hat, one of the traditional items of clothing of Prague's Jews. In certain periods Jews were not allowed to leave the ghetto without this mark of their religion.

The receptacle for the Torah (Aron ha-Kodesh), the holiest place in the synagogue, walled-in in the eastern wall, fulfils a religious mission. This receptable has a special architectural form consisting of two Renaissance columns on fluted consoles of the 16th century. Of the greatest artistic value is the tympanum of the tabernacle, set with crabs and culminating with a bunch of flowers. The surfaces of the tympanum are filled with vine leaves and clusters of grapes.

Pews are placed round the almemor and the walls. Their location and order played a great role in the life of the community. The seats in the synagogue were bought and inherited by one generation from another. One of them deserves special attention. It bears the number 1 and it is situated on the right of the almemor. It differs from the others due to the fact that the star of David is located on the wall above it. It is alleged that the legendary rabbi Loew sat here.

The main nave was reserved for men. Not until the end of the 17th to the 18th century was a side corridor added for women from where they could observe the services and rites through small windows only. This limitation applied only in the case of orthodox rites, when women were allowed to enter the synagogue only on the occasion of a wedding.

The interesting features of the Old-New Synagogue include the small window situated between two bigger windows in the frontal wall. This orifice is oriented in eastern direction and it makes it possible to observe the first signs of daybreak, which signals the beginning of a new day and thus also the time for morning prayer.

The Old-New Synagogue was a massive bulding of stone. Contrary to all the other buildings in the ghetto, it survived all the medieval catastrophes and pogroms and resisted destructive fires.

*The Old-New Synagogue
– the rib vault.*

A number of rabbis (Elija ben Jitzhak, Jitzhak Margalita, Abraham ben Avigdor, Jitzhak Meling) worked at the synagogue before the most illustrious rabbi of the 16th century, Yehuda ben Bezalel (Maharal mi Prag). After rabbi Loew his pupil Yom Tov Lipmann Heller worked here and after him the illustrious Jonathan Eybenschütz, Ezechiel Landau and Solomon Juda Rapoport, one of the founders of the science of the Jewish faith.

In 1883 the synagogue underwent substantional repairs, supervised by the architect Josef Mocker, who reconstructed other monuments in Prague in the same period. It was subjected to further restorations in the years 1921 to 1926 and 1966 to 1967.

The Old-New Synagogue is one of the most frequented historical monuments in Prague. It still serves as a house of prayer of Prague's Jewish community, but apart from Saturdays and Jewish holidays it is open to the public.

The Old-New Synagogue – the Torah scroll receptacle (Aron-ha-kodesh) in the centre of the east wall.

The High (Vysoká) Synagogue, Červená Street

This synagogue is also called the Town Hall Synagogue and it belongs to the circle of Renaissance buildings of the Jewish Town, founded along with the Jewish Town Hall by its patron, the primate of the community, Mordecai Maisel. The present entrance to the building is situated opposite the entrance to the Old-New Synagogue and the whole synagogue adjoins the Jewish Town Hall, with which it forms one whole. Originally access was gained to the synagogue directly from the first floor of the Town Hall.

The two buildings, the Town Hall and the synagogue, feature the same building elements at least in their initial, basic characteristics and their origin is dated approximately in 1568. The original façade of the Town Hall was even simpler, without any form of decoration, similarly as the later façade of the synagogue.

The High Synagogue fulfilled the function of the house of prayer of the Town Hall. At first it was intended for the chief representatives of the community and perhaps also for sessions of the rabbi's court.

The architect concerned was Pankratius Roder, a man of Italian or South Tyrolean origin, who was assisted by the Czech master mason by the name of Rada.

The front part of the High Synagogue has two interiors on the ground-floor: a corridor with a cross vault with two fields and the main space with a barrel vault with lunettes. (The original Renaissance vaults have also been preserved in three rooms lying in the north-west corner of the Town Hall, mostly barrel-vaulted with lunettes.

The same architectural conception of the two buildings can also be observed in their halls which are both built in one plane on a square ground-plan.

The most important part of the Renaissance building period is the central space of the High Synagogue on its first floor. It is lit on the northern side by three windows and originally also by two windows on the eastern side. A receptacle for the Torah is situated between them. This was formerly marked on the façade by means of a Renaissance gable on consoles.

The eastern façade of the High Synagogue terminated with a high, horizontally articulated gable.

Similarly as in the case of other

Renaissance interiors, excessive attention was also devoted here to the stucco decoration of the ceiling and the rich and complicated vaulting of the main hall. The vault and the whole hall of the synagogue prove that even church buildings can be lent a wholly secular character. At the same time, however, the vault is one of the most important examples of the Renaissance combination of surviving Gothic elements with endeavours to create an ideal interior. The work of Czech master masons manifested itself here. In decorating the vault they modelled a rich ornament from the ribs with turned scrolls and rosettes and an eight-pointed star in the centre.

In 1689 the synagogue was damaged by fire. It is most likely that the building serving as the women's gallery was built-on to the southern side during its repair. A new receptacle for the Torah was built at the same time. During the repair of the High Synagogue, supervised by the architect Pavel Ignác Bayer and completed in 1693, a new entrance was built on the ground-floor.

After the return of the Jews after their banishment by Maria Theresa and after the fire of 1754 it was merely necessary to repair the burnt-out trusses of the roof.

Langweil's model of Prague affords us a picture of the then contemporary appearance of the High Synagogue, especially of its eastern façade before it was walled-up in the slum clearance period.

In 1883 the reconstruction of the

124   *The interior of the High Synagogue – the exhibition hall of the Jewish Museum.*

*The High Synagogue –
the Torah scroll
receptacle
(Aron-ha-kodesh) on the
east wall of the main
hall.*

synagogue was entrusted to the architect J. M. Wertmüller. In the course of this work the entrance to the synagogue from the Town Hall was walled-up for all time and the synagogue was provided with an inside staircase and new furnishings.

In the period of slum clearance activity, when it had already been decided which of the old buildings were to be preserved for the next generations, the façade of the High Synagogue was to have been newly designed and enriched. In addition, the gable was to have been modified and the entrance portal rebuilt in Neo-Renaissance style. However, these alterations were never realized.

The High Synagogue was then incorporated in a block of new buildings. In 1907 the entrance in the eastern façade was walled-up and a new one was built in the form of the present entrance from Červená Street. The years 1961, 1974–1979 and 1982 were marked by the realization of further restoration works, the revealment of the original appearance of the receptacle for the Torah and modifications of the whole interior of the building for the exhibition purposes of the Jewish Museum.

The Maisel (Maislova) Synagogue, Maislova Street

Practically no building in the Jewish ghetto is the subject of such precise chroniclers' records as the Maisel Synagogue. It has already been mentioned that the rich primate of Prague's Jewish community Mordecai Maisel acquired a plot of land for a synagogue in 1590 in order to build his own house of prayer on it. It was an empty space between the houses of Salamún the physician and Salamún Muna and two years later, in 1592, this house of prayer or school was consecrated.

Apart from the previously quoted information of the chronicler David Gans in the book ZEMACH DAVID, a commemorative poem by Jacob ben Izaac Segré, an Italian-Jewish scholar and poet who wrote Hebrew poems and elegies and died in 1629, was placed in the foundation stone of the Maisel Synagogue. This poet was probably also the author of the inscription in the synagogue itself, of which only a fragment has been preserved. In the foreword to the commemorative poem it is stated that Maisel spent 12,000 denars on the building and that its foundation stone was laid on 14 adar, 5350 (1590).

"And there were other builders whose endeavours now mean nothing,
their proud buildings now stand in ruins,
their silver is waste and held in contempt,
but the house which Maisel built is constantly protected by safety
because the strength of the power in it is raised to the poor."

This fragment of the inscription celebrates Maisel's many charitable deeds and the good characteristics of his wife and it ends with the following wish: "... May this synagogue never be demolished."

The fact that the synagogue was exceptionally richly furnished is witnessed not only by the words of David Gans, but also by the splendour of the drapes and sculptures bestowed on it by its founder and his wife. The original building was perhaps of the triple-nave type, supported by twenty columns. There can be no doubt that at its time it was the most imposing house of prayer of Prague's Jewry. The plans for the building of the

*The Maisl Synagogue –
view of the east wall of
the nave.*

synagogue were the work of the Jewish architect Juda Coref de Herz (we shall come across his name later in connection with the plans for the Pinkas Synagogue) and the construction work was supervised by Josef Wahl. It is most likely that the original building did not have a women's gallery on the first floor, a side nave on the ground-floor being intended for women.

Like the Old-New Synagogue, the Maisel Synagogue had a similar banner of its own. Mordecai Maisel had it made on the basis of a special privilege granted by Rudolph II.

The synagogue was destroyed by fire in 1689 and rebuilt in a simpler form up to 1691. In the course of this reconstruction activity the building was shortened by about one third of its original length. Further reconstructions were carried out from 1862 to 1864 (J. M. Wertmüller) and from 1893 to 1905, when the architect Alfréd Grotte widened the synagogue and modified it in Neo-Gothic style in connection with the clearance of the whole quarter. The transfer of the main entrance to the building to the western façade represented a fundamental change in the layout of the synagogue.

Before the Second World War services were held in the synagogue in a somewhat reformed ritual and an organ was also installed in the building. During the occupation the Nazis

confiscated from the homes of deported persons.

In 1950 the depository of the collections of the Jewish Museum was situated here and later, from 1965, a permanent exposition of synagogal silver was installed in the synagogue.

However, after the elapse of several years the synagogue had to be subjected to another radical restoration and in the same period a new exposition of synagogal silver was prepared.

The unique collections of "Silver of Czech Synagogues" acquaint visitors with silver and other cult and ritual articles used in the 153 Jewish communities and in hundreds of Jewish households for religious purposes.

Visitors can see in particulart art products of silver from the Czech Lands and samples of the work of masters in Augsburg, Nuremberg and Vienna. The oldest works date in the period of the Late Renaissance, in the 16th century, and come from southern Germany, where they were a model and source of inspiration also for home craftsmen. All these articles are fairly small in size and have rich, floral orgnamental decorations. In some cases their decoration has more complicated figural themes.

A large part of the collection consists of Torah roll decorations such as Torah crowns, stands, shields and pointers or rare filigree spice containers, cups, Levite sets and the most varied types of candlesticks. These works of silver represent the Bohemian and the Moravian Baroque and originated after 1700.

In accordance with their own style

View of one of the showcases of the exhibition "The Silver of Bohemian Synagogues": a silver Torah shield.

converted the house of prayer as well as other parts of the building into a place of storage for the furniture

Overall view of the main hall of the Maisel Synagogue, now used for exhibition purposes by the Jewish Museum.

principles, Bohemian, Moravian and Viennese workshops mostly produced articles for individual religious communities.

The collection of silver articles made by members of the Jewish goldsmiths' guild in Prague, which was founded in 1805 and existed until 1859, is very interesting.

Apart from silver articles, pewter products (wedding plates, seder plates), mosaic goods (candlesticks, hanuka candlesticks, table lamps) and ceramics and glass jugs can also be seen here.

The exhibition is a valuable contribution also to the history of the silversmith's and goldsmith's crafts in the European context.

259

the present synagogue fall approximately in 1564, in the period marked by Maisel's public activity. Apart from Mordecai Maisel, two rabbis, Eilieser Ashkenazi and Judah ben Bezalel Loew, participated in the realization of this publicly beneficial building.

The building consisted of three smaller, separate structures, one of which was Loew's school, where the scholar explained the Talmud, while another was the house of prayer, the synagogue. These smaller buildings were called "klausen" – hence the later name of the synagogue.

The Klausen (Klausová) Synagogue, U starého hřbitova

The Klausen Synagogue, a small building and one of the oldest synagogues in the ghetto, stands in front of the entrance to the Old Jewish Cemetery. The original building was situated on the edge of the Jewish Town, in a quarter with a bad reputation, where ill-famed houses had stood since the Middle Ages. The street was originally named Hampejzská accordingly (hampejz = brothel) (in Gallimordio). After the death of Václav IV, however, these brothels were gradually demolished and at the time when the synagogue was founded and when the cemetery already existed here the locality already had a respectable character.

The beginnings of the original building which stood on the site of

The Klausen Synagogue – the interior after the restoration of 1978–1984.

Apart from fulfilling church and school functions, the synagogue later served also as a socio-cultural centre, becoming what might be called the assembly room of the first public corporation of the ghetto – the Prague Jewish Burial Society.

The original buildings fell victim to a fire in 1689 and so the first more precise records about the new synagogue, built on the site of the three "klausen", date in 1694 and 1696.

From 1694 the Klausen Synagogue was the second main synagogue of Prague's Jewish community. Well-known personalities such as Baruch Jeiteles, Eliezer Fleckeles, Samuel Kauder, Efraim Teweles and others, all members of the community, worked here.

In the years 1883 to 1884 the synagogue was radically restored and modified by the architect Bedřich Münzberger. In the course of this work the house of prayer was extended, an empora being built-in into the new part.

After further modifications (carried out in 1960, 1979, 1981 and 1984) the interiors of the synagogue were adapted to meet the exhibition purposes of the Jewish Museum. A permanent exposition acquaints visitors with the development and history of old Hebrew prints and manuscripts and rare manuscripts of Jewish religious philosophers can also be seen here. Old Czech notes and glosses have been preserved in certain medieval Hebrew texts, this witnessing the fact that the Jews knew the Old Czech language.

The first floor of the synagogue is used for short-term exhibitions devoted to Jewish art, culture and customs.

The Pinkas (Pinkasova) Synagogue, Široká Street

The Pinkas Synagogue has been closed for over twenty years, specifically since 1968. In the course of its restoration (how many times has it been restored?) the oldest underground interiors, an old well and most likely the oldest ritual bath were discovered. Archeological research has dated these finds in the 13th or the early 14th century.

Everything points to the fact that one of the oldest synagogues of the Jewish Town of Prague stood here. However, this presumption must be confirmed by further proofs. The results of research carried out to date show that the synagogue was first mentioned in 1492, when the name Pinkas also appeared in the complicated property relations of the corner house called U Erbů.

The house of prayer was owned by the esteemed Horowitz family and through the heritage of Yeshai Horowitz the house fell into the possession of Aaron Meshulam Horowitz in 1519. The latter had the synagogue in the house reconstructed in 1535. Aaron Meshulam Horowitz was the grand-nephew of the original founder of the synagogue, rabbi Pinkas, of the clan of "recalcitrant, sharp-tongued Pinkases, who probably waged some kind of dispute with the old settlers round the Old-New Synagogue and in 1479 founded a private synagogue on uncultivated barren land near St. Valentine's Church".

As regards the building of 1535, it was most likely a new one, although another, smaller house of prayer was still in use. Only the original ground-plan, which affords a picture of the artistic penetration of Renaissance elements also into ghetto buildings, has been preserved to the present.

Today it can only be presumed that the unattractive and inconspicuous exterior of the building concealed a rich interior in which the single-naved hall had a net vault in the style of the Jagiello Gothic. According to fragments found during later reconstructions and also to the remains of paintings preserved on the ribs, the interior of the building was richly polychromed, the capitals beind decorated with gold. The receptacle for the Torah was also richly decorated similarly as the entrance portal, which already bore strong marks of Renaissance art.

In the early 17th century (between 1607 and 1625) a Renaissance assembly hall was added to the synagogue. It had cross vaults with flat, stone ribs and with compound windows

decorated on their outside with finely profiled tracery. A women's nave and gallery, opening through arcades into the hall of the main house of prayer, originated.

The reconstruction was designed by one of the few Jewish architects. His name – Judah Goldschmied de Herz (Judah Coref de Herz) – has been preserved in the following inscription on a tombstone in the Old Jewish Cemetery:

"Tuesday 2 tishri 5386 (= 1625). Here lies the wise and skilled man Judah Goldsmith de Herz. He was always careful and always said his prayers devoutly. He kept himself through the work of his hands and the whole building of the Pinkas Synagogue and a part of the Maisl Synagogue were realized after his plans. Glory be to him."

As time passed a small quarter grew up round the Pinkas Synagogue and a larger street running to one of the gates of the ghetto was later named Pinkasova after it. The number of seats in the main prayer hall indicates its size. In the lower part, in the men's department, there were 177, while in the women's part there were 100. On the gallery, intended exclusively for women, there were 143 seats.

The Pinkas Synagogue, standing on the very edge of the Old Jewish Cemetery near the river and, due to its age, the second synagogue of the

Jewish ghetto, was often the victim of a flood causing its masonry to get lost in the soil. In consequence of the floods which occurred in the 17th and 18th centuries the synagogue had to be repaired more frequently, losing a part of its decoration on each occasion, so that in the 18th century it corresponded only partly to its original appearance. In the years about 1775 modifications of the receptacle for the Torah were carried out and later, in the early 19th century, a new pewter receptacle was provided for it. Furthermore, the seats were replaced with pews.

The modifications carried out about 1862, especially the wasteful raising of the floor, led to further deformation of the original appearance of the whole building. At that time relics of the Spanish Jew Solomon (Shlomo) Molcho, a mystic burned at the stake in Mantua in 1432, were still kept in the synagogue. Solomon Molcho, allegedly secretary to King John III of Portugal, was possessed with the idea of the Messiah and considered himself to be and presented himself as Elijah, the Messiah's predecessor. On two occasions these ideas along with the faith of Israel led him to prison and the threshold of death. The first time he was saved by the intervention of Pope Clement VII, but on the second he was condemned to death by burning. Before being burned at the stake he was asked whether he regretted his sins and whether he would like to return to Christianity and with the words that he regretted only the one year in his life during which he was not a Jew he entered the flames.

(Solomo Mochlo's caftan and red

The Pinkas Synagogue – the women's gallery, added at the beginning of the 17th century.

banner with the embroidered text of psalms have been preserved in the Pinkas Synagogue).

After the First World War, in 1922 and 1925, the first results of archeological research appeared: fragments of the foundations of the medieval building were unearthed and in the years 1950 to 1953 the original plaster was revealed. In the seventies the Jewish ritual bath (mikve) was discovered and later the receptacle for the Torah, the bimah and the portal were restored.

Due to the penetration of ground water, the renewed synagogue, whose interior was modified for the

purpose of the Monument to Victims of Nazi Persecution, was threatened with complete destruction. For this reason the monument was closed in 1968 and subjected not only to new, thorough archeological research, but also to general architectural restoration. It was newly opened in 1991.

In 1960 the "Monument of 77,297" victims of Nazi persecution, now known throughout the whole world, was opened here. The names of the victims are written on all the walls of the synagogue – in the main nave and in all the adjoining interiors. The records of the names of all those tortured to death were based on preserved transport files. The main nave contains the names of Prague Jews, arranged alphabetically and accompanied by their date of birth and the date on which they were transported to liquidation camps in the east. The names of victims from other towns and communities than Prague can be seen in the adjoining interiors. It should be added that only the names of inhabitants of Bohemia and Moravia are inscribed here and not the names of Slovak victims. During the Second World War Slovakia was a separate state.

The wall which once bore the receptacle for the Torah contains the names of the concentration camps set up by the Nazis.

The monument of 77,297 names inscribed on the walls of the Pinkas Synagogue is the biggest epitaph in the world.

The Pinkas Synagogue – the names of the victims of Nazi persecution – The Memorial of 77 297 – on the walls.

The Spanish (Španělská) Synagogue, Vězeňská Street

Apart from the name of one of the little streets – U staré školy (At the Old School) – nothing here brings to mind the existence of Prague's oldest community of Jews of eastern Byzantine origin.

It is not known when they arrived in Prague, but it is presumed that it was in the course of the 11th to the 12th century. Here, by their Old School, they formed their community, their ghetto, which never combined or merged with the ghetto round the Old-New Synagogue. Perhaps it was directly symbolic that it was the Christian Church of the Holy Spirit that separated the two Jewish districts. It is remarkable that the Jews remained here for such a long time, because the Church of the Holy Spirit, a Gothic single-naved building of the second quarter of the 14th century, was also a part of the bigger complex of the convent of Benedictine nuns which stood on the western side of the church until 1420.

The little Jewish houses of the community round the Church of the Holy Spirit literally crouched round what was allegedly Prague's oldest synagogue, the so-called Old School. Later history tells us how the Jews stuck to this piece of land and refused at all costs to join their brothers in the ghetto. They adhered to their inherited traditions and to their special Byzantine religious rite. (These specialities were preserved for a very long time and were finally recorded in book form in the collection of prayers of Prague Jews, called Selihot, of the early 17th century.) Also dating from that time are reports to the effect that Jews from the "Alt Shul" (Old School) district refused to move to the more easterly territory round Cikánská Street. The community lived its closed, characteristic life until the 17th and the early 18th century The street called U staré školy (At the Old School) was a "strange zig-zagging one, more interesting than any other in the Jewish Town", says Professor František Ruth in his Kronika Královské Prahy (Chronicle of Royal Prague). The group of houses was called Portugese Island, perhaps to commemorate the fact that Jews from Portugal perhaps settled here for a short time. Later there was another smaller synagogue, the house of prayer of the Fischell-Hönigsberg family, in the community.

The Simon Lämmel (a wealthy Jewish nobleman) foundation exist-

The Spanish Synagogue – the richly decorated interior.

ed here and the former house No. 187 contained the Babetta Lämmel home for the poor where twenty-five poverty-stricken Jews were fully cared for. The Chronicle of Royal Prague tells us that until 1785 "the Jews had to pay the bell-ringer of the Church of the Holy Spirit for ringing against heavy clouds and contributed to the purchase of bells destroyed by fire".

The first mentions of the existence of the "Old School" date in 1142, when the orignal house of prayer in the Little Quarter was destroyed by fire. Opinions exist to the effect that Jewish scholars, rabbis with a knowledge of the Czech or a Slavonic language, worked just in the circle of

this synagogue, referred to as "Old" in contradistinction to the new building (now the Old-New Synagogue). This is documented by the wealth of Czech glosses preserved in Hebrew religious books. A source of knowledge of the life of Prague's then contemporary Jewish community lies in the work mentioned in the introductory part of this guide. During the reign of Přemysl Otakar II Isaak ben Moshe wrote his work "OR ZAR-UA", which in the first place concerns the life of Jews living in the Old School district.

Not much is known about the Old School itself. In the course of anti-Jewish riots the synagogue was demolished several times (in 1389,

271

The abolished exposition of synagogal textiles.

1516, 1604, 1622), but it was always repaired and rebuilt. In 1693, on the basis of an imperial order, it was closed, but shortly afterwards, in 1703, it was reopened. In 1744, in the period marked by the expelling of Jews from Prague, the synagogue was deserted and greatly damaged by fire only to be repaired once again, however.

A true picture of the appearance of the synagogue, where, as the first in Prague, the modern reformed religious service was introduced in 1837, is afforded by Langweil's model of Prague. It was a long building with a saddle roof, with five windows along the sides and two windows in the eastern façade. This tells us that it was not a very complicated building. Nevertheless, it was interesting due to the fact that, as the first in

a Jewish house of prayer, an organ was installed here and that the first organist was the Czech composer František Škroup, who wrote the song "Kde domov můj" (Where Is My Home), which later became the Czech national anthem.

František Škroup, who worked at the synagogue from 1836 to 1845, also composed several synagogical compositions to liturgical texts in that period. The example of František Škroup's activity in a Jewish synagogue not only confirms the positive attitude of non-Jewish Czech patriots towards their Jewish fellow-citizens, but also signalled the new assimilation tendencies in Czech-Jewish relations.

The radical Neo-Gothic reconstructions and gradual modernization of the old building proved to be inadequate and so it was decided to demolish it and build a new synagogue on its site – one which would fully correspond to the growing influence of the reform (neological) part of Prague's Jewry.

In 1868 the construction of a new synagogue was started after a design by one of the best-known Czech architects of the time, Vojtěch Ignác Ullmann (1822–1897), who also designed, among other buildings, the Czech Savings Bank in Národní Street (now the Czechoslovak Academy of Sciences), the Czech Technical University in Charles Square and the High School for Girls in Vodičkova Street. The design of the interior of the building was entrusted to the equally well-known architect of the period of historicism, Josef Niklas (1817–1877). The ostentatious and unusual decoration of the interior

Detail of an embroidered synagogal curtain.

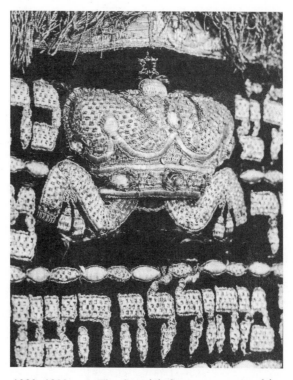

was designed in the years 1882–1893 by the architects A. Baum and B. Münzberger. The synagogue was erected on a square ground-plan and represents a classical Neo-Renaissance formation with a huge cupola. Its interior was richly decorated with ornamentally conceived and gilded stucco imitating Alhambra interiors in Spain – hence its present name – the Spanish Synagogue. Decorative elements were also applied in other details, for example, in the adornment of the doors and the wall panelling. The windows were glazed with stained glass.

At its time the interior of the synagogue was one of the most original of the cult type.

The Spanish Synagogue served its purpose up to the outbreak of the Second World War. In 1955 it was handed over to the Jewish Museum and after it had undergone essential repairs and modifications an exposition, unique even on the world scale, of synagogal textiles, both woven and embroidered, from the Renaissance period up to the 20th century was installed in it. The collections contain synagogal drapes, curtains and Torah mantles.

Due to the necessity of realizing technical works the Spanish Synagogue has been closed for a number of years. After undergoing a new general reconstruction it will serve the Jewish Museum as an exhibition hall.

The Jewish Town Hall, Maislova Street

Present-day Maislova Street, which runs in parallel with Pařížská Street, was one of the main streets of the Jewish Town. It was originally called Zlatá (Gold) or Úzká (Narrow) Street (in the south), Malá Masařská and later Bellesova Street (between the Old-New Synagogue and Josefovská street), Rabínská Street (further north), Velkodvorská Street (northernmost part along the eastern side of Pařížská Street of the present). The Jewish Town Hall was built in Rabínská Street, which from the mid-19th century spread to Velkodvorská and Bellesova Streets. After the slum clearance activity after 1901 the whole street was named after Mordecai Maisel – Maislova Street. Precise reports of the origin and period of origin of the Jewish Town Hall do not exist. The Town Hall was connected with the development of Jewish autonomy and with the transfer of certain administrative powers whose concentration in the hands of elected or appointed Jewish officials was a gradual process. In the ghetto first place always belonged to the synagogues which, apart from their religious purpose, also fulfilled economic, judicial and administrative functions. The Jews did not devote very much attention to dwelling-houses for a very simple reason, namely that the king regarded Jewish houses as his own property and could dispose of them as he wished.

Only later, in the Renaissance period, when the Jews also gained a more important economic func-tion, manifested also beyond the boundaries of the ghetto, was a part of the competence of the synagogues transferred to the municipal buildings, the forerunners of the Town Halls, similarly as in Prague's other towns.

Later still the synagogues retained only their religious, educational and, in the person of the rabbi, judicial function.

In the 16th and 17th centuries separate councillors' buildings originated in the ghettos of some Czech communities, including, of course, the biggest Czech ghetto – the one in Prague.

The exact date of the origin of the

Jewish Town Hall in Prague is not known. No proof exists of whether such a building existed already before 1567, when Maximilian II issued an Imperial Charter according to which Jews were not to be banished from either Bohemia or Prague.

In the same year a fire occurred in the ghetto and no precise proof exists as to whether a building fulfilling the function of a Town Hall was destroyed.

The first mention of a Town Hall building (the Jewish "rathouz") dates approximately in 1577. It tells us that at that time "the burned councillors' building is being enlarged. The neighbouring house on the right, which belonged to Joachym Nosek, is being purchased for 37 and a half k."

Built simultaneously with the Town Hall, in fact as a part of it, was the High Synagogue which from then on was to fulfil the function of the Town Hall's house of prayer. Both buildings were financed by Mordecai Maisel, the architect concerned being Pancratius Roder with Václav Rada, a master mason living in Prague.

The original appearance of the Town Hall differed considerably from its present one. Its façade was plain, not articulated in any way. With its simple character it resembled the façade of the High Synagogue, without, however, a sloping façade wall. The original parts of the Town Hall include its barrel-vaulted cellars. The original vaults and three rooms in the north-west corner have been preserved of the Renaissance parts.

The great fire which occurred in 1689 also affected the Town Hall,

The main hall of the Town Hall used also as a "kosher" restaurant.

Detail of the ceiling decoration of the main hall of the Town Hall.

which was practically burnt to the ground. Its renewal, this time in Baroque style, was entrusted to the ar-

The Jewish Town Hall with the clock with Hebrew figures and hands moving in anticlockwise direction.

chitect Pavel Ignác Bayer, who collaborated with other well-known architects such as Haffenecker and Canevalle.

When the Jews were expelled from Prague during the reign of Maria Theresa (1745) the Town Hall became more or less deserted and after the damage which it sustained during the fire of 1754 it was subjected to a fundamental Rococo reconstruction in the years 1763 to 1765. According to guild books the work involved was supervised by the architect Josef Schlesinger. During the reconstruction a document was placed in the tower which tells us that the Jews borrowed 200,000 fl. r. for the restoration of the ghetto and the work was completed within eleven years. In the course of the Rococo period the Town Hall acquired a new street façade and a turret on the mansard roof.

The tower of the Town Hall has a gallery with a rich Rococo grille and cupola with a lantern and the Jewish star on its summit.

A Jewish clock with a Hebrew dial and hands moving in anticlockwise direction was placed in the dormer window of the main façade. The other clock on the tower has a Roman dial. Both clocks were made in 1764 by Sebastian Landensberger, a citizen of Prague who held the function of clockmaker to the royal court.

During the Rococo reconstruction of the building the main councillors' room was newly decorated with stucco with the star of David and a Jewish hat. The main portal was located on the long side of the façade in Rabínská (Maislova) Street and there is a similar masked portal in the left corner

The Town Hall houses also the office of the Rabbi of Prague.

formed with Červená Street.

The Town Hall was also to have been demolished during the slum clearance activity, but it was later decided to preserve the building and extend it in southerly direction. This was done in 1910. The new entrance with a vestibule runs along the right side to the main hall where a gallery was built in 1934.

The Jewish Town Hall has a rich past.

As a public building it was the seat of the administration of the Jewish Town where originally the Jewish court sessions were also held even though it was not until 1627 that the Emperor Ferdinand raised the Jewish Town to a special town formation with its own town council and judicial competence. This was transferred here from the synagogue.

In 1850 the Jewish Town was made a part of Prague and the Town Hall be-

The kosher restaurant at No. 18, Maislova Street.

came the seat of the administration of the Jewish Religious Community.

During the occupation the Nazis instituted the Council of Jewish Elders here which was to assist in the registering and liquidating of Jews from Bohemia and Moravia. And so once again the Town Hall was a witness to the tragedy of Czech Jews during the years of the Second World War just as it had been so often in the course of their history.

Nowadays the Town Hall once again serves its original purpose as the administrative centre of the Jewish Religious Community. It is the seat of the representatives of the community, the rabbi and a number of cultural and educational institutions. The editors of the Bulletin of Jewish Religious Communities work here and a publication entitled Information Bulletin for Foreign Countries is also published here. The Town Hall also contains a filing department with the transport documents of Jews deported during the Second World War and a library serving study purposes.

From 1954 the councillors' room was converted into a ritual kosher dining-room where hundreds of mid-day meals are served daily except Sundays. The councillors' room also serves cultural and festival purposes.

278

The Old Jewish Cemetery, U starého hřbitova

The most remarkable features of Old Prague include the Old Jewish Cemetery, a unique monument of world importance and one of the most memorable Jewish graveyards in the world.

The cemetery originated in the first half of the 15th century as a replacement for the original Jewish cemetery lying outside the periphery of the town on the territory of Vladislavova and Spálená Streets. The previous cemetery spread out on territory which was called the Jewish Garden (hortus, cimeterium Judaeorum). Burials took place in this original cemetery of all Prague Jews, founded about 1270 during the reign of Přemysl II, until 1478.

In the course of the passing centuries the cemetery of the Jewish Town was enlarged by new areas in the south-west, the north and the south. Apart from a small piece of land cut off at the turn of the 19th and 20th centuries during the construction of the Arts and Crafts Museum and the surrounding buildings the cemetery has been preserved in its medieval size.

However, in spite of all the endeavours of the community to get the area of the cemetery enlarged the demarcated ground did not suffice with the result that it is characterized by superimposed burial strata. The lack of space was the main reason for the accumulation of gravestones and there are over 12,000 on the relatively small area. In the course of the stratification of graves already existing gravestones were always raised, so that in places groups of gravesto-

Plan of the Old Jewish Cemetery
1 – the oldest tombstones of the 14th century, brought here from the abolished cemetery in Vladislav Street, 2 – the Nephele mound. Tombstones: 3 – Aron Meshullam Horowitz (Salomon Horowitz), 4 – Avigdor Kara, 5 – David Gans, 6 – Mordecai Zemach and his son Becalel (printers), 7 – David Oppenheim, 8 – Mordecai Maisel, 9 – Rabbi Loew, 10 – Hindel Bashevi, 11 – Joseph Salomon del Medigo of Crete.

community. It is a source of cultural and historical knowledge and the history of the ghetto speaks to us from the style and artistic character of the symbols on the gravestones and from the inscriptions on them.

Apart from the name and the date of birth and death on the gravestones of the deceased, we can also learn many interesting things about their life and the Jewish society in which they lived. As is the custom in the case of gravestones, we do not encounter realistic prose only, but also poetic inscriptions which truthfully characterize the atmosphere of a certain period. Very often gravestones bear carved symbols indicating that the deceased was a member of a certain family belonging to the hierarchy of priests in biblical times. Concerned in particular in this respect is the Cohen family, whose members held religious functions. The Levites were another family whose members enjoyed the privilege of serving in the temple in biblical times. Their symbol has the form of the jug from which they poured water on the hands of the priest during religious rites.

Apart from family symbols, various symbols executed in different styles according to the time of origin of the gravestones can be seen in the cemetery. A frequent symbol is a cluster of grapes, whose meaning different researchers interpret in different ways. Some consider a cluster of grapes to be the common symbol of the Jewry in general, while others regard it as a mark of abundance, whether concerning work and diligence in the case of men or fertility and motherhood in the case of women. A pine cone has a similar

nes correspond to as many as twelve burial strata. The cemetery occupies an irregular area between 17. listopadu and Břehova Streets and blocks of houses in Maislova and Široká Streets. The greater part of its periphery is enclosed by a wall built after a design of the architect Bohumil Hybšman in 1911.

The Old Jewish Cemetery is one of the most valuable sources for study of the history of Prague's Jewish meaning. A symbol in the form of a crown can be seen on numerous gravestones. It may, perhaps, have been the symbol of learned, cultured men well-versed in the Torah and high learning. A special poetic effect is created by the symbols of names in the form of an animal, a plant or a bird. We can see a carp, a stag, a fox, a lion, a bear, a wolf, a cock, a dove, a rose and other representatives of the animal and vegetable kingdoms. Contrary to other Jewish cemeteries, a number of reliefs portraying human figures can be seen in the Old Jewish Cemetery. The artistic portrayal of a human figure represents a deviation from the traditional ban placed on the representation of Man.

Very often human activites and forms of employment are depicted in gravestone symbols. For example, scissors symbolized a tailor, a lance a physician, a mortar a pharmacist and a violin a musician.

The inscriptions on the gravestones contain the name of the deceased and that of his father, while the name of married women is accompanied by the name of their husband. Very often the deceased's calling or another characteristic is indicated, for example, his function or rank in the community. The formulation is usually poetic and the inscriptions on the gravestones often draw attention to good characteristics, a devout life, regular attendance at the synagogue, charity, etc.

Most of the given names are Hebrew, but we also come across quite a number of names of Czech origin as well as names derived from the place of origin and form of employment of the deceased. Many names

are connected with physical or other properties.

Cultural and art currents can be traced according to the style and artistic value of the gravestones.

The oldest gravestones are usually the simplest. They are sandstone slabs with a straight, rounded or gable-shaped top, decorated merely with carved script. Elongated Gothic gravestones are represented here only by fragments brought to this cemetery from the abolished cemetery in the New Town. The decisive aspect for the division of the gravestones into style epochs is the method of work of the masons concerned and not the ornamental style elements. Relief script is carved on both Late Gothic and Renaissance gravestones. Formal modifications can also be observed. The Late Gothic is characterized by a trefoil, while a profiled frame separating the script from the edge of the stone is typical of the Early Renaissance. Sometimes the inscription runs into the frame and from time to time it is hewn in a high relief, so that the surface of the stone has a greater plastic effect. This period is marked by the most frequent occurrence of an oblong or square sandstone gravestone with deeply carved script creating a plastic effect.

In the 16th and 17th centuries sandstone was replaced with white or pink Slivenec marble and wider use was made of a Renaissance ornament for the artistic decoration of gravestones. Four-walled tombs (in Hebrew "ohel", tabernacle), kinds of sarcophagi, began to be built by the gravestones of rich citizens. The oldest of them were built to commemorate the miraculous rabbi Loew and the financier Mordecai Maislel.

The 17th and 18th century graves in the central part of the Old Jewish Cemetery have the most imposing gravestones with richly decorated marble tombs featuring Renaissance ornaments portraying simple articles and sometimes a whole story. The marble tomb of the rich Jewess Hendel Bashevi and the gravestones of the Spiro family of rabbis are examples of such a tombstone.

The later Rococo period was characterized artistically by a flat relief and a wealth of small figural elements. Most frequently seen is the figure of a woman or young girl and in one case two figures are portrayed and stylized – Adam and Eve in Paradise. Rather than as a violation of the biblical prohibition, these symbols can be regarded as an expression of naive folk art and an endeavour to preserve loving persons at least in the stylized form of a portrait or symbol.

From the artistic aspect the gravestones in the Old Jewish Cemetery do not represent high art. Above all else they are expressions of folk art, a historical testimony to past times.

A small street called U starého hřbitova leads to the cemetery.

The building on the left is the Klausen Synagogue, while the somewhat strange building on the right (No. 243) is a kind of pseudo-Romanesque castle built in 1908 by the architect Gerstl. It belongs to the Jewish Museum and children's drawings from the Terezín concentration camp are installed in it. This exposition of artistic and literary creations from this concentration camp commemorates the children who were murdered in Nazi concentration and extermination camps during the Second World War. In those war years approximately 15,000 children were deported to Terezín, where they lived in so-called children's homes. In the autumn of 1944 most of the Terezín children were deported to Oswieczim, where they died.

Before their deportation the children in the Terezín ghetto drew pictures and painted. Their naive, often shocking drawings reflect the cruel reality of the place where they were forced to live. Apart from drawings and paintings, their literary works, letters and poems have been preserved, still representing the most moving heritage of their short life.

* * *

The present size of the cemetery corresponds approximately to the area of the medieval burial ground even though it was constantly enlarged in the course of the passing centuries. Plots of land were purchased for the needs of the cemetery in 1526 and in 1573 the territory between the Pinkas and Klausen Synagogues up to Sanytrová Street was attached to it.

In Mordecai Maisel's time the cemetery area was enlarged by its present northern part. In 1768, twenty years before the cemetery was abolished, its area was further enlarged on the southern side, in the vicinity of the Pinkas Synagogue. Apart from the short period of the plague epidemic in 1680, when a new Jewish cemetery was established at Olšany, the Old Jewish Cemetery continued to be the biggest Jewish cemetery in Prague until 1787.

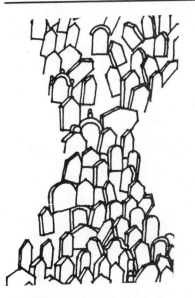

A Visit to the Cemetery and Its Most Important Graves

The entrance to the Old Jewish Cemetery is situated next to the Klausen Synagogue (this entrance has been used since the 19th century, the original entrance gate lying in its easternmost corner).

Our tour of inspection begins immediately beyond the entrance to the central part, which began to be used for burials in the 17th century. Situated opposite the entrance are the gravestones of the physician Beer Teller and his son Loew of the late 17th century. They are decorated with symbols of their names and calling.

In the corner by the Klausen Synagogue we can see the memorial of the physicians Solomon Gumperz and his son Bendit († 1729), and the latter's son Moses († 1742). An in-scription tells us that Solomon remained in the ghetto even when the plague raged in it.

Walled-up in the wall on the left side are the remains of the oldest Gothic gravestones from the abolished cemetery in Vladislavova Street. The oldest legible date can be deciphered as 1346 or 1351.

On the left, behind the Klausen Synagogue, is a hillock, called "nephele", where children who had not attained one year of age were buried. Opposite this small hill (on the right), inside the burial field, is the simple, black gravestone of Aaron Meshulam Horowitz who reconstructed the Pinkas Synagogue in 1535. The memorial of its founder, rabbi Pinkas, is situated next to it and dates in 1495.

The next field on the right side (on the path leading to the original entrance to the cemetery) contains the gravestone of Moses Lipman Beck, whose burial was the last to take place in the Old Jewish Cemetery. This Jew died on 17 May, 1787.

Standing below the hillock "nephele" is the pink gravestone of Abraham, son of Jacob, who died as a martyr in 1476.

From here let us proceed in southerly direction in order to reach the oldest part of the cemetery. The memorial of rabbi Avigdor Kara, author of the elegy about the devastation of the ghetto in 1389, is situated here. The date of the rabbi's death inscribed on the stone is 25 April, 1439 and the memorial is thus the oldest in the cemetery.

From here let us make our way across the cemetery to the Pinkas Synagogue, where burials began to take

The oldest tombstones (14th century) brought from the abolished Jewish cemetery in Vladislavova Street.

place approximately in the mid-16th century. In 1543 Abraham, son of Avigdor Kara, was buried here and towards the end of the 16th century members of the Horowitz family, founders of the Pinkas Synagogue, were laid to rest here.

Along the path, on the right, we can see the printed gravestone of David Gans (1541–1613), whose name is symbolized by the star of David and a relief decoration in the form of a goose. David Gans wrote a general history ("Zemach David") and he was also a mathematician and astronomer who maintained contacts with Johann Kepler and Tycho Brahe.

The following gravestones commemorating certain outstanding personalities can also be seen:

The square gravestone of the printers Mordecai Katz († 1592) and his son Bezalel († 1589), continuators of the family traditions of Prague's Jewish printers.

The Rococo gravestone of Majer Fischl († 1769), head of the Talmudistic school.

The grave of the Jewish judge, the chief jurist, Nehemiáš Feibel Dušenes († 1648).

The grave of chief rabbi Zeeb Auerbach († 1632) with a relief in the form of a wolf.

The grave of David Oppenheim (1664–1736), the chief rabbi of Prague whose memorable Jewish library is now installed in the library of Oxford University.

The grave of Samuel Lichtenstadt

(† 1752), a rabbi of the Klausen Synagogue.

From here we turn twice to the right and come to the Renaissance tomb of Mordecai Maisel (1528–1601), the primate of Prague's Jewish community, who did so much to secure its enhancement.

The most frequented grave in the cemetery is that of the "miraculous rabbi Loew" (1520–1609) who, as a legend has it, created Golem. He founded a school for rabbis and was a scholar whose name is interwoven with many legends.

The gravestone of the rabbi's grandson Samuel, son of Bezalel († 1655), whose narrowness is explained by a legend according to which he wanted to be buried next to his grandfather's grave. There was not sufficient space for this, but rabbi Loew's gravestone allegedly moved to one side by itself, thus making room for his grandson's grave.

The group of gravestones above the graves of rabbi Loew's pupils contains the small tomb of chief rabbi Shelomo Ephraim Luntschitz († 1619). Also situated here is the gravestone of Fruma, daughter of Isaak the physician and second wife of Mordecai Maisel († 1625).

On the right of the place where the wall breaks off to the left there is a marble gravestone whose front panel bears a lion holding the emblem of Hendel, daughter of Eberl Geronim and wife of Jacob Bassewi

The tombstone of David Gans with the symbol of a goose (Gans) and the star of David (1613).

of Treuenberk († 1628), who was buried in 1634 in the Jewish cemetery at Mladá Boleslav.

Then there is a group of graves of members of the Spira family of rabbis. A Baroque tomb stands above the grave of the chief rabbi of Prague, Aron Simon Spira († 1679), called Šimon Zbožný (the Devout).

Next we see the grave of his great-grandson, Simon Frankl Spira († 1745), primate of Prague's Jewish community, and, on the other side of the tomb, the gravestone of Wolf Spira († 1715), the provincial rabbi.

The gravestone with hands raised in blessing belongs to the butcher David Koref († 1656), who on the occasion of every Jewish festival allegedly gave the poor an amount of meat equalling the weight of his wife and children.

Standing in the direction to the centre of the northernmost part of the cemetery is the tomb of Joseph del Medigo de Candia (1591–1655), a philosopher and physician and a pupil of Galileo of Cretic origin.

* * *

The characteristic, unique and wholly inimitable atmosphere of the Old Jewish Cemetery, often nourished by the dramatic destinies of deceased inhabitants of the ghetto, soon found a place for itself in numerous myths, legends, literary works and paintings. The environment of the cemetery was intensified by the long history of one of the oldest Jewish settlements in Europe. It is just the Old Jewish Cemetery that of all the places connected with the common fate of Prague's Jews concentrated the greatest attention. Efforts were made to increase the importance of the cemetery by placing its beginnings in the time even preceding the foundation of Prague. The Baroque period in particular inclined towards these ideas and unfounded fabrications. According to the erroneous reading of the dates of the death of the respective deceased on some gravestones, where, in accordance with a Jewish custom, the thousand figure was omitted, the oldest grave was dated 606.

And it is interesting that it was just a Jew, Prague's chief rabbi Solomon Judah Rapoport (1790–1867), who on the basis of a philological-historical study of gravestone texts ascertained that the given dates were wrong and that the gravestones were actually one thousand years younger. Rabbi Rappoport arrived at this finding without personally visiting

the cemetery because, as a member of the Kohen clan, he was forbidden to spend time in the cemetery. The oldest grave in the Old Jewish Cemetery is dated in 1439. However, this did not prevent the Prague legends which originated in the 18th century from maintaining that the illustrious rabbi Salamon ben Isaak, called Rashi, who most likely died about 1105 in France, was, as a false Messiah, murdered and later buried in the Old Cemetery.

The legends about the Old Jewish Cemetery are not specifically concerned with either time or persons. All their originators added something and enriched them according to their own fantastic ideas of old folk tales and legends. The most frequent protagonist is rabbi Loew with whose name horrifying and moving tales are connected. It is said that in one corner of the cemetery there is a strange gravestone whose inscription alludes to a dog. How would a dog find itself in the cemetery? According to a legend someone threw its carcass on the sacred soil of the cemetery out of a feeling of hatred for Jews. The rabbi decided that everything that was dead must remain in the cemetery regardless of how it got there. And so the carcass of the dog was piously buried and has remained in the cemetery to the present.

A Polish queen is also allegedly

The tombstone of Mordecai Maisel (Mayzl, d. 1601).

The tombstone of Rabbi Löw (d. 1609).

The tombstone of David Oppenheim (a. 1736).

buried in the cemetery. She is supposed to lie under a single gravestone bearing a noble coat-of-arms. This gravestone is a magnificent marble one and inscribed on it is the name Anna or Hendel, wife of the first Jewish nobleman Bassewi of Treuenberk, who died in 1628. This name is not, however, her correct one and it was inscribed on the gravestone in order to prevent anyone from disturbing the peace of the Polish queen laid to rest here. After her royal husband had repudiated her, the queen fled from Poland to Prague. Before her death she converted to the Jewish faith in order to be able to be interred in the local Jewish cemetery.

Another legend tells us about a young man who, out of love for a young lady, converted to Christianity and even became a priest and organist at St. Vitus's Cathedral. Before his death he returned to his original faith and was buried in the Old Cemetery, which he leaves every night in the company of a skeleton which ferries him across the river so that he can play the organ in the cathedral.

A legend is also attached to the grave on whose gravestone Adam and Eve are portrayed as a young married couple whom the angel of death struck down on their wedding day.

The gravestone with two hens facing each other with their beaks oriented to a woman's head is said to belong to a grave containing the remains of an adultress whose eyes were pecked out by the hens as a punishment.

Legends and myths inspired a number of writers to treat them artistically, their number including Jiří Karásek, Vladimír Holan and Jaroslav Seifert.

The atmosphere of the Old Jewish Cemetery also captivated creative artists, among them Antonín Mánes in particular. Others included August Bedřich Piepenhagen and Bedřich Wachsmann. Apart from other Old Prague themes (Čertovka – The Devil's Stream, Helm's Mills), motifs from the Old Jewish Cemetery were also used by the painter and graphic artist Bedřich Havránek who in his compositions from about 1855 to 1865 portrayed gravestones and their romantic grouping in an almost documentary way. Another painter of the cemetery was the landscapist Matyáš Wehli, now unjustly forgotten, and themes characterizing the cemetery can also be found in the paintings of Jaroslav Čermák and Vojtěch Hynais.

Jewish Monuments in the Old Town

Apart from the synagogues and the Old Jewish Cemetery there are also other monuments in Prague marked by the moving history of the Jewish past.

Standing in front of the small park by the Old-New Synagogue in Pařížská Street is an interesting **statue of Moses,** a work of the Czech sculptor František Bílek (1872–1941), the most outstanding representative of the symbolists among sculptors. This statue survived the Nazi occupation of Czechoslovakia thanks only to the courage of the people who kept it hidden from the Nazis.

Another interesting Jewish monument is the monumental **statue of rabbi Loew** (Maharal) on the corner of the building of the New Town Hall in Prague.

The patriarchal figure of Maharal is carved in stone along with the figure of a young woman and depicts one of the many legends connected with the rabbi. This learned man who knew only religious duties was to remain alive as long as he did not avert his eyes from the holy script. The group of statues shows how the great rabbi rejects the temptations of the beautiful woman with his hands. The group is the work of Ladislav Šaloun (1870–1946), one of the most striking representatives of Czech Art Nouveau sculpture whose most outstanding work is the Master Jan Hus (John Huss) monument in nearby Old Town Square. This statue was also hidden from the Nazis.

Rabbi Loew in the artistic concept of Ladislav Šaloun.

On the other corner of the building there is a statue portraying the Iron Knight, another imaginary figure featured in old Prague legends.

* * *

Occupying third place on the right side of Charles Bridge is a group of statues Calvary-Crucifix of the 17th century. It has the form of a lifesized Corpus Christi cast in bronze in 1629 by H. Hillger after a model created by the Saxon sculptor W. E. Brohn. The work was originally intended for a bridge in Dresden, but it was purchased by Prague's town council and in 1657 installed on Charles Bridge in the place where a Gothic cross had stood already in the 14th century. The gilded Hebrew inscription on the cross "Kadosh, kadosh, kadosh" – the first

The Calvary with the Hebrew inscription on Charles Bridge (17th century).

three words of the sanctification "Holy, holy, holy is the Lord", was executed in 1696 and paid for from a financial fine imposed on an unknown Jew for mocking the cross. The statues of the Virgin and St. John of 1861 are the work of the sculptor E. Max.

Whether we have here a legend or a real event, the combination of a cross with a Hebrew inscription is in every case a unique monument of Jewish Prague.

Jewish Monuments in Other Towns and Communities of Prague

Jewish monuments can be found throughout the whole of Prague as well as beyond the cadastral territory of the historical towns of Prague. After the economic emancipation of the Jews in 1848, Jewish inhabitants moved to nearby and more remote suburbs. And they left traces – synagogues and cemeteries – of their presence everywhere.

Jews settled in the New Town of Prague from the time of its foundation, i. e. from 1348. Charles IV permitted them to live here on condition that "they build of stone and thoroughly there". Jews made their way here from all over Bohemia with the exception of the Old Town, from where they were not allowed to move to the New Town. They settled round the old Jewish cemetery on the territory of Vladislavova and V jámě Streets of the present. They had their own private houses of prayer here and still have their own synagogue here.

The Jubilee (Jubilejní) Synagogue, Jeruzalémská Street, Nové Město (New Town)

The consequences of the slum clearance activity included the liquidation of both large and small synagogues owned either by societies or privately. In the years 1905 to 1906 the so-called Jubilee Synagogue was built in Jeruzalémská Street under the auspices of the Society for the Building of a New Synagogue and with the exception of the war years it has served the purpose of the Prague religious community ever since. It is an interesting building characterized by then contemporary Art Nouveau elements and inspired, moreover, by eastern, Moorish architecture. Alois Richter was responsible for the construction of the synagogue, built by Wilhelm Stiastny. The painted decoration of the interior, designed by F. Fröhlich, also corresponds to the Art Nouveau style of the time.

The Jubilee and Old-New Synagogues are two of the many scores of formerly existing houses of prayer which served the original purpose of Prague's small Jewish religious community.

Synagogues which originated in many quarters of Prague after 1900 were demolished or abolished, or now serve a different purpose.

The most ostentatious and the biggest of them, the **synagogue in Královské Vinohrady**, built from 1896 to 1897 in Sázavská Street, fell victim to one of the few air raids on Prague during the last months of the Second World War.

Earlier photographs acquaint us with the appearance of this representative Neo-Renaissance building, proudly designed with two high steeples in its eastern façade. The interior of the synagogue also had a pompous character. The women's gallery with arcades opening on to the main nave, the receptacle for the Torah, indeed everything bore testimony to the wealth of the Jews residing in Vinohrady, one of Prague's most prosperous quarters.

In vain would we seek former synagogues, which became alive every Friday with the prayers of believers, in decaying buildings in Prague's suburbs. The former synagogue of the old Prague Jewish community in Koželužská Street in **Libeň** serves the purposes of the Na Palmovce Theatre, while the former synagogue in the street U Michelského mlýna (No. 27) in **Michle**, a modest building with a simple façade and pseudo-historical elements of the first half of the 19th century, now serves the needs of the Czechoslovak Hussite church.

The Hebrew inscription on the façade of building No. 32 in Stroupežnického Street in **Smíchov** suffices to remind us that a synagogue for the Smíchov community has stood here since 1863.

Nowadays the ecumenical council of the churches of the Czech Republic has its seat in **Karlín**, in building No. 13 in Vítkova Street, once a synagogue built in 1861 in Moorish-Neo-Romanesque style.

Other smaller Jewish houses of

The former synagogue in Smíchov is no longer used for its original purpose.

prayer of the past in **Košíře** (building No.160 in the street Na Popelce) and in **Žižkov** (building No. 48 in Seifertova Street) all serve other churches.

✳ ✳ ✳

A similar fate was shared by old **historical Jewish cemeteries** belonging to Prague's individual Jewish religious communities.

Fragmentary reports about the oldest of them, the cemetery in the Újezd locality in the Little Quarter and the Jewish Garden in the New Town, can be found in chronicles. The **old Jewish cemetery in Libeň,** with gravestones preserved from the early 17th century, has also become extinct. Apart from other notable personalities, the Czech-Jewish writer Vojtěch Rakous (1862–1935, proper name Albert Österreicher), who described the every-day life of the Czech-Jewish population in a hu-

The principal (western) façade of the Jubilee Synagogue.

A part of the old Jewish cemetery in Žižkov (Fibich Street) has been reverently restored.

mourous way, is buried in the no longer used cemetery in Davídkova Street in **Ďáblice.** Situated in the street U starého židovského hřbitova on the cadastral territory of **Radlice** is an old Jewish cemetery, maintained in order by the institute concerned with the care of historical monuments, which spreads out picturesquely on a mild slope on the edge of a forest and is surrounded by a stone wall. The mortuary, serving also as the entrance gate, is built in Classical style and the gravestones date in the 18th, 19th and early 20th centuries.

The **Malvazinky** Jewish cemetery, located between the streets Liebknechtova and U smíchovského hřbitova, adjoins the western side of a catholic cemetery. Valuable gravestones of the late 19th century can be seen here and outstanding among them is the grave of the Porges family of Portheim, whose wealthy members resided in Prague. Spreading out between the streets Ondříčkova, Fibichova, Kubelíkova and Čajkovského in the Žižkov quartter is the **old Olšany Jewish Cemetery,** cared for as a historical monument. A part of the cemetery disappeared in 1958 in the course of building works carried out in its environs during which it was converted into a park. The cemetery was used from 1680, when Prague was afflicted by a big plague epidemic. The greatest number of infected persons lived in the Jewish Town. The dead increased in number and so the community of the New Town purchased a garden near the Olšany community, on the site of former vineyards, in order that they might bury plague victims here. At the same time they built a hospital, intended for provisionary use only, by the cemetery.

The entrance gate to the New Jewish Cemetery at Olšany.

During the ten months of the plague epidemic about three thousand persons were buried here. Until 1713, when Prague suffered another plague epidemic, the former garden was not used for burials, but in the course of the eight months of its duration the number of new burials here again exceeded three thousand.

Burials took place here regularly from 1787. During the reign of Joseph II a decree was issued to the effect that cemeteries were to be established outside the boundaries of the city of Prague. From then on, i.e. from 1787, when the Old Jewish Cemetery in the former ghetto ceased to be used, the Žižkov cemetery was the chief Jewish burial-place in Prague until 1890.

(In 1713 a Jewish cemetery was established in the Christian plague cemetery, where some six thousand persons of French nationality were buried in 1741 and about two thousand Prague citizens who died during the influenza epidemic in 1771.)

Of the most prominent personalities buried here let us mention at least a few: rabbi Ezechiel Landau (1713–1793), his son Samuel Landau (1750–1834), Eleazar Flekeles (1754–1826) and Solomon Yehuda Rapoport (1790–1867).

In 1986 several gravestones of the greatest importance from the architectural and historical aspects were concentrated on ground newly laid out in a park-like manner and that is all that has remained of the old Jewish Olšany cemetery.

* * *

Our short journey through the history of the ghetto and the monuments of Jewish Prague will now come to an end at the **new Jewish cemetery in Žižkov,** in Jan Želivský Street, which can be easily reached by means of the underground railway (line A – Želivského Station).

Let us first halt at the most sought-after grave in this cemetery, i.e. at the **grave of the writer Franz Kafka** (1883–1924). This grave bearing the number 21-14-21 has the form of a sexagonal, truncated crystal and apart from the writer, his parents are also buried here.

Set in the wall opposite this grave is a bronze memorial tablet commemorating Dr. Max Brod (1884–1968), a friend and propagator of the works of Franz Kafka.

This cemetery, where Jewish burials still take place, was founded in 1890. The Neo-Renaissance hall of ceremonies with a house of prayer, the administrative building and the wall surrounding the cemetery, intended for about one hundred thousand graves, date in the same period.

A number of artistically valuable gravestones – Neo-Gothic, Neo-Renaissance, Art Nouveau and modern ones – representing the work of leading Czech sculptors and architects such as Jan Kotěra (1871–1923), Josef Zasche (1871–1957), Josef Fanta (1856–1954), Čeněk Vosmík (1860–1944) and others can be seen in the cemetery.

Of the gravestones of prominent personalities buried here let us mention those of rabbi S. I. Kaemps (1818–1892), Dr. Nathan Ehrenfeld (1843–1912), the work of architect Paul Albert Kopetzky, and rabbi Gustav Sicher (1880–1960). The painter Max Horb (1882–1907) and the writer Ota Pavel (1930–1973) are buried in the cemetery.

An urn grove, where, apart from others, the poet Jiří Orten (1919–1941) is buried, forms a part of the news Jewish cemetery in the Žižkov quarter.

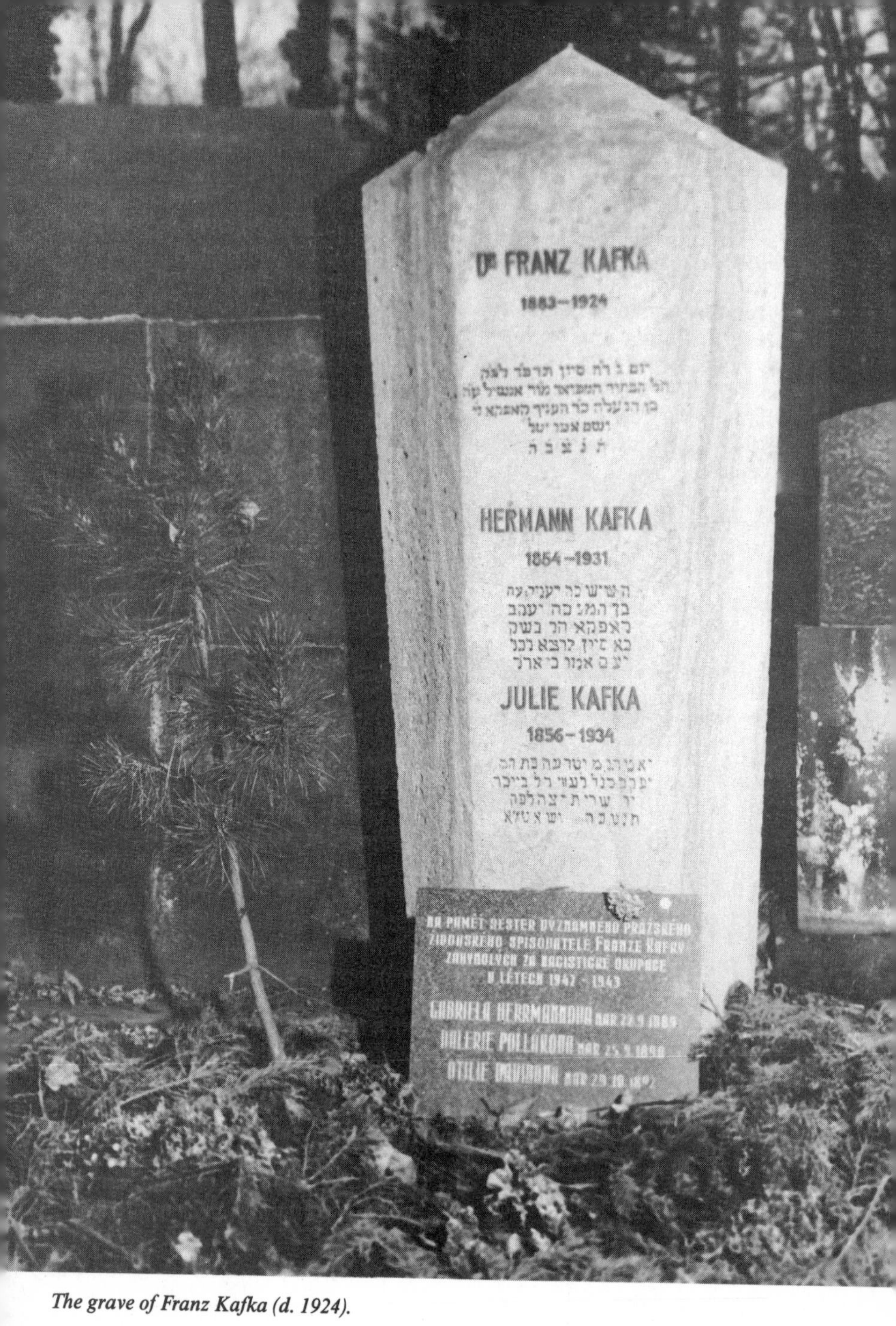

The grave of Franz Kafka (d. 1924).

BIBLIOGRAPHY

(Selection of basic sources only)

ALTSCHULER, David: *The Precious Legacy* (Summit Books, New York)

BENDA, Vilém: *Die Prager jüdischen Sehenswürdigkeiten* (Olympia, 1968).

BERGER, Natalia: *Where Cultures Meet* (Bet Hatefutsoth, Tel Aviv, 1990)

BONDY, DVORSKÝ: *K dějinám Židů v Čechách od r. 906–1620 (The history of the Jews in Bohemia 906–1620),* (Prague 1906)

FEDER, Richard: *Židovská tragedie (The Jewish tragedy),* (LUSK, Kolín 1947)

HERRMANN, I., TEIGE, J., WINTER, Z.: *Pražské ghetto (Prague ghetto),* (Prague 1902)

JANÁČEK, Josef: *Malé dějiny Prahy (A short history of Prague),* (Orbis, 1977)

DIE JUDEN IN PRAG *(B'nai B'rith,* Prague 1927)

KIEVAL, Hillel J.: *The making of Czech Jewry* (Oxford University Press, 1988)

KOSMOVA KRONIKA ČESKÁ *(Cosmas'Bohemian chronicle),* (Svoboda, Prague, 1972).

JIRÁSEK, A.: *Staré pověsti české (Old Bohemian tales),* (SNDK, Prague 1953)

RUTH, František: *Kronika královské Prahy (The Chronicle of royal Prague)* (Pavel Körbr, Prague, s. a.)

STÁTNÍ ŽIDOVSKÉ MUZEUM V PRAZE *(State Jewish Museum in Prague)* (Olympia, Prague, 1967)

PRAGUE GHETTO IN THE RENAISSANCE PERIOD (Orbis, Prague, 1965)

PRAŽSKÉ SYNAGOGY *v obrazech, rytinách a starých fotografiích (Prague synagogues in paintings, engravings and old photographs),* (State Jewish Museum in Prague, 1986).

STARÝ ŽIDOVSKÝ HŘBITOV V PRAZE *(The Old Jewish Cemetery in Prague),* (Umělecká Beseda, Prague, 1947)

TOMEK, Václav Vladivoj: *Dějepis města Prahy (The history of Prague),* Vols. 1–XIII (Prague 1987).

VOLAVKOVÁ, Hana: *Zmizelá Praha. Židovské město pražské (The disappeared Prague. The Jewish Town of Prague),* (Václav Poláček, Prague, 1947).

VOLAVKOVÁ, Hana: *Příběh Židovského muzea v Praze (The Story of the Jewish Museum in Prague),* (Odeon, Prague, 1966)

VOLAVKOVÁ, Hana: *Zmizelé Pražské ghetto (The disappeared ghetto of Prague),* (STN, Prague, 1961).

VOLAVKOVÁ, Hana: *Židovské město pražské (The Jewish Town of Prague),* (STN, Prague, 1959).

Periodicals:
– Kalendář česko-židovský, Židovská ročenka, Věstník ROŠ CHODEŠ Židovských náboženských obcí v České republice

CTIBOR RYBÁR

JEWISH PRAGUE

**(Notes on History and Culture
Guidebook)**

Published in 1991 by TV SPEKTRUM
in cooperation
with AKROPOLIS Publishers
Editor: Jiří Tomáš
Cover (using a painting by Karel Chaba)
and graphic design by Milan Maršo
Printed by
Severografia Most
1st edition